LOVECRAFTIAN PROCEEDINGS 3

HIPPOCAMPUS PRESS LIBRARY OF CRITICISM

S. T. Joshi, *Primal Sources: Essays on H. P. Lovecraft* (2003)

————, *The Evolution of the Weird Tale* (2004)

————, *Lovecraft and a World in Transition: Collected Essays on H. P. Lovecraft* (2014)

Robert W. Waugh, *The Monster in the Mirror: Looking for H. P. Lovecraft* (2006)

————, *A Monster of Voices: Speaking for H. P. Lovecraft* (2011)

Scott Connors, ed., *The Freedom of Fantastic Things: Selected Criticism on Clark Ashton Smith* (2006)

Ben Szumskyj, ed., *Two-Gun Bob: A Centennial Study of Robert E. Howard* (2006)

S. T. Joshi and Rosemary Pardoe, ed., *Warnings to the Curious: A Sheaf of Criticism on M. R. James* (2007)

Massimo Berruti, *Dim-Remembered Stories: A Critical Study of R. H. Barlow* (2011)

Gary William Crawford, Jim Rockhill, and Brian J. Showers, ed., *Reflections in a Glass Darkly: Essays on J. Sheridan Le Fanu* (2011)

Steven J. Mariconda, *H. P. Lovecraft: Art, Artifact, and Reality* (2013)

Massimo Berruti, S. T. Joshi, and Sam Gafford, ed., *William Hope Hodgson: Voices from the Borderland: Seven Decades of Criticism on the Master of Cosmic Horror* (2014)

Donald R. Burleson, *Lovecraft: An American Allegory–Selected Essays on H. P. Lovecraft* (2015)

Mark Valentine and Timothy J. Jarvis, ed., *The Secret Ceremonies Critical Essays on Arthur Machen* (2019)

Lovecraft Annual

Dead Reckonings

Lovecraftian Proceedings

LOVECRAFTIAN PROCEEDINGS 3

Select Papers from the Dr. Henry Armitage Memorial Scholarship Symposium, NecronomiCon Providence: 2017

Edited by Dennis P. Quinn

Hippocampus Press

New York

Cover illustration "The Shadow of His Smile" © by Pete Von Sholly.

Published by Hippocampus Press
P.O. Box 641, New York, NY 10156.
www.hippocampuspress.com

Cover illustration by Pete Von Sholly
Cover design by Barbara Briggs Silbert.
Hippocampus Press logo designed by Anastasia Damianakos.

First Edition
1 3 5 7 9 8 6 4 2

ISBN 978-1-61498-274-6 (paperback)
ISBN 978-1-61498-282-1 (ebook)

Contents

Preface: The Dr. Henry Armitage Memorial Scholarship Symposium

Niels-Viggo S. Hobbs
Arch-Director, Lovecraft Arts and Sciences Council
Providence, Rhode Island

In the early days of 2012, when NecronomiCon was just a twinkle in the eyes of several of us here in Providence, I do not think any of us could have envisioned the remarkable successes ahead . . . or, certainly, some of the bumps and bruises along the way. Several years, and three conventions later, and I still look to the Dr. Henry Armitage Memorial Scholarship Symposium as the greatest success of all. First named the Emerging Scholarship Symposium to highlight new research brought to the field of Lovecraftian and weird academia, the research presented has covered a variety of topics, some retreading old assumptions and some forging into unexplored regions. The work has come from scholars of all levels from new independent researchers to tenured university faculty. Although the content may have varied in topic and form, the research that has emerged over the past three conventions has been something for which we are exceedingly proud. The revised name, with reference to the librarian-gatekeeper of knowledge at fabled Miskatonic University, is meant to signify that all contributed work sits upon the same vaunted dais of weird academia.

As the proceedings of the third symposium is brought to print, I wish to express my greatest appreciation and undying admiration for all who have contributed to the growing corpus thus far—including papers presented by nearly ninety scholars around the country and beyond. Their hard work, curiosity, and desire to share their passion for knowledge is central to the success of the Armitage Symposium. I must also heartily thank our patron and most dedicated admirer of the symposium, Ken Birdwell. In ways beyond simple financial patronage, his support is the very life-blood of this endeavor. My final and ultimate thanks goes to the chairman of the symposium and the editor of the proceedings here, Professor Dennis P. Quinn. Shepherding this band of scholars has been no easy task, I'm sure, but for the past two—and, mercifully, the fourth one to come in 2019—Prof. Quinn has accomplished it with aplomb, professionalism, and remarkable patience. My gratitude is boundless.

To the reader now, and to all who attend and support both the Armitage Symposium, and NecronomiCon Providence in general, I hope you find the work presented here both illuminating and encouraging of your own interest in plumbing the depths of Lovecraftian and weird fiction.

Advert for NecronomiCon Providence 2019.
Used with kind permission of the artist, Dean Kutha.

Introduction: Writing Under the Shadow of Dr. Armitage

Dennis P. Quinn
Chair of the Dr. Henry Armitage
Memorial Scholarship Symposium
Professor and Chair of the Interdisciplinary
General Education Department
Cal Poly, Pomona, California

The essays contained in this volume of Lovecraftian Proceedings are taken from papers presented at The Dr. Henry Armitage Memorial Scholarship Symposium at NecronomiCon Providence, RI, 17-20 August, 2017. But who is Dr. Henry Armitage, and what's in a name?

The librarian of Miskatonic University and hero of "The Dunwich Horror," Dr. Henry Armitage, "the same erudite Henry Armitage (A.M. Miskatonic, Ph. D. Princeton, Litt. D. Johns Hopkins)" (CF 2.433), is in some ways the quintessential Lovecraft protagonist. But in some ways he is different. An academic and bibliophile, expert in ancient languages, and possessed by keen interests in arcane and esoteric knowledge, Dr. Armitage's profound scholarly abilities and interests gets him into trouble. Trouble much like so many academics in Lovecraft's fiction. Consider Dr. George Gammell Angell, in "The Call of Cthulhu," who begins the story already dead, was Professor Emeritus of Semitic Languages widely known as an authority on ancient inscriptions, learns more than he can survive. But unlike Dr. Angell, Dr. Armitage survives his eldritch interests and saves the world from the terrors he was ultimately able to discern.

So many of Lovecraft's consummate book-lovers put themselves in great danger by what might seem an otherwise noble, if on the surface a rather dull, pursuit: collecting and reading books. This is because among their more innocuous volumes, their dusty shelves contain such frightful tomes as Trithemius' *Poligraphia*, Giambattista, Porta's *De Furtivis Literarum*

De Vigenère's *Traité des Chiffres*, Falconer's *Cryptomenysis Patefacta*, or even perhaps Klüber's *Kryptographik*. They may also have in their dark libraries old Ludvig Prinn's hellish *De Vermis Mysteriis*, the infamous *Cultes des Goules* of Comte d'Erlette, or the sinister *Liber Ivonis*—not to mention the *Unaussprechlichen Kulten* of von Junzt. But more often they have access to accursed, abhorred and abhorrent, dreaded, forbidden, hideous, objectionable, and unmentionable, *Necronomicon* by the mad Arab Abdul Alhazred, which threatens a gruesome undoing to all who turn its horrific pages. But Dr. Armitage survives, and becomes one of the archetypal savior-librarians and scholars in literary history.

The "old, white-bearded Dr. Armitage" (CF 2.460) can easily decipher alphabets which "might be something esoterically used by certain forbidden cults which have come down from old times" (CF 2.448-49). But unlike Lovecraft's often fainting assemblage of all-too curious characters, "Armitage had a sound physique despite his seventy-three years" (CF 2.452). He prevents Wilbur Whateley from checking out the *Necronomicon*, knowing something was seriously amiss with the strange fellow, who later tries, but dies failing, to steal it. In the climactic encounter near the end of "The Dunwich Horror," when they confront Whateley's hideous invisible twin brother, colleague Professor Rice "wholly lost consciousness for an instant." This was right after the bevy of academics first arrived and "[one] of the three—it is not certain which—shrieked aloud at what sprawled before them among disordered tables and overturned chairs." (CF 2.438). Whoever it was, it was certainly not Dr. Armitage.

He is not only physically more fit than his younger and weaker-nerved colleagues, he is also clearly a better scholar. Armitage has "wide linguistic learning and skill in the mystical formulae of antiquity and the Middle Ages" (CF 2.448). "Dr. Armitage knew, from the repeated failures of his colleagues, that the riddle was a deep and complex one; and that no simple mode of solution could merit even a trial." He knew he was the one to find out what was going on with the Whateley Family. Indeed, Dr. Armitage comes off in "The Dunwich Horror" as quite the erudite scholar. The following section from the text is a good example of Dr. Armitage's hermeneutical dexterity and vast learning needed to interpret Wilbur Whateley's quizzical and frightening annals:

> He interspersed his study of the books with attacks on the manuscript itself,
> and in time became convinced that he had to deal with one of those subtlest

and most ingenious of cryptograms, in which many separate lists of corresponding letters are arranged like the multiplication table, and the message built up with arbitrary key-words known only to the initiated. The older authorities seemed rather more helpful than the newer ones, and Armitage concluded that the code of the manuscript was one of great antiquity, no doubt handed down through a long line of mystical experimenters. Several times he seemed near daylight, only to be set back by some unforeseen obstacle. Then, as September approached, the clouds began to clear. (CF 2.449–50)

He conquered the text as he would later conquer Whateley's even more hideous twin brother, thereby saving the world from "the truths and menaces to man's existence that he had uncovered" (CF 2.451), for the time being at least. Lovecraft seems to revel in writing of the scholarly prowess and exegetical gymnastics of Dr. Armitage. One might even envision Lovecraft imagining such an exciting day of study for himself. This may not be as far-fetched as one might think.

What does Lovecraft say about Dr. Henry Armitage outside of "The Dunwich Horror"? Not very much. Certainly the character speaks for himself in the tale. But the few things Lovecraft does say about his uber-scholar and hero of the story are telling. In a letter to J. Vernon Shea in 1931, he explains one way he crafts his characters. Lovecraft attempts "to have my various shadowy figures (Wilmarth, Akeley, Armitage, &c) as normal and undistinguished as the average passive agents in a weird happening would be likely to be. Nor do I make them all young and prepossessing. On the other hand, I seek to have them of varying ages and types, just as any assortment of people culled at random would be likely to be" (JVS 295).[1] Certainly, Dr. Armitage is not young; but much of what Lovecraft says to Shea seems a bit understated if we go back to an earlier letter he wrote in 1929 to August Derleth. In it, Lovecraft writes about using first person in stories, which, admittedly, he used quite a bit. "The first person seems to me the easiest of all persons to write in—so cursedly easy that one has to be on guard against monotonously using it all the time. I steered clear of it in "The Dunwich Horror", yet even so *found myself psychologically identifying myself with one of the characters (an aged scholar who finally combats the menace) toward the end*" (Emphasis mine) (*Essential Solitude*

---

1. Many thanks to David E. Schultz for pointing this letter out to me.

158). So, more than simply seeing Dr. Armitage as perhaps one of the greatest of Lovecraft's "various shadowy . . . normal and undistinguished . . . average passive agents," we might see him more as a literary figure whom Lovecraft enjoyed creating and held a special place in his imagination. The Armitage Symposium is named after the one person in his fiction that he said that about.

And it is right and fitting that the symposium, from which this collection of essays arose, is named after him. It would also be safe to say that, although none of the scholars have yet reached the great age of Dr. Armitage, I have a suspicion that none of them would be among the shrieking or fainting scholars who might come across the weird and horrific happenings that are common to a Lovecraftian setting; and they all show some signs of the erudition and textual-analytical prowess of our librarian from Miskatonic. I also wouldn't be surprised if they had a number of those frightful tomes mentioned at the beginning of this introduction—or at least wished they had, despite the well-known potential for dreadful consequences.

Indeed this third collection of presentations from the 2017 Armitage Symposium, which have all been revised and double-blind peer reviewed by some worthy scholars in their own right, continues the tradition of the other two by containing some of the most novel and cutting edge scholarship in Lovecraftiana. Some have taken familiar topics down unfamiliar paths, such as Karen Joan Kohoutek, who asks us to look again at two of Lovecraft's lesser known tales, "He" and "The Horror at Red Hook," to argue that they have had more resonance in modern popular culture than is often realized. Paul Neimann explores the familiar short story, "The Unnamable," and shows us that it may be time to reconsider the relationship between Lovecraft's theoretical understanding of weird fiction, as outlined in "Supernatural Horror in Literature," and his actual literary method.

Some have asked brand new questions and proposed answers in which it would be beneficial for scholars to take notice. For example, Ian Fetters argues how one of Lovecraft's most famous stories, and arguably one of his most challenging—*At the Mountains of Madness*—has been mostly neglected in scholarship and challenges us to place the work front and center for its great contributions to what he terms "polar realism" and other works that place an exacting attention to scientific and geographical detail within a fictional context. Further, Heather Poirier challenges us to see Lovecraft within the constellation of the great detective story writers of the twentieth century, among the many other distinctive genre hats worn by the Old Gent from Providence.

There have no doubt been many controversies swirling about Lovecraft's legacy, and some of these are duly addressed here. Troy Rondinone examines "Imprisoned with the Pharaohs" and "Out of the Aeons" within the context of contemporary Egypto-mania of his day, after the discovery of King Tut's tomb, to expose the overtly orientalist threads that undergird these works and reflect Lovecraft's preconceptions. Ray Huling explores Lovecraft's flirtations with fascist themes in his writings, and, by comparing and contracting him to the left-leaning Georges Bataille, offers a reevaluation of Lovecraft's value for modern progressive thought. Fiona Maeve Geist and Sadie Shurberg chisel out Lovecraft's homophobic/erotic statements and racist sentiments in stark relief in an essay that challenges critics and scholars to face these issues anew.

Some have demonstrated how Lovecraft's influence has traveled to places and resonated with people far from his hometown Providence— places perhaps even Randolph Carter could not have dreamed. We can see this in Elena Tchougounova-Paulson's treatment of Lovecraft's kinship with the Russian poet Alexander Blok, Lúcio Reis Filho's journey into Lovecraftian Brazil, and Edward Guimont demonstrating that Lovecraft's characters did not even have to set foot on Mars to have made a footprint in many of the subsequent authors' works whose protagonists have traversed the Red Planet. Circling an orbit that has collected many satellites, Sean Moreland's Lovecraft is shown to have included spiral imagery in many of his early work that both draws from and impacts many literary figures and artists who have gone before and after, particularly the popular magna artist Junji Ito. Beyond the visual arts, Nathaniel R. Wallace traces the surprisingly great volume of musicians, particularly in psychedelia and the drone musical genre, who invoke the hideous and mighty Azathoth in their songs, creating musical landscapes that try to capture the "maddening beating of vile drums and the thin monotonous whine" (CF 2.211) that is the soundtrack of this ominous creator deity.

As stated at the beginning of this introduction, papers published here are only a sample of the excellent works presented at The Dr. Henry Armitage Memorial Scholarship Symposium. Papers not included here are absent not necessarily because they were of inferior quality. Far from it. Several authors decided to retain their work because they were parts of other projects, such as books they had in progress or other collections where they planned to publish. Others wanted more time to refine and expand upon what they presented and have published or are working to publish them in other journals or media. This is why we have included a full list of authors and abstracts from everyone who presented at the Symposium so readers might find the many other fascinating topics that were covered and track down where the work has gone from here. The Armitage Symposium is still going strong with no end in sight. In fact we only see the popularity of this facet of NecronomiCon Providence growing and expanding, attracting many more that Lovecraft has inspired, and continues to inspire. We see no end in sight for that either.

I wish to thank many people who helped bring this volume of *Lovecraftian Proceedings* to light. John Michael Sefel, the first and original Chair of the Armitage Symposium (at first called Emerging Scholarship Symposium), and editor of the first *Lovecraftian Proceedings*, has been a great resource and exemplar in chairing the Symposium, as well as this and the previous volume. So too, Niels-Viggo S. Hobbs, the founder and patriarch of NecronomiCon Providence who intended from its inception to have a part of the convention that showcased the latest scholarship on Lovecraft and weird fiction as a prominent facet of the whole experience. His vision and endurance to see NecronomiCon Providence every two years to such phenomenal success is a great inspiration to me. I thank him for his boundless support, encouragement, and trust. David E. Schultz, whose excellence as an editor and expert on Lovecraft's fiction and voluminous letters need not be mentioned here (he's one of the greatest ever, there I said it!), was essential in putting these proceedings through to completion and to a much higher quality than I could have accomplished without him. Derrick Hussey has been fantastic to work with over the years and I admire him for all he has done to ensure the continual expansion of the Lovecraftian universe. He is responsible for much of the growing recognition of Lovecraft as one of the pillars of American literature. S. T. Joshi, who has influenced so many of us in this volume, should be thanked in any contemporary work on Lovecraft and his legacy. His work has stimulated and challenged scholars to follow in his ceaseless rigor and erudition and, if we might live two or three more lives, we could someday come close to matching his vast and almost innumerable works. But even then, we might never match his inestimable imprint on the field. Lastly, a tremendous thank you to the unnamable, unanimous peer reviewers who were so generous with their time and intellect, who, I think I can speak for the authors in this volume, helped make what were already fine papers even better. I look forward to working with you all again on the next Lovecraftian Proceedings, and beyond—that is if I can summon the courage and stamina (if not the erudition) of Dr. Armitage.

Works Cited

Lovecraft, H. P. *Essential Solitude: The Letters of H. P. Lovecraft and August Derleth.* Edited by David E. Schultz and S. T. Joshi. New York: Hippocampus Press, 2008.

Abbreviations

AG   *Letters to Alfred Galpin* (Hippocampus Press, 2003)

AT   *The Ancient Track: Complete Poetical Works* (Hippocampus Press, 2013)

CE   *Collected Essays* (Hippocampus Press, 2004–06; 5 vols.)

CF   *Collected Fiction* (Hippocampus Press, 2015–17; 4 vols.)

CLM   *Letters to C. L. Moore* (Hippocampus Press, 2017)

DS   *Dawnward Spire, Lonely Hill: The Letters of H. P. Lovecraft and Clark Ashton Smith* (Hippocampus Press, 2017)

IAP   S. T. Joshi, *I Am Providence: The Life and Times of H. P. Lovecraft* (Hippocampus Press, 2010)

JFM   *Letters to James F. Morton* (Hippocampus Press, 2011)

JVS   *Letters to J. Vernon Shea, Carl F. Strauch, and Lee McBride White* (Hippocampus Press, 2016)

MF   *A Means to Freedom: The Letters of H. P. Lovecraft and Robert E. Howard* (Hippocampus Press, 2009)

MWM   *Letters to Maurice W. Moe and Others* (Hippocampus Press, 2018)

SL   *Selected Letters* (Arkham House, 1965–76; 5 vols.)

Lovecraft's Dark Continent: *At the Mountains of Madness* and Antarctic Literature

Ian Fetters
Cal Poly San Luis Obispo

Antarctica is a place of great importance in H. P. Lovecraft's mythos, and *At the Mountains of Madness*, one of Lovecraft's longer prose works, occupies just as important a spot in his body of work.[1] Though the novel's history is fraught with rejection and even the writer's own uncertainty about its merits, the text remains to this day a narrative triumph and an early science fiction masterpiece.[2] However, the Antarctic novel garners little attention in the critical sphere. Despite a resurgence of general scholarly interest in Lovecraft, *At the Mountains of Madness* seems to be neglected. Worth noting is the relative absence of scholarly articles that address the novel as a primary text; it is more often used as a supporting or subsidiary text in research. For example, John Navroth's article "Lovecraft and the Polar Myth" includes the novel in an analysis of "coldness" as a distinctly Lovecraftian theme, but ultimately the novel is introduced only as an example, a reference point for the theme at play, not the focus. Very little is said about the Antarctic continent itself, let alone any potential import

1. This project was funded by The Aeroflex Foundation as part of the 2017 S. T. Joshi Endowed Research Fellowship. The research took place over an eight-week period at Brown University in Providence, R.I. Manuscripts, correspondence, and other archival materials from the H. P. Lovecraft Papers and the Swan Antarctic Collection were consulted when putting this essay together. Thanks are due to the staff at the John Hay Library, John D. Rockefeller Library, and John Carter Brown Library for their assistance in with archives.

2. Farnsworth Wright of *Weird Tales* rejected *At the Mountains of Madness*, and HPL never resubmitted the story. *Argosy* also rejected the story when submitted surreptitiously by Donald Wandrei in 1935, but *Astounding Stories* published it as a serial in 1936. HPL was highly disappointed with the result (*IAP* 2.788–90).

that one might take away from Lovecraft's only story set at the southernmost point of the world. Granted, Antarctica is not the stated focus of the article, but one cannot help but think of coldness as the province of the Antarctic: the coldest place on Earth.

The scholarship that takes the novel as its primary text tends to narrow its focus on the nascent science fiction elements, particularly the "demythologizing" factor that Robert M. Price was first to point out in *Lovecraft and the Cthulhu Mythos* (1990)—that the novel represents Lovecraft's move away from the gods of the mythos to favor instead explicitly extraterrestrial beings, like the famously barrel-shaped Old Ones (100). Likewise, S. T. Joshi makes it fairly clear in his own assessment of the novel's significance that the Old Ones are the focus, their transformation from "objects of terror to symbols of the best in humanity" constituting the major thematic shift in the novel and for the mythos at large (*IAP* 2.784).

And while the demythologized take on the Old Ones and their evolutionary narrative are indeed worthwhile, the Antarctic setting of the novel has largely been passed over by scholarship. Though Lovecraft is no stranger to writing exotic or fantastic locales—Australia, Venus, the Dreamlands, the deep sea, etc.—and having his protagonists suffer their various and, usually, unpleasant demises in those settings, Antarctica stands out above the rest. *At the Mountains of Madness* is set in one of the last unexplored regions of the Earth (as of the early twentieth century, when Lovecraft is composing his epic adventure-horror science fiction novel)—an icy, dark continent in one of the harshest and remotest environments in the world. But Antarctica is not merely a setting: the continent defines the entire novel from beginning to end.

This essay pinpoints what I call an essential *Antarcticness* in the novel, which is encoded into every aspect of the novel's identity but most apparent in its polar realism: the engagement with the Antarctic space and its temporality. Polar realism is defined herein in the context of Jason Eckhardt's essay "Behind the Mountains of Madness: Lovecraft and the Antarctic in 1930," wherein his analysis of the heightened verisimilitude of the expeditionary elements of the protagonist's narrative grants the novel an extraordinary "ability to capture the real and to make us believe the unreal" (38). It is the unity of narrative form, constructed relationship to Antarctica's storied expeditionary past, and consummate attention to scientific, geographical, geological, and historic detail that produces the effect Eckhardt observes and I call polar realism. And when this polar realism is at play in the novel—which is sent spiraling into pure cosmic horror by the climax in the novel's third act—the consequence is an Antarctic setting and identity that is at once earthbound and situated beyond "some accursed ultimate abyss," a liminal space where awe and horror exist in equal measure (MM 21). After penning the final draft of the novel, Lovecraft would come to theorize the feeling reader's experience, when balancing awe and horror, compulsion and repulsion, as a sense of "adventurous expectancy," which his Antarctic novel represents, then, as an ideal praxis of that theory and prose. At the Mountains of Madness is, at its icy core, a work of Antarctic fiction, its identity going beyond simple setting or a culminating showcase of Lovecraft's juvenile polar obsession[3]—it becomes instead a defining work in a larger Antarctic literary tradition.

Antarctic Fiction

There is a long-standing tradition of Antarctic fiction, to which At the Mountains of Madness belongs. From Satan's flight down to the pole in search of passage into the Garden, to the frozen underworld survived by Coleridge's mariner in his fraught southern voyage, to more contemporary tales of awe and horror such as John W. Campbell's Who Goes There? (1938), which generated two film adaptations in 1951 and 1982, Antarctica has been a force in popular cultural and literary production.[4]

---

3. HPL admits to an obsession with the Antarctic continent from an early age in a letter to Rheinhart Kleiner in 1916: "About 1900 [at the age of 10] I became a passionate devotee of geography & history, & an intense fanatic on the subject of Antarctic exploration. The Borchgrevink expedition, which had just made a new record in South Polar achievement, greatly stimulated this study" (Letters to Rheinhart Kleiner 70). Not only did the juvenile HPL study the region, he also wrote "many fanciful tales about the Antarctic Continent, besides composing 'learned' treatises on the real facts" (13). This early interest in Antarctica shows an appreciation for the pole's imaginative qualities right alongside the "real facts," as it were. Thirty years later, HPL's passion for Antarctic exploration emerged in At the Mountains of Madness, showing no less a dedication to representing the real facts of the far South alongside the cosmic horrors of his developing mythos. All this from a man who would never set foot on the south polar continent.

4. "From Eden over Pontus, and the pool / Mæotis, up beyond the river Ob; / Downward as far antarctic; and in length / West from Orontes" (Paradise Lost 9.77–80); Samuel Taylor Coleridge, The Rime of the Ancient Mariner (1798); The Thing from Another World (1951), dir. Howard Hawks; The Thing (1982), dir. John Carpenter.

The list does not stop here, but what exactly is Antarctic fiction? How is it defined as a genre or a body or work or a style guide? In *Antarctica in Fiction*, Elizabeth Leane explores the tradition's foundations and its most obscure corners—what constitutes Antarctic fiction. A text is considered Antarctic when the following is observed:

> Strict criteria are applied—for example, that a title can only be Antarctic if it is substantially set in the region . . . or engaged with its history or politics. The corpus is not only larger than expected, but it is also more diverse. . . . As a landscape category describing that which instills awe mixed with a pleasant frisson of terror—which humbles the subject by its incomprehensible scale even while giving him/her a sense of exhilaration—this seems the most obvious aesthetic term to apply to Antarctica. (11)

This wide-ranging definition seems to encompass hundreds of literary works, from novels to dramas to poems, and even other media, such as film—but it is the latter part of Leane's working definition here where foundational works of Antarctic fiction, such as Edgar Allan Poe's *The Narrative of Arthur Gordon Pym of Nantucket* and *At the Mountains of Madness*, come into their own—with terror and awe in equal measure.

In fact, the connections between Poe and Lovecraft's Antarctic novels are well documented: Lovecraft's protagonist and narrator makes explicit references to Poe's novel—"the disturbing and enigmatical *Arthur Gordon Pym*"—virtually bringing Poe into the realm of his fiction. Additionally, the infamous cry "Tekeli-li," first recorded in *Pym* as intoned by the native Antarcticans and sea-birds of the continent, appears in *Mountains*, extrapolated by Lovecraft's host of scientists to be the dread-inducing musical piping of the imitative shoggoth from the novel's climax. Claims that *At the Mountains of Madness* is just a sequel to Pym, an attempt by Lovecraft to continue Poe's polar misadventure, do not pan out. As S. T. Joshi puts it, "except for the cry 'Tekeli-li,' as unexplained in Poe as in Lovecraft . . . the various references to *Pym* throughout the story end up being more in the manner of in-jokes. It is not clear that *Pym* even influenced the work in any significant way" (*IAP* 2.787).[5] Jeffrey Weinstock takes the connection a

---

5. Clark Ashton Smith, an underappreciated and incredible writer of fantastic weird fiction in his own right, expresses his opinion on *Mountains* in relation to *Pym*, writing, "I read the story twice—parts of it three or four times—and think it is one of your masterpieces. For my taste, anyway, it is vastly superior to Poe's Antarctic opus, 'Arthur Gordon Pym.' I'll never forget your descriptions of that tremendous non-human

bit further. Weinstock takes on a socio-political reading of the Antarctic texts, claiming that "the tabula rasa of the Antarctic provides a blank white page for the inscribing of racial anxieties" as they appear in both novels ("Tekeli-li!" 51). And while that interpretation has merit, the essay tends to have more to say about the "gothic" nature of Lovecraft's novel—an argument obviously developed in deference to Poe's work—than its Antarctic nature. So, although the Poe–Lovecraft polar connection has been made before, it fails to account for the "Antarcticness" of either work.

Criticism focused on Antarctic works of fiction, such as Weinstock's, often echoes a "blank" or "empty" interpretation of the Antarctic space— that the continent is a white canvas upon which Lovecraft is variously said to paint his anxieties about race, the collapse of western civilization, his well-documented fear of extreme cold, and so on. Elizabeth Leane disputes the blank slate trope, arguing for a different kind of Antarcticness, one that is much more about what *is there* rather than what can be inscribed or overlaid on the continent. That said, Leane falls into the camp of critics accusing *At the Mountains of Madness* of being a *Pym* sequel, relegating Lovecraft's novel to a minor position in what she dubs the "Legacy of Pym," a convenient category error that dismisses the novel's larger-than-life Antarcticness so crucial to its identity (64).

Poe's shadow seems to loom large over Lovecraft's polar tale, but *At the Mountains of Madness* is much more than just a black streak of cosmic horror across an icy white canvas, or a reverential tribute to Poe's legacy. It is a true work of Antarctic fiction, a centerpiece novel in the polar literary tradition.

The Antarctic Space

The depictions of the Antarctic continent's space and geography are a significant element in developing a sense of Antarcticness in *At the Mountains of Madness*. The effect of the spatial polar realism is most appreciable in the descriptions of the titular mountains themselves. During an early observation flight past Beardmore Glacier, Professor Dyer, the narrator, remarks that the titanic mountain range ahead of him is vast beyond Lake's previous observations: "starting as a low range at Luitpold Land on the

---

architecture, and the on-rushing *shoggoth* in the underworld cavern! Wright's rejection was certainly a piece of triple-dyed and quadruple-plated lunacy" (*DS* 315). And with that, the Sorcerer has spoken.

coast of Weddell Sea and virtually crossing the continent" (MM 52). In the original manuscript of the novel, "Luitpold Land" appears to be an additive edit to the text—the writer substitutes the landmark's name after striking through the first iteration of the passage, which is now unintelligible. This may be evidence of Lovecraft revisiting Antarctic maps—perhaps even his own nonextant "Antarctic Atlas" manuscript—to revise the name of the region or even just its spelling during one of many editing stages of this draft.[6] Luitpold Land, named for a Bavarian benefactor, was discovered and named during the Antarctic summer of 1911 by a German expedition, so Lovecraft would have been privy to the coastline's title long before the initial drafting of the novel (Riffenburgh 454). It is possible that maps Lovecraft referenced to situate the Antarctic continent had been updated to reflect more accurate location names at some point between initial drafts and a later stage of editing. Whatever the case, Lovecraft takes great care in describing the Antarctic space; the convention of naming explored or claimed regions of the continent is critical to his realist sensibilities. He knows that if there is any way to "capture the real," as Jason Eckhardt reminds us, and to make readers believe in the horrors that wait just beyond the mountains, it is by an accurate and detailed depiction of the setting: the half-explored Antarctic continent as it was between 1929 and 1932 (Eckhardt 38).

But does referring known Antarctic landmarks (circa early 1930s) by name really establish a distinct Antarcticness in spatial terms? Not quite; but Lovecraft is not yet finished with his tour of the awe-inspiring Antarctic geography. The first physical description of the mountains reaching from Weddell Sea on the far west coast all the way to the other side of the continent would be enough to give readers a sense for their vastness, but Lovecraft's meticulous attention to spatial detail, in service of polar realism, goes far beyond just that, even giving students of geology and geography a scare.[7]

---

6. "I want to date HPL's three lost [Antarctic] treatises to around 1900, since it would seem odd for HPL not to have chosen to write up the Borchgrevink and Scott expeditions, so fresh as they would have been in his mind . . . 'Antarctic Atlas' must have been an interesting work, and presumably consisted largely of a map of the continent; but so little exploration of the land mass had been done by this time that large parts of it were utterly unknown and unnamed" (*IAP* 1.75–76).

7. HPL writes the following in a letter to J. Vernon Shea, a student: "Glad you have a brilliant pedagogical staff to deal with—& hope the 'Mts. of Madness' didn't scare you

One particular passage in the manuscript depicts the location and span of the mountains down to minute coordinates. Dyer makes his in-flight observations before ascending the mountainous pass, saying that the largest part of the range stretches "from about Latitude 82°, E. Longitude 60° to Lat. 70°, E. Long. 115° with its concave side toward our camp and its seaward end in the region of that long, ice-locked coast," with the highest peaks—the "abhorred things" far surpassing the Himalayas in height—residing between 70° to 100° Longitude (MM 52). The coordinates here are impressive not just for their detail but because they represent a literal blank space on an Antarctic map. When the mountain range coordinates are, as presented in the passage, plotted on a map, such as Scott's famously incomplete coastal map of East Antarctica, the range appears to occupy a place that is seemingly empty, a featureless space whose edges expand off the map itself, signifying a region yet to be explored.[8] In drafting At the Mountains of Madness Lovecraft knew that the vast section of East Antarctica in which the mountains are purported to reside was, in 1930, relatively unknown in its geographical and topographical composition. Even when comparing the mountains on a modern-day map of the continent, fully described now due to satellite imaging, the coordinates still correspond to a region that is one of the least explored, least defined areas in the east of the continent.

The detailed coordinates and landmarks represented in the text exist at an intersection between Lovecraft's consummate polar realism and his speculative imagination. On the one hand, Lovecraft presents coordinates for a mountain range that can only be described as "accurate," in that they appear in a large enough region on the continent to invoke speculation about their *potential* existence; on the other, the region in question is just that—a question. Between 1929 and 1936 (the years from the novel's conception to its publication), the eastern coastline was only glimpsed at, until in 1931 a Norwegian explorer by the name of Christensen successfully mapped the coast by plane. David Day recalls the historic moment in Antarctica: A Biography:

---

off from geology!" (JVS 31).

8. Captain Robert F. Scott produced a map of the Antarctic coastline, the edge of which disappears as it approaches East Antarctica, an ice-locked region that at the time was inaccessible by ship. Scott produced the map in an attempt to lay claim to the area for Britain. Found in the Antarctic Scrapbook (1946) in the Swan Antarctic Collection at the John Hay Library.

[Christensen] had mapped the principle features of the Antarctic coastline all the way from 20° W to 100° E. Much of what had been blank or conjectured on Antarctic maps was now filled in, and Christensen invited people to compare his maps with the much less detailed British maps that had been published in 1926 [e.g., Scott's map]. (256)

By setting the titular mountains in the East Antarctica "badlands," Lovecraft created a liminal space for them—one that is simultaneously said to exist but is untouched by humanity and preserved in its primeval, frozen state. It is the recognition on Lovecraft's part of known and unknown spaces coexisting on the continent that helps established the novel's spatially linked Antarcticness. The definitive landmarks—Luitpold Land, the Weddell Sea, etc.—pair with the unknown potential of the eastern ice wastes, creating a convincing portrait of a darkened continent, one where titanic mountains and cosmic horrors could indeed be found, if one were to look for them.

The Heroic Age of Exploration and Antarctic Space

Decades after the novel's publication, explorers from the Soviet Union, Australia, and the United States would attempt to lay claim to the eastern territory of the Antarctic continent, but few had actually set foot onto the region. And though Lovecraft's narrator mentions by name almost every significant explorer from Antarctica's Heroic Age of Exploration, two names stand out in connection with the eastern region.[9] Charles Wilkes (1798-1877), the American naval officer, and Douglass Mawson (1882-1958) of Australia are significant allusions in the text for their supposed sightings of mountainous geographic features off the eastern coast of Antarctica. Although Wilkes's name is anathema to the exploration community, both explorers are linked in the text, according to Dyer's observation from a passage describing the mountain range's eastern end: "the region of that long, ice-locked coast whose hills were glimpsed by Wilkes and Mawson at the Antarctic Circle" (MM 52).[10] Lovecraft uses

---

9. HPL mentioned by name Carsten Egeberg Borchgrevink, Robert F. Scott, Roald Amundsen, Sir Ernest Shackleton, Admiral Richard E. Byrd, James Clark Ross, Charles Wilkes, and Douglass Mawson. This venerable roll call of early explorers of Antarctica during what is known as the Heroic Age of Exploration further cements the text's polar realism.

10. It is no coincidence that HPL pairs Wilkes and Mawson in this section. Mawson

the shared space of the "half-known, half-suspected" coastline as a way to establish polar realism through the allusion to Wilkes and Mawson's quarrel and mountain sightings, and to suggest a parallel Antarctic space that is more speculative than real. Lovecraft's Antarctica is a blurred, liminal space where real Heroic Age explorers and fictional characters alike spot mountains where there are none, imagining a continent half real and half speculative. So, when the narrator claims to be ascending the mountains that Mawson supposedly glimpsed, it should come as no surprise that Mawson's expedition to discover the Antarctic eastern edge of the continent is working concurrently—that is, at the same time as the fictional Miskatonic expedition, as Dyer proclaims in the manuscript, from 1929 to 1931—in Mac. Robertson Land (now Queen Mary's Land), 1000 miles away from Dyer and his party (Day 246; MM 78).

Just as Lovecraft blurs the lines between the real and the speculative, he also blurs storytelling and nonfiction in an attempt to characterize the Antarctic space in the novel. Admiral Byrd (1888–1957), whose experiences on the continent are recorded in a nonfiction account of his harrowing Antarctic winter, rivaled the popularity of accounts written by Scott and Shackleton at the time of its publication. And though Byrd is invoked only three times, typically in passing, his nonfiction book *Little America* (1930) has a far greater impact on *At the Mountains of Madness*'s narrative structure than is evident in the novel. Jason Eckhardt is one of the first critics to point out Byrd's influence. Byrd's extensive use of Navy airplanes on the southernmost continent no doubt inspired the Miskatonic University expedition's reliance on airplanes during their own ill-fated expedition. For Eckhardt, the influence is benign: "Thus we have two expeditions, fact and fiction. It is clear that Lovecraft, though not intending to 'cash in' on the popularity of Byrd's exploits, certainly admired the man

---

disputed Wilkes's egregious claim that he discovered the eastern coastline; after investigation, the exploration community determined that Wilkes had lied, his assertions proven impossible at the time of his claim, and ultimately sided with Mawson. "[Wilkes] had sailed some 1300 kilometers and reached 112° E by February 1839, when Wilkes climbed the mainmast to see a snow-covered mountain range rising in the distance above the ice-barrier . . . he wrote in his journal how the sightings of the mountains 'settles the question of our having discovered the Antarctic continent.' . . . Where Wilkes claimed to have sailed over open sea, Mawson [in 1911] encountered the ice barrier that indicated the edge of the continent" (Day 74, 154).

enough to use his travels as a basis for his own flights of fancy" (37). A closer look at the two texts, fiction and nonfiction, reveals just how indebted Lovecraft's narrative structure is to the real-life struggles of the Byrd expedition. In *Little America*, Byrd recalls an incident in which a reconnaissance plane crashes at the foot of a mountain in the East, just past Beardmore Glacier; the same "plot point" is echoed in *At the Mountains of Madness*. From *Little America*:

> There was no word from Gould [Byrd's geologist on the flight] on the 15th. Nor the 16th. Nor the 17th. And on the 17th, which was a Saturday, I became genuinely alarmed [. . .] Only a crash could have disabled both sets [of radios] beyond repair [. . .] We stirred up nothing but reckless theories. (Byrd 174)

And of Lake's downed plane incident in *At the Mountains of Madness*, Dyer reports the following passage:

> Throughout the day we all listened anxiously and tried to get Lake [a biologist] at intervals, but invariably without results [. . .] Reflecting that he had had four planes, each provided with an excellent short-wave outfit, we could not imagine any ordinary accident capable of *crippling all his wireless equipment at once*. Nevertheless the stony silence continued; and when we thought of the delirious force the wind must have had in his locality we could not help *making the most direful conjectures*. (MM 19; my emphasis)

Though Byrd's incident ends with all plane crew members alive and accounted for, and Lovecraft's narrator makes a most grisly discovery at Lake's camp-crash site, the structural similarity between the two passages is remarkable. Textual analysis of the Lovecraft manuscript reveals that the similarity is no coincidence—a large section of Dyer's passage describing the days before discovering Lake's crash site is an additive edit to the original handwritten text. This suggests that the edit was made at some point in the drafting stages after 1930, when Lovecraft would have had an opportunity to read *Little America* or pore over collected excerpts of it in weekly journals.

Lovecraft infuses the Byrd plane crash incident into *At the Mountains of Madness* in an effort to achieve a spatial polar realism. In other words, when the plane crashes in Byrd's account, a real-life tension is created: a lack of communication, the intense weather conditions, and the real fear that without rescue, the crew would quickly die of exposure to eastern Antarctica's climes. Lovecraft effectively mirrors this tension by establishing the same stakes produced by the harsh weather conditions and unknown geographical obstacles that Byrd's crew experienced. And beyond that, he sets up the same technological failures (the radios) to further those same stakes. Narratively and spatially, Lovecraft sets up a life-or-death tension in the same vein as his nonfiction counterpart without ever having set foot onto the icy wastes of the southern continent or wintered over at McMurdo Sound.[11] His experience may be second-hand, but Lovecraft demonstrates in this passage a fundamental understanding of what makes the Antarctic so averse to human life, what makes it unforgiving and horrific in the extreme—the vast distances between flights, the incalculable unknowns, the near impossibility of rescue in the middle of a blinding white desert. The polar realism in the narrative, borrowed in part from nonfiction contemporaries, is nigh indistinguishable from real accounts of Antarctic adventure and terror, producing an effect of verisimilitude that rivals any other Antarctic fiction text in the tradition.

Antarctic Temporality

Lovecraft's consummate polar realism goes beyond merely nodding to Heroic Age exploration and his lifelong interest in Antarctic geography. The temporality at play in At the Mountains of Madness brings the dark continent to life in a very real and horrific sense. Lovecraft treats temporality—the details and mechanics of time and narrative chronology in the Antarctic—with the same verisimilitude as the spatial-geographical elements. The manuscript of the novel contains numerous temporal edits and extra-textual markings that show a Lovecraft obsessed not only with getting right the time intervals in Antarctica, but also making that work serve the horrific themes that gradually play out in the second half of the novel.

Take, for example, Lake's ice-boring mission and the first sighting of the titular mountains. Lake first reports his discovery from the air, sending the following message to the base camp party: "10:05 p.m. On the wing. After snowstorm, have spied mountain-range ahead higher than any hitherto seen. May equal Himalayas allowing for height of plateau" (CF 3.27). The seemingly small detail of the time in the passage (10:05 P.M.) begs an important question: If Lake's subexpedition was flying at night, how could it spot the mountains from the air? In other words, why does Lovecraft seem to select a time that would not work with the realism of the scenario

---

11. No doubt the Antarctic winter would have been far too cold for the Old Gentlemen, reaching a temperature of -130° F in the dark, polar winter months (Borunda).

put forth by Lake and his crew? It is here that the Antarctic setting, and its constituent temporality, come into play—for it is no "normal" setting. There is, according to authorities, a special time period in the Antarctic when the sun never truly sets, as it were—it shines bright over the ice at its peak or bathes the continent in a perpetual twilight at its lowest.[12] That period occurs during the apex Antarctic summer months, meaning that Lake's 10:05 P.M. discovery on January 22 would likely have been illuminated by a brilliant twenty-four Antarctic sun ("Weather–Sunlight Hours").

Other strikethroughs and additions of temporal details in the manuscript seem to suggest hesitation on Lovecraft's part: page 8 exhibits a number of issues with time and day that are edited at a later stage. Take, for example, the same passage from Lake's ice-boring mission and the following extra textual annotations that appear in the manuscript margins but not in best text published versions of the novel: "10 pm Jan 22," "10:35 pm Jan 22," "in about an hour and a half later," and several others (MM 8). These represent an attempt to keep the temporal beats of the passage linear and objective, as would be consistent with the character Lake, who is a scientist and therefore would need to provide up to the minute details as part of his observations. Furthermore, ever the realist and man of science himself, it is possible that Lovecraft altered the timing of this particular passage (editing in specific times at a later date) after conducting further research on the Antarctic twilight. Prior evidence, such as the references to Byrd's 1930 flights over East Antarctica and Mawson, suggests that Lovecraft was well aware of the unique temporality of the Antarctic setting at the time of drafting, if not at a later stage of editing before completing the typescript on May 1, 1931. What is ultimately demonstrated here, from simple annotations and edits to the linear time-sequence of this passage and others, is an impressive polar realism, made all the more impressive in that this kind of attention to Antarctic temporality can be found nowhere else in the tradition of Antarctic literature, let alone in a work of fiction.

Critics have made note of perceived flaws in Lovecraft's Antarctic timing. Donald R. Burleson points out in *H. P. Lovecraft: A Critical Study* (1983) that the novel is rather skewed in its pacing; by his estimates, nearly sixty-five percent of the plot occurs over the sixteen hours that Professor Dyer and the graduate student, Danforth, explore the alien city ruins be-

---

12. According to the Antarctic Division of Australia's Department of Energy and Environment (www.antarctica.gov.au/about-antarctica/environment).

yond the mountain peaks. Burleson argues that the drawn-out pacing of the final parts represents a break from the conventional temporality of previous parts of the novel, saying, "as if, in those brief but portentous hours, time itself has been frozen as the polar wastes in which the final revelations come" (166). Though the thought of time freezing into an unwieldy chunk of narrative for the second half of the novel is quite attractive, analysis of the manuscript suggests that the novel is in fact governed by a strictly conventional temporality: a linear chronology and a realistic distribution of story beats. For example, though they do not appear in best text versions of the novel, Lovecraft annotates the margins of the manuscript with reminders on the locations and time spent in the alien city ruins. Just before the appearance of the infamous "bulky white shape," Lovecraft makes a note of Dyer and Danforth's progress in an annotation: "start 10:05 / see peng[uin]. 10:20" (MM 65). And just before the two bewildered scientists enter the stinking cavern in the "primordial celestial dome," he writes, "–½ mile in / 11pm," and again when they stop to record more bas-reliefs: "11:15–¾ mile in" (MM 68-70). As in the Lake passage, the narrator maintains an objective and linear temporality that is consistent with the progress that the two characters make on their way through the city. Granted, extra-textual annotations are just that—extratextual, beyond the text. They do not appear in any published version of the novel. But what they demonstrate is a consistent effort on the part of the writer in constructing a convincing Antarctic, one that is governed by a realistic temporality.

Though conventional temporality is a common feature of Lovecraft's other prose works, it is a uniquely Antarctic feature of the novel, contributing to its overall Antarcticness. The novel's Antarcticness is, in other words, directly linked to the realist depiction of time. Elizabeth Leane explains that most works in the Antarctic fiction tradition are governed by a conventional temporality—that a realist mode is often employed over "the contortions of modernist and postmodernist novels" (154). She puts it best when she claims that "fiction writers find it difficult to describe an experimental world through an experimental style" (154). Lovecraft is no ordinary fiction writer, but Antarctica still presents the challenge of being a thoroughly "experimental world," just as alien and unknown as any of the outré settings of other mythos tales. His conventional, realist framing helps to stabilize the Antarctic continent as much as possible in order to better contrast the horrific, cosmic revelations of the climactic escape from the shoggoth at the novel's close. Time, even as it unfolds in a conventional sense, becomes a major contributing factor to the Antarcticness of the novel.

Adventurous Expectancy

In a letter to J. Vernon Shea, shortly after finishing the final draft of *At the Mountains of Madness*, Lovecraft responds to his young penpal's question about his gravitation toward weird fiction:

> Why did I happen to land on weird fiction? Haven't the least idea—was merely built that way. Since I could talk & walk nothing has ever interested me so much as the imaginative liberation of fantastic fiction—the casting off, in fancy, of all the chafing limitations of time, space, & natural law, & the achievement (on paper) of *an unbounded sense of opened vistas fraught with adventurous expectancy*. (JVS 19–20; my emphasis)

There can be no better way to describe the literary effect of *At the Mountains of Madness* and its Antarcticness than in terms of "adventurous expectancy." For Lovecraft, the notion of adventurous expectancy—a concept of his own coinage appearing once in the text of *Mountains*—is related directly to the dark southern continent, its spatial and temporal elements being simultaneously committed to realism as well as fantastic and alien horror at turns. The novel perfectly encapsulates the thrill of writing about the unknown South Polar region in the early twentieth century; it asks the brooding question of "What if? . . ." and eagerly awaits the primal continent's response. Lovecraft's early pursuit of this quality—of provoking anxious excitement in both reader and writer—is certainly what prompted him to write to Shea in 1934: "Much of the universe baffled me . . . Geography—just *what* would Scott & Shackleton & Borchgrevink find in the great white Antarctic or their next expedition. . . . . which I could—if I wished—live to see described?" (JVS 222). Though both Scott and Shackleton made their notable discoveries and broke polar records before *At the Mountains of Madness* was conceived and written, the inherent thrill of the novel reflects that same spirit of wonder at the landscape and world of the South Pole—with its attendant awe and horror of a continent not yet fully discovered or filled in on maps.

Make no mistake: Antarctica is not a blank space so much a rough geography rich with potential. Just the notion that in 1931 no human eye had ever gazed upon certain vast regions of the Antarctic is intoxicating to the writer of weird and speculative fiction; certainly it is the same feeling Lovecraft describes when speaking of "an unbounded sense of open vistas fraught with adventurous expectancy." What a fine place Antarctica is to let adventurous expectancy roam free, where vast mountains are merely glimpsed at in reality and speculated at with horrific dimensions in fiction! All told, *At the Mountains of Madness* has come to occupy an important position in the tradition of Antarctic fiction, seamlessly blending absolute polar realism found almost exclusively in nonfiction Antarctic literature and cosmic horror that takes advantage of the Antarctic's inherent quality of adventurous expectancy—that "half-glimpsed, half-suspected" notion that fills readers with awe and dread. And in this sense, Lovecraft has found in Antarctica a dark continent to call his own.

Works Cited

Borunda, Alejandra. "Coldest Place on Earth Found—Here's How." *National Geographic News* (6 June 2018).

Burleson, Donald R. *H. P. Lovecraft: A Critical Study*. Westport, CT: Greenwood Press, 1983.

Byrd, Richard E. *Little America—Aerial Exploration in the Antarctic: The Flight to the South Pole*. New York: G. P. Putnam's Sons, 1930.

Day, David. *Antarctica: A Biography*. Oxford: Oxford University Press, 2013.

Eckhardt, Jason C. "Behind the Mountains of Madness: Lovecraft and the Antarctic in 1930." *Lovecraft Studies* No. 14 (Spring 1987): 31-38.

Leane, Elizabeth. *Antarctica in Fiction: Imaginative Narrative of the Far South*. Cambridge: Cambridge University Press, 2012.

Lovecraft, H. P. *At the Mountains of Madness*. Manuscript A32500, Box 20, H. P. Lovecraft Special Collection, Brown University, 1931. Cited in text as MM.

———. *Letters to Rheinhart Kleiner*. New York: Hippocampus Press, 2005.

Navroth, John M. "Lovecraft and the Polar Myth." *Lovecraft Annual* No. 3 (2009): 190-99.

Price, Robert M. *H. P. Lovecraft and the Cthulhu Mythos*. Mercer Island, WA: Starmont House, 1990.

Riffenburgh, Beau. *Encyclopedia of the Antarctic*. Vol. 1. New York: Routledge, 2007.

Scott, Robert F., and Bradford F. Swan. "Chart of the Antarctic Ocean." *Antarctic Scrapbook*. Bradford F. Swan Antarctic Collection, John Hay Library, Brown University, 1946.

"Weather–Sunlight Hours." *The Australian Antarctic Division*. www.antarctica. gov.au. 2017.

Weinstock, Jeffrey A. "Tekeli-li!: Poe, Lovecraft, and the Suspicion of Sameness." In *The Lovecraftian Poe*, ed. Sean Moreland. Bethlehem, PA: Lehigh University Press, 2017. 51–68.

Alexander Blok and H. P. Lovecraft: On the Mythopoetics of the Supernatural

Elena Tchougounova-Paulson
Independent Scholar, Cambridge, UK

> Everything is already full of accords in the lilac twilight of the crushing worlds, although their laws are essentially different than before, because there is no golden sword anymore.
> —Alexander Blok, "O sovremennom sostoyanii russkogo simvolizma"[1]

> And then it was that my former high spirits received their damper.
> —H. P. Lovecraft, 16 November 1916

This essay analyses the vivid resemblance between the literary works of the Russian Symbolist poet Alexander Blok and American horror writer H. P. Lovecraft from the perspective of their mythopoetics. Such an approach is entirely original; although scholars have studied both authors extensively, none has attempted a comparative assessment of their aesthetic worldviews. I address not only the writings of Blok and Lovecraft but also their extra-textual ontology (their imagined universes), including the evolution of Blok's and Lovecraft's *Weltanschauung* as reflected in their heritage. The analysis proceeds in two stages. First, I classify the most significant publications on which a comparative study can be based; second, I establish the actual conception on the structural and typological levels, using primarily comparative and intertextual methods.

We might begin by asking both what mythopoetics is and where the genesis of its supernatural exceptionality lies. Although the number of interpretations of the term is wide,[2] we understand mythopoetics as an entirety of symbolic projections that anticipate the author's vision within his

---

1. All translations of quotations hereinafter are by the author.

2. For example, in works of Alexander Veselovsky and Mikhail Bakhtin.

lifetime and form the basis of his creative perception. The aesthetics of the supernatural, and myth as its major manifestation, have been an integral part of a continually evolving literary canon for a long time. Every historical era is connected with the phenomena of the supernatural, and its extent depends on the current period and territory, i.e., the actual reality *as is*.

At the same time, myth, as a transhistorical, archaic, continuous entity, with its supernatural metamorphic consequences, explicitly connects different cultural subjects, as Deleuze and Guattari show in their collective work, *A Thousand Plateaus*:

> The twofold idea "series-structure" crosses a scientific threshold at a certain moment; but it did not start there and it does not stay there, or else crosses over into other sciences, animating, for example, the human sciences, serving in the study of dreams, myths, and organizations. The history of ideas should never be continuous; it should be wary of resemblances, but also of descents or filiations; it should be content to mark the thresholds through which an idea passes, the journeys it takes that change its nature or object. (235)

In other words, to reveal supernatural discourse is to decipher the mythology of the author, to name it, to cross a threshold. Proceeding from that understanding, we seek to uncover the internal similarity between Blok's and Lovecraft's poetics of the supernatural, and to compare the evolution of the mythological elements in their works. Why, exactly, these two writers? Because there is a striking resemblance in the depth of their world perception and their philosophical development. Given the extensiveness of this topic, we offer here only an introductory commentary.

The works dedicated to Blok and Lovecraft (separately rather than comparatively) are voluminous. Of the two, only Blok has received significant attention in both Russian and Western literary studies, largely as the key figure in the literature of the Russian Silver Age. Lovecraft's work has remained primarily the domain of Western scholars, who have addressed his influence on modern American literature, fine art, and cinema. Although Lovecraft and his works are well known in Russia, few Russian scholars have addressed him or his place in American literature of the twentieth century. Existing work in Russian is preoccupied with the artistic methods used in his fiction, the structure of the Cthulhu Mythos, and Lovecraft's unquestionably substantial role in American neo-Gothic culture.

Comparing the poetics of the supernatural in Blok's and Lovecraft's works demands an examination of their entire *oeuvre*, including poetry, fiction, articles, and correspondence. Historians of twentieth-century literature regard Alexander Blok as one of the most substantial poets and essayists of the Russian Silver Age, part of the Modernist movement covering roughly the period of the late 1870s to 1917. What was the Silver Age? As Sibelan Forrester and Martha Kelly point out,

> it is the most fascinating period in Russian culture [. . .] Russian Silver Age poetry engages with classical Antiquity and Western European writings, of course, but also with Africa, the Far East, and the Americas. The Silver Age witnessed an unprecedented degree of collaboration of writers with visual artists, musicians, dancers, and other creative individuals. (x)

Blok began his literary career in the early 1900s, when he published his book *Verses on a Beautiful Lady*. It included his early poetic experiments named "Ante Lucem." As a poet, he undoubtedly belonged to the Symbolist circles and was connected with his elder contemporaries, the so-called Senior Symbolists Vyacheslav Ivanov, Innokenty Annensky, Valeriy Bryusov, Dmitry Merezhkovsky, and Zinaida Gippius, and with the Young Symbolists, such as Andrei Bely. As I have noted previously:

> It is clear that the specific character of Blok's influence on writers from the same generation was systematic; as a type of an artist, Blok cannot be called *poeta doctus* (i.e. an author whose poetry is academic per se); it is rather fair in regard to Vyacheslav Ivanov, Valery Bryusov and, somewhat, to Andrei Bely. But the most essential thing in Blok's poetic persona, the combination of conceptual, which could be referred to mind (intellect), and confessional, gave him the status of an indisputable authority. (Tchougounova-Paulson, "Alexander Blok and the 'Seal of Decadence'" 187)

Blok's works were heavily influenced by classical Greek philosophy (Platonism and, especially, Neoplatonism and Gnosticism), German Romanticism (Heinrich Heine), and, later, Nietzsche's works. The author whose impact on Blok was particularly profound was Vladimir Solovyov. (Blok was indirectly related to him.) Solovyov was a Russian mystical thinker, who created the concept of All-Unity (Всеединство). According to this conception, a whole perceptual world is preparing for a cosmic transformation where the redemption of Sophia-Eternal Wisdom, a central idea in Hellenistic philosophy and religion, Platonism, Gnosticism, and Christian theology, from the "ocean of world evil," and its manifestation to the people will be a central moment. That is how the Ecumenical Church will be made, and that is how a person will approach the perfect harmony in the unity of "immaculate" and "mundane." Solovyov, a poet, adopted and presented Gnostic ideas for the wider circles of Russian Dec-adent intellectuals, and he was known as a modern eschatological prophet who could predict a turbulent future for Russia and, broadly, for the whole world:

> Although the Symbolists and especially the Decadents often advanced the idea of art for art's sake, they never doubted the importance of a writer's civic mission and, therefore, of writing *publitsistika* (passionately committed journalism) for various media outlets: newspapers, journals, almanacs: "Vladimir Solovyov's poetry and religious philosophy ... helped set the tone for the period's exploitations of sex, love, and beauty." (Forrester and Kelly xiv)

Solovyov's ideas and *solovyovstvo* as a system of philosophical principles had an obvious and strong effect on Blok during nearly all his literary life: that was spotted by Blok's contemporaries and was widely discussed. It was done, for instance, by one the poet Zinaida Gippius, a Senior Symbolist, who wrote in her review of *Verses on a Beautiful Lady* (1904) that "Solo-vyov's shadow" was in Blok's book (Gippius 271).

Blok himself divided his literary heritage into three large phases; he called the process "a trilogy of incarnation" (Трилогия вочеловечения). Solovyov profoundly affected the first phase. Blok named the second "the period of antithesis" (Blok, *Sobraniye sochineniy* 5, 428):[3] it was affected by tremendous changes in Russian political life (the Russian-Japanese war 1904-05, the Russian Revolution of 1905, further political instability, which led to the beginning of World War I and the October Revolution) that were reflected in art, literature, and music. This period of Blok's prolif-ic activity roughly covered 1905-16 (until the start of his civil service in the 13th Engineering and Construction Brigade during World War I). And the third phase connected directly with the October Revolution, the beginning of the civil war in post-revolutionary Russia, and includes Blok's final years in Petrograd under the first Soviet government until his death in 1921.

During those two periods Blok created his most famous works, such as the poetry volumes *The Snow Mask* (1907), *Homeland* (1907-16), *Iambs* (1907-14), *The Harps and the Violins* (1908-16), *Retribution* (1908-13), *Ital-ian Poems* (1909), *The Terrible World* (1909-16), and *Danse Macabre* (1912-

---

3. "The whole pattern of feelings is changing drastically, the 'antithesis' is about to start, the 'change of an image,' which was already anticipated from the very beginning of the 'thesis'" (Blok, "On a Current State of Russian Symbolism," 428).

14); dramas such as *A Puppet Show* (1906), *The Unknown Woman* (1906), and *The Rose and the Cross* (1912–13); essays such as *Stagnation* (1906), *Nature and Culture* (1909), *People and Intelligentsia* (1909), *On the Current State of Russian Symbolism* (1910), and *Decline of Humanism* (1919); and the poems "The Twelve" (1918) and "The Scythians" (1918). We can say that in these two prolific decades Blok showed his full potential as a complex Modernist poet, dramatist, and essayist, whose mythopoetics could be associated with Nietzsche's philosophy directly and indirectly (through Wagner's opera symbology).[4] Nietzschean discourse can help to make an ontological juxtaposition of Blok's aesthetic and Lovecraftian overview. (In my work, I focus more on Lovecraft's prose than his poetry.)

As noted, Blok's mythological poetics, as in his early poetic cycles such as "Ante Lucem" and "Verses on a Beautiful Lady" (1900–04), originate from Platonism, Neoplatonism (Plotinus), Gnostic philosophy, and the doctrine of the Russian religious thinker Vladimir Solovyov. Indeed, the subject of Blok's early cosmological worldview versus ancient philosophy and Solovyov's ideas has been studied thoroughly. That being said, the primary idea of Blok's early Symbolist aesthetics—the Fair Lady–Sophia-Demiurge, Soul of the World–das Ewig-Weibliche (Eternal Feminine)—has an ambivalent, chaocosmic nature, and its ambiguity makes the poet think about the hidden, monstrous part of it, as he explained to his fiancée Lyubov Mendeleeva in a letter dated 21 November 1902: "This has happened to me—something that didn't obey my magic. Before, I collected the multitude inside me, having the power to lull some monsters and to rouse the others" (RGALI 39–40).

Why did things start changing so radically for the poet? There were very real and external reasons. As Dina Magomedova and Irina Prihodko argue,

> Eschatological predictions, the sense of *the end of time*, the expectation of the Antichrist, promises of "new skies and new lands" marked for contemporaries the inevitable and final end of the drama of human essence. The apocalyptic prophesy of Vladimir Solovyov in his last work "Three Talks" and the lecture "On the End of World History" ("О конце всемирной истории") that also got wide attention, had significant influence on the Symbolist mind. That ideological basis in forming a new mysteria was reinforced by philosophy and aesthetics; continuing Wagner and Nietzsche's doctrine, Symbolists were creating the theory of myth. (436)

---

4. See, for example, Kluge.

Blok felt those changes, expressing them in a letter to his colleague, friend, and rival Symbolist-poet Andrei Bely, dated 9 January 1903:

> Like never before, our poetic times perceived the dual nature of the Universe as far as the prophetic insight, and they did it in a musical way, in a way that spatial images were rejected for the sake of more sensitive listening to "the rhyme." (Blok, 1990, 102)

I have referred to these changes in "Alexander Blok and the 'Seal of Decadence.'" The fact that traces of Vladimir Solovyov's *irony* became faintly visible in Blok's "Majestic Eternal Wife" (*Величавой Вечной Жене*) gives evidence that Blok's poetic method was developing not only as a reduction of Solovyov's All-Unity (*Всеединство*), but also as a distinctive expression of the constant duality of Blok's main character, the Fair Lady-Sophia (Eternal) Wisdom–Das Ewig-Weibliche, which in this connection took other names, such as "the Mysterious Maiden of Sunset" (*Закатная Таинственная Дева*), Faceless (*Безликая*), etc. As Veronika Shenshin has said, "Blok blamed Vadimir Solovyov, calling it a disease, the destructive, inane and desperate laugh of the possessed" (139–40).

Blok's self-identification with Russian Symbolism, with its main prophet Vladimir Solovyov, turned out to be quite excruciating: the power of a dark side, seductive and dangerous, which essentially is the matter of Decadence, which means decline and decay, attracted Blok and at the same time repelled him; that's why Blok's close friend and second cousin, the poet Sergey Solovyov,[5] in his letter to Blok on 29 September 1903 wrote about "this impression of horror" (341) from his poems. At the same time, young Blok himself was very critical of his colleagues of this genre, whose fame was inseparably connected to the Symbolist/Decadent movement—Zinaida Gippius, Dmitry Merezhkovsky, Alexander Dobroliubov[6]—and we can see the signs of his anger and disappointment with their ideas, for instance, in his letter to Sergey Solovyov of 23 December 1902:

> Mme Merezhkovsky expressed once that Solovyov has become obsolete and that "we" have to go further. The more she talks about these things (and also

---

5. Solovyov Sergey Mikhailovich (1885–1942), Russian Symbolist poet, a nephew of Vladimir Solovyov.

6. Dobroliubov Alexander Mikhailovich (1876–1944?), Russian Symbolist poet, who became a god-seeker and founded a cult of *dobroliubovtsy* (Free Christians). In the early 1900s, he was famous in St. Petersburg for his religious strivings.

about lots of others), the more I feel angry at her, and sometimes I feel it so strongly that it's just too much, and I start to remind myself of her undisputable talents. [. . .] To crown it all, there is Mr Dobroliubov, who comes out from the stage and who is "recovered." Our place is sacred. (Blok, *Sobraniye sochineniy* 48-49)

The other—dark and destructive—side of Blok's mythopoetic universe is far more distinguishable in his later poetic cycles (roughly starting from 1904), critical essays, and dramas. The motives of the universal consent of powers of chaos, the long vacillation between harmony and dissonance created a new system of consistency of these changes in Blok's aesthetic position. In his point of view, Symbolism determines the initial recognition of the creative personality of its unchallenged power, and constant in-depth study of its dark sides reveals the individual world of the artist (Tchougounova-Paulson, "Alexander Blok and the 'Seal of Decadence'").

Blok dubbed his retreat from Gnostic-Solovyovian mysticism and move to Wagneresque and Nietzschean aesthetics as "the period *of* antithesis": in poetical series such as *Bubbles of the Earth* (*Пузыри земли,* 1904-05), *The City* (*Город,* 1904-08), *The Snow Mask* (*Снежная маска,* 1907), *The Terrible World* (*Страшный мир,* 1909-16), *Iambs* (*Ямбы,* 1907-14), and *The Harps and the Violins* (*Арфы и скрипки,* 1908-16), Blok searched for new forms and patterns, and his myth (or, more precisely, his mythopoetics) became ever more complicated and ambivalent. Seeking a definition in his manifesto "On the New State of Russian Symbolism" ("О современном состоянии русского символизма," 1910), he wrote:

And here is the end of "the thesis." And now, the miracle of the lonely transfiguration is beginning. [. . .] The tempest has already touched the Fair Face, it has been nearly incarnated, and *the Name is almost unraveled.* Everything has been foreseen except one: *the dead spot of a feast.* This is the hardest moment of the transition from the thesis to the antithesis which has been already defined a posteriori and which I am able to describe only by adding the fictional presence of some outsider. (a person whom I don't know). (Blok, Sobraniye sochineniy 5, 423; emphasis mine)

On the one hand, Blok's new phenomenology with its transvaluation of all values granted him more aesthetic freedom, yet on the other, it emphasized his sense of catastrophe and made his poetic world simultaneously more powerful and more macabre. The dual and ambivalent nature of Blok's lyrical world has vividly manifested itself in the poems from the second book of his works, *Unexpected Joy* (Chugunova 9).

Thus Alexander Blok in *Unexpected Joy* and the essays of that time is a spontaneous creator of myths, for whom

> myth is a "figurative disclosure of the immanent truth of spiritual self-affirmation of public and universal." Myth is a disclosure of embodiment. . . . the dark element of a symbol is painfully necessary step to sunny music, to light universal myth. (Blok, *Sobraniye sochineniy* 5, 10)

The motifs of "sunny music" that might have helped to create the "light universal myth" were gradually but inevitably replaced by new, demonic ones. Moreover, the variety of poetic meters Blok used at that time, including free verse and so-called *taktovik*, or the strict accentual verse, helped to accentuate these motifs. The iconic example of this poetic transfiguration of the supernatural elements in Blok's worldview is his poem "The Puppet Show" ("Балаганчик," 1905). Here Blok defines his new principles, which we would term as principles *Post Lucem*.[7] As Magomedova argues,

> motifs of a sin (betrayal of the previous values, self-betrayal as an attempt to obtain new, positive, values, to break the borders of a previous, harmonious, but closed, world of the Beautiful Lady) occupied an extremely substantial place in [Blok's] lyrics in the period of "antithesis" . . . the denial of an absolutized ideal of Immobility was definitely positive for Blok, bringing his poetry to new fields of natural and social reality, . . . to creation of a new, disharmoniously unstable world view. (142, 143)

In other words, Blok rejects his overly abstract and academic structure of Gnostic and Neoplatonic doctrines in favor of a new, more diverse image of his mythopoetical universe, and his phenomenology has evolved from thesis to antithesis. And we find a striking resemblance between Blok's aesthetical transformations and the philosophical explorations of H. P. Lovecraft.

Let us then turn to Lovecraft and his own aesthetic transformation. Before Lovecraft created his outstanding mythology of the Great Old Ones (or anti-mythology,[8] as David E. Schultz has dubbed it and about which we shall

---

7. As an opposition to Blok's first lyrical cycles, "Ante Lucem" (1899–1900) and "Verses on a Beautiful Lady" (1902–04).

8. HPL's comment shows that his "pseudo-mythology" is not so much a "false" or made-up mythology, but an anti-mythology—the only kind of mythology that could be possible in this day and age. It is not a mythology of the kind invented or believed in by previous cultures—lore or legend intended to explain or account for the history of humankind, the history of the universe, the exploits of heroes, and so on. See Schultz 222.

say more below), let us see how his world perception and his mythopoetics had developed. Like Blok in his early years with his commitment to the ancient era (not only to specific philosophers, but to the ambiguous Gnostic aesthetics), Lovecraft also demonstrated a vivid interest in Greco-Roman mythology at quite a young age, in later years even calling himself a "pagan" in his "A Confession of Unfaith":

> When about seven or eight I was a genuine pagan, so intoxicated with the beauty of Greece that I acquired a half-sincere belief in the old gods and Nature-spirits. I have in literal truth built altars to Pan, Apollo, Diana, and Athena, and have watched for dryads and satyrs in the woods and fields at dusk. Once I firmly thought I beheld some of these sylvan creatures dancing under autumnal oaks; a kind of "religious experience" as true in its way as the subjective ecstasies of any Christian. (CE 5.146)

To be sure, Lovecraft's interest in antiquity was prominent but not entirely consistent. Moreover, he acquired it through contact with modern, rather than ancient, sources. Nevertheless, similarities with Blok are evident.[9] As S. T. Joshi has noted,

> Lovecraft is certainly to be commended for his brief citations of fantasy in ancient literature (even though some of these were derived from second-hand sources), although I find it a little surprising that he does not cite Greek epic [. . .], Greek and Roman tragedy [. . .], and other random works such as Lucian's *True History* of Catullus 63 (the "Attis" poem), which he must have read. (*Lovecraft and a World in Transition* 426–27)

A significant amount of Lovecraft's writings bears clear traces of ancient doctrines, including the occult and Gnostic (though primarily Greek

---

9. Blok adopted Platonic, Neoplatonic, and Gnostic doctrines through Solovyov's works: being a student, he read a lot of the ancient sources, such as Plato, Pythagoras, Thales of Miletus, Anaximander, Aristotle etc., and it is well known that Solovyov was not only the most important Gnostic philosopher of the *fin de siècle*, but a professional historian and translator of Hellenistic philosophy. Blok started studying Greek philosophy from the book *Plato: Selected Works* (*Платон: Творения,* 1899), which Solovyov translated, and wrote about to his father on 1 December 1900: "My philosophical study, Plato primarily, aren't moving that fast. I am still reading and re-reading the first volume in Solovyov's translation—Socratic dialogues." Cited in Tchougounova-Paulson, "The Letters of A. Blok as a Historical Source and a Literary Phenomenon of the Russian Fin De Siècle," *Reshaping the Boundaries of the Epistolary Discourse*, The Inter-Disciplinary Press (2016), e-book, np

and Egyptian). Among these works are "The Tomb" (1917), "The Doom That Came to Sarnath" (1919), "The Cats of Ulthar" (1920), "Celephaïs" (1922), and "Nyarlathotep" (1920). In his article "A Confession of Unfaith," Lovecraft himself offered a curious description of his own encounters with antiquity during his formative years:

> I read much in Egyptian, Hindoo, and Teutonic mythology, and tried experiments in pretending to believe each one to see which might contain the greatest truth. I had, it will be noted, immediately adopted the method and manner of science!" [. . .] The most poignant sensations of my existence are those in 1896, when I discovered the Hellenic world. (CE 5.146, 147)

All the ancient traces in Lovecraft's world outlook could easily come under the umbrella of cosmicism, a concept that furthermore connects him to Blok's ambivalent or "chaocosmic" system of views. Remarkably, even the term cosmicism, which Lovecraft maintained was a guiding principle in his work, is closely related to Symbolist "cosmism." This concept derived, at least in part, from Vladimir Solovyov's writings, although Solovyov's predominantly Gnostic doctrine conveys the idea that humankind personifies living Logos (see Kurakina 91–113), whereas cosmicism considers humankind insignificant (i.e., anti-Logos, chaocosmic *par excellence*). In the years of his literary activity, Lovecraft is developing his understanding of cosmicism, outgrowing the influence of his elder contemporaries Ambrose Bierce and Lord Dunsany[10] and pretty much elaborating the idea of cosmicism in his most essential work, "The Call of Cthulhu" (1926). As Joshi writes, defining the term, "In particular, he [Lovecraft] points out the 'cosmicism'—the central principle in his fiction, involving the suggestion of the vast gulfs of space and time and the consequent triviality of the human race—of many authors whose actual sense of the cosmic was probably very small" (Lovecraft, *Annotated Supernatural* 5).

Lovecraft's cosmicism transforms itself into a mythology of a new

---

10. See Joshi, *Lovecraft and a World in Transition* 427. See also "Some Notes on a Nonentity" (1933), wherein HPL states that he got the idea of the artificial pantheon and myth-background represented by Cthulhu, Yog-Sothoth, Yuggoth, etc. from Dunsany, who in *The Gods of Pegāna* and *Time and the Gods* (and in those volumes alone) wrote a linked series of tales involving an invented pantheon in the imaginary realm of *Pegāna*. HPL wrote a lecture read before an amateur journalists' group, "Lord Dunsany and His Work" (1922). HPL also discusses Dunsany in "Supernatural Horror in Literature" (1927).

kind, where the main component is horror as a model of the perception of the supernatural. Lovecraft's symbology—which includes his conceptions of the Great Old Ones, the ageless creatures documented (yet not explained) in the *Necronomicon*—describes the universe as incompatible with mundane existence and incomprehensible to the human mind. As consequence of the latter, the universe remains dark and ultimately anti-human, which looks very much like the duality of Blok's interpretation of Sophia (Logos) that began in his *Verses on a Beautiful Lady* and developed later, portraying Blok's post-Gnostic cosmogony as "damned," unpredictable, and "demonic."[11] As Ramsey Campbell describes,

> The Mythos was conceived as an antidote to conventional Victorian occultism—as an attempt to reclaim the imaginative appeal of the unknown—and is only one of many ways his tales suggest worse, or greater, than they show. It is also just one of his means of reaching for a sense of wonder, the aim that produces the visionary horror of his finest work (by no means all of it belonging to the Mythos). (155-56)

We see this "imaginative appeal of the unknown" as the precise intersection of two mythopoetics of the supernatural in Lovecraft's and Blok's legacies. This intersection, moreover, exists regardless of the differences between the cultural sources of the writers' development, the foundations on which their works had to grow and progress, and even the languages in which they wrote. That distinction remains something, we argue, as typical of the whole culture of the *fin de siècle* era, with its eschatology and absolutely new way of aesthetic self-representation in all its dramatic and linguistically complicated aspects, which "addressed class enmity or cultural decline à la Oswald Spengler, themes that had been important in Realism, with fresh aesthetic power" (Forrester and Kelly xiv). In that sense, Lovecraft, like Blok, was a writer in ideological transition from the *fin de siècle*, with its typical demand for transcendent insights, to a later Modernist turn with its eerie, or chthonic, aesthetics, heavily impacted by World War I.

Both Blok's and Lovecraft's mythopoetics went through several stages of evolution, a progression motivated by an aspiration to uncover the fear of the unknown, to decipher its symbolic language, and to embody it in artistic forms. Significantly, although Blok was a religious person[12] and Lovecraft

---

11. See, for example, the feedback on Blok's "demonology" from Russian religious thinkers, such as the Russian Orthodox theologian Pavel Florensky. See Pyman 54-70.

12. Not in a traditional way, because at the time the relationship between the Russian

was not, their aesthetic perceptions bore a striking resemblance. Their mythologies were dramatically different from the literary mainstream, as Blok's
was genuinely alien and new even for the Symbolist circles, and Lovecraft's
was unique amidst all the works of his American contemporaries. Lovecraft elucidated his creative method in his emblematic work "Supernatural
Horror in Literature," wherein he also defined horror literature:

> The oldest and strongest emotion of mankind is fear, and the oldest and
> strongest kind of fear is fear of the unknown. These facts few psychologists
> will dispute, and their admitted truth must establish for all time the genu
> ineness and dignity of the weirdly horrible tale as a literary form. [. . .] The
> appeal of the spectrally macabre is generally narrow because it demands from
> the reader a certain degree of imagination and a capacity for detachment
> from everyday life. (Lovecraft, *Annotated Supernatural* 25)

In Blok's prose, we detect a similar dramatic approach, particularly
when he writes about this peculiar, suggestive and fearsome effect of the
literary work:

> People, beware, don't get closer to a lyric. "He doesn't sting a heart like a
> snake, but sucks it like a bee." He has come out of that damned lair that you
> are slipping past, crossing yourself, and he is now ready, putting the pipe to
> his lips, this innocent flute, to tell you about something that you'd better not
> listen to; otherwise, being overwhelmed, you, the meek, shall wander all
> around the world. (Blok, *Sobraniye sochineniy* 5, 131-32)

Blok's works of the era of antithesis, especially the article "Stagnation"
("Безвременье," 1906), and poetic cycles such as *The Terrible World*
(*Страшный Мир*, 1909-16), *Danse Macabre* (*Пляски смерти*, 1912-14),
and *The Life of My Companion* (*Жизнь моего приятеля*, 1913-15)
demonstrate the dehumanized world's horrific and tragic impact on
human existence.[13] If we look at Blok's poems and essays written between
1906 and 1916 (when he was involved in the civil service during the World

---

intelligentsia and the Orthodox Church was quite complicated. There was a time
when intellectuals were trying to modernize religion, among them Vladimir Solovyov,
Dmitry Merezhkovsky, Nikolay Berdyaev, and others. As I have pointed out in "The
Letters of A. Blok as a Historical Source and a Literary Phenomenon of the Russian
Fin de Siècle," "So-called White Synthesis of the Kingdom of the Third (and the final) Testament" proclaimed Dmitry Merezhkovsky in the vast majority of his philosophical works. See, for example, Merezhkovskiy 24-25.

13. See Tchougounova-Paulson, "Alexander Blok and the 'Seal of Decadence'" 187-97.

War I), we can say that they vividly demonstrate what Blok described later as the "decline of humanism." Blok's characters at that time are mostly ambivalent "anti-heroes" and Doppelgängers ("The Song of Hell," "Demon," "Danse Macabre," "Humiliation," "Black Blood," etc.), which makes his mythopoetic infernal, mythopoetic "De Profundis." As Rita Spivak writes,

> The state in Chaos ("awe of Chaos") for Blok means that "the world is sinking in wickedness." Blind fate dominates there as well as the "dark (vulturous) principle", disorder, and formlessness. . . . That state of "madness and the vicissitudes of life", which is unable to distinguish goodness from evil that could be absolute and relative. In Blok's articles and notes the world embraced by Chaos, has got the image of a terrible "world's wheel", where the movement is losing its progress and turning into something aimless, chaotic. (29–30)

The poems "Night, street, street-light, apothecary . . ." ("Ночь, улица, фонарь, аптека . . ."), "The worlds are flying, the years are going . . ." ("Миры летят. Года летят. Пустая. . ."), and "The day was going as always. . ." ("День проходил как всегда. . .") are especially revealing in this sense. The notion of the circle as a frightening "world's wheel" that turns the dehumanized world around pointlessly essentially has the same meaning as Lovecraft's dark universe and its anti-mythology:

> Now all my tales are based on the fundamental premise that common human laws and interests and emotions have no validity or significance in the vast cosmos-at-large. [. . .] To achieve the essence of real extremity, whether of time or space or dimension, one must forget that such things as organic life, good and evil, love and hate, and all such local attributes of a negligible and temporary race called mankind, have any existence at all. (SL 2.150)

Compare the preceding with the following fragment from Blok's "Stagnation":

> Now, a new species of people has developed, who turned these ideas [nature, art, literature] upside down and, despite that, announced themselves as normal. They became fussy and pale. Their passions died, and nature is alienated and not comprehensible for them anymore. [. . .] They lost eventually, while walking along paths of languishing, first God, then the world, and finally themselves. (Blok, *Sobraniye sochineniy* 5, 68)

The fatality of the transformation of Blok's and Lovecraft's mythopoetics (anti-mythological in the case of Lovecraft, chaocosmic in Blok's case), the essence of their supernatural, and their claim to the monstrous side of life make them eschatologists *par excellence*:

> Ben Woodard invokes Lovecraft in 2012's *Slime Dynamics* to paint a picture of a universe crawling with life repugnant to human taste and sensibility that not only calls into question human assumptions about evolution and forces us to consider the degree to which higher intelligence is a significant advantage, but also prompts the very Lovecraftian realization of a universe inhospitable to human beings. This leads Woodard to postulate a philosophical principle he refers to as "dark vitalism," a rethinking of traditional philosophical vitalism that strips humanity of its exceptionalism and resituates it as the fragile product of cosmic coincidence. (Sederholm and Weinstock 7)

The "world's wheel" metaphor is another link Blok and Lovecraft, one that is clearly related to Friedrich Nietzsche's "Eternal Recurrence." In Blok's case the brightest implementation of Nietzschean ideas can be seen in his famous article written in 1906, "Stagnation" ("Безвременье," 1906), which, as it turns out, has much in common with *Also Sprach Zarathustra: Ein Buch für Alle und Keinen* (*Thus Spoke Zarathustra: A Book for All and None*). The title itself, "Stagnation," also could be the evidence of a Nietzschean context of Blok's poetry and prose of this time, the era of the antithesis. Though Nietzsche himself didn't use this word very much to describe the pointlessness of "mechanical existence," he used his own terms, such as "disappeared time," "non-existing time." In "Stagnation" we can see how the idea of eternal recurrence appeared in Blok's poetics. For example, writing about the tragic fate of Russia, he said in particular that

> Time doesn't exist anymore. [. . .] I think, everything, which had to happen on this long way, has already happened. No aim, because everything was attained; everything contains the sign of accomplishment. The cross was out inside a soul, and a soul in its eternal aspiration every moment feels its limits" (Blok, *Sobraniye sochineniy* 5, 75).

In this sense, Lovecraft's Decadent ideas of cosmic (and blind) fate and horror are absolutely consonant with Nietzschean discourse. Not for nothing does Lovecraft contend in his "Nietzscheism and Realism" that

> There are no absolute values in the whole blind tragedy of mechanistic Nature—nothing is either good or bad except as judged from an absurdly limited point of view.
>
> The only cosmic reality is mindless, undeviating fate—automatic, unmoral, uncalculating inevitability. (CE 5.167)

That is to say that Blok and Lovecraft were fearless enough to face that unwelcomed world, to describe its madness, to anticipate its myths and its power.

Despite the introductory nature of the analysis in this essay, five initial conclusions are evident. First, despite their obvious differences (first and foremost, linguistic and geographical), Blok's and Lovecraft's cultural resemblance is evident in a deconstruction of their personal mythology. Second, the identification of the supernatural and its development in their aesthetic worldviews is a function of the evolution of their mythopoetics. Indeed, this connection is the key to theoretical comprehension of their literary biographies. Third, Blok's and Lovecraft's mythopoetics each underwent considerable changes. In Blok's case, it was the period of antithesis; in Lovecraft's, it was the creation of anti-mythology. Fourth, Blok's period of antithesis introduced the possibility of Chaos as a state of world madness (reflected in poetic cycles such as *The Terrible World* and *Iambs,* and in various critical essays, for instance); Lovecraft considered world madness as a turning point for creating cosmic horror ("Cthulhu Mythos," the conception of the Great Old Ones). Finally, Blok's aesthetics of the period of anti-thesis and Lovecraft's anti-mythology have clear links to the philosophy of Friedrich Nietzsche in general and to the notion of Eternal Recurrence in particular. Without doubt, there is much more to discover about the worlds of Alexander Blok and H. P. Lovecraft and their interconnectedness.

Works Cited

Bagauv, Y. D. "Neogotika kak fenomen sovremennoy khudozhestvennoy kul'tury." Dis kand. kul'turologii. Chita: Zabaykal'skiy gos. un-t, 2013.

Blok Aleksandr. *Sobraniye sochineniy v vos'mi tomakh.* Moscow: GIKHL, 1960.

———. *Polnoye sobraniye sochineniy i pisem v dvadtsati tomakh.* T. 6 Kniga 1. *Dramaticheskiye proizvedeniya (1906–1908).* Moscow: Nauka, 2014.

———. *Issledovaniya i materialy.* Moscow: Nauka, 1991.

———. *Issledovaniya i materialy.* St. Petersburg: Izdatel'stvo Instituta russkoy literatury (Pushkinskiy Dom) 'Dmitriy Bulavin,' 1998.

Blok, Aleksandr, and Andrey Bely. *Dialog poetov o Rossii i revolyutsii.* Moscow: Vysshaya shkola, 1990.

Blokovskiy sbornik. Trudy Vtoroy nauchnoy konferentsii, posvyashchennoy izucheniyu zhizni i tvorchestva A. A. *Bloka.* Tartu: Izdatel'stvo TGU, 1972.

Campbell, Ramsey. "H. P. Lovecraft." In *Morphologies: Short Story Writers on Short Story Writers.* ed. Ra Page. Manchester: Comma Press, 2013.

Chugunova, Ye. Ye. "Problema 'stikhiynosti' v tvorcheskom opyte Aleksandra Bloka." Dis. . . . Kand. filol. nauk. Moskow: Institut mirovoy literatury RAN, 2003.

Deleuze, Gilles, and Félix Guattari. *A Thousand Plateaus: Capitalism and Schizophrenia.* Trans. Brian Massumi. Minneapolis: University of Minnesota Press, 1987.

Forrester, Sibelan E. S., and Martha M. F. Kelly, ed. *Russian Silver Age Poetry: Texts and Contexts.* Boston: Academic Studies Press, 2015.

Gippius, Z. N. "Literaturnye zametki. 'Stikhi o Prekrasnoy Dame.'" *Novy Put* No. 12 (1904): 271.

Joshi, S. T.. *Lovecraft and a World in Transition: Collected Essays on H. P. Lovecraft.* New York: Hippocampus Press, 2014.

Joshi, S. T., and David E. Schultz. *An H. P. Lovecraft Encyclopedia.* 2001. New York: Hippocampus Press, 2004.

Kluge, R.-D. *Westeuropa und Russland im Weltbild Alexandr Bloks.* Munich: Otto Sagner, 1967.

Koval'kova T. M. "Goticheskaya traditsiya v amerikanskoy proze 1920-30-kh godov: novellistika G. F. Lavkrafta." Dis Kand. filol. nauk. Saransk: Saranskiy gos. un-t, 2001.

Kurakina O. D. "Sofiynaya estetika russkogo kosmizma." *Oriyentiry.* Vyp.2. Pod red. T.B. Lyubimovoy. M.: IF RAN, 2003. 91–113.

Lovecraft, H. P. *Against Religion: The Atheist Writings of H. P. Lovecraft.* Ed. S. T. Joshi. New York: Sporting Gentlemen, 2010.

———. *The Annotated Supernatural Horror in Literature.* Ed. S. T. Joshi. New York: Hippocampus Press, 2nd ed. 2012.

Magomedova D. M. *Avtobiograficheskiy mif v tvorchestve* A. *Bloka.* Moscow: Izdatel'stvo "Martin," 1997.

Merezhkovskiy, D. S. *Ne mir, no mech. K budushchey kritike khristianstva.* St. Petersburg: Izdanie M.V. Pirozhkova, 1908.

Nalitova Y. "Problema mifa i antimifa v tvorchestve Govarda Fillipsa Lavkrafta." www.bogoslov.ru/text/3340846.html. Accessed 29 October 2016.

Oriyentiry. Vyp.2. Pod red. T. B. Lyubimovoy. Moscow: IF RAN, 2003.

"Perepiska Bloka s S.M. Solovyovym (1896–1915)." Vstup. Statya, publikatsii i kommentarii N. V. Kotrelyova i A. V. Lavrova. *Literaturnoe nasledstvo.* T.92. Kniga 1. Moscow: Nauka, 1980. 308–407.

Pyman, Avril. "Tvorchestvo Aleksandra Bloka v otsenke russkikh religioznykh mysliteley 20–30 gg." *Blokovsky sbornik*, XII. Moscow: Tartusky universitet, Kafedra russkoi literatury, 1993.

Reshaping the Boundaries of the Epistolary Discourse. Oxford: Inter-Disciplinary Press, 2015. Ebook. www.academia.edu/

Schultz, David E. "From Microcosm to Macrocosm: The Growth of Lovecraft's Cosmic Vision." In *An Epicure in the Terrible: A Centennial Anthology of Essays in Honor of H. P. Lovecraft*, ed. David E. Schultz and S. T. Joshi. 1991. New York: Hippocampus Press, 2011. 208–29.

Sederholm, Carl H., and Jeffrey Andrew Weinstock, ed. *The Age of Lovecraft.* Minneapolis: University of Minnesota Press, 2016.

Solovyev, V. S. *Soch.<ineniya>*: V 2 t. Moscow: "Pravda," 1989.

Spivak, R. S. A. *Blok. Filosofskaya lirika 1910-kh godov. Uchebnoye posobiye po spetskursu.* Perm: Permskiy Universitet, 1978.

Tchougounova-Paulson, E. "Alexander Blok and the 'Seal of Decadence.'" In *The Proceedings of the Sixth Conference "Language, Culture and Society."* London: Senate House, University of London, 2015. 187–97.

———. "Gnostic Motives in the Early Correspondence Between A. Blok and L. Mendeleeva." Theses for BASEES-2014. www.academia.edu/6671079/ Gnostic_Motives_in_the_Early_Correspondence_Between_A._Blok_and_ L._Mendeleeva Accessed 29 October 2016.

———. "The Letters of A. Blok as a Historical Source and a Literary Phenomenon of the Russian Fin De Siècle." *Reshaping the Boundaries of the Epistolary Discourse.* The Inter-Disciplinary Press 2016. e-book, np.

At the Mountains of Mars: Viewing the Red Planet through a Lovecraftian Lens

Edward Guimont
University of Connecticut

Introduction

No planet in the solar system has been the subject of more baseless speculation than Mars" (*CE* 3.24). Thus begins "Is Mars an Inhabited World?," an article published in the *Pawtuxet Valley Gleaner* (7 September 1906) by the sixteen-year-old H. P. Lovecraft. Although referring to contemporary scientific debates over the existence and meaning of the supposed "Martian canals" first observed in 1877, Lovecraft's comments were equally applicable to the science fiction of his time. Lovecraft's own first published work—a letter to the editor of the *Providence Sunday Journal* on 3 June 1906 in response to basic errors in an astrology column—had come only three months earlier, and itself focused on the astrologer's lack of understanding of Mars' orbit (*CE* 3.16). At seventeen Lovecraft met Percival Lowell, the astronomer who from 1892 to 1910 popularized the notion that the canals were the constructs of a dying civilization.

Lovecraft fiction is filled with real astronomical objects and contemporary discoveries, most famously the 1901 GK Persei nova in "Beyond the Wall of Sleep" (1919) and the discovery of Pluto in 1930 in "The Whisperer in Darkness." The novella "The Shadow out of Time" mentions intelligent aliens from Mercury, Venus, a moon of Jupiter, and several extrasolar planets. Mars, however, and any potential inhabitants are absent from Lovecraft's fiction, being mentioned only once in "Through the Gates of the Silver Key." Why might this be?

The reasons for the absence of Mars in Lovecraft's fiction cannot be known for sure, but given his political, scientific, and literary views, several reasons can be postulated. Although Mars itself is almost completely absent, contemporary theories about Mars, especially those of Lowell, can be seen as influencing Lovecraft's late fiction—as can Mars-related works of fiction by the likes of Edgar Rice Burroughs, G. P. Serviss, and especially H. G. Wells in *The War of the Worlds*. But despite its terrestrial setting, *At the Mountains of Madness* is a work that draws the most from the Martian themes of prior science and science fiction alike. With its depiction of a realistically planned expedition to an inhospitable environment, it marks a sort of transition between the more fantastic planetary romances of earlier authors and the more scientific bent of later writers of both fiction and nonfiction, who speculated on what expeditions to Mars might resemble. And from Lovecraft's own lifetime up until the present, there has been no shortage of pasticheurs willing to bring the Cthulhu Mythos and its themes—and sometimes even Lovecraft himself—to the Red Planet.

Searching for Mars

Scholarship on the role of Mars in science and science fiction during Lovecraft's time provides some circumstantial reasoning for its absence in Lovecraft's works. Lovecraft identified himself as a "Verne enthusiast [and] many of my tales showed the literary influence of the immortal Jules" (*Letters to Rheinhart Kleiner* 29), and Jules Verne ignored Mars almost completely (Harpold 29-35). Or perhaps Lovecraft's anti-communism (Joshi, "Political and Economic Thought") was a reason, turning him off of Mars due to its adoption by socialist authors, who took its nickname of the Red Planet to heart (Lane 170-85; Schroeder 13-14). Mars was particularly prominent in Soviet science fiction, most notably Aleksandr Bogdanov's *Red Star* (1908) and *Engineer Menni* (1913), both influenced by H. G. Wells, and Aleksei Tolstoi's *Aelita* (1923), influenced by Edgar Rice Burroughs and in 1924 adapted into the first Soviet blockbuster film (Crossley 174-76; Yudina 51-55). Meddy Ligner used this combination to great effect in his short story "Trajectory of a Cursed Spirit" set in an alternate history where the Soviets relocated their gulags from Siberia to Mars. The story follows a purged Party official who falls under the sway of the Great Old Ones once resident on Mars, and who caused the once-lush world to waste away to the airless desert it now is. Lovecraft's typical Cyclopean monoliths are replaced by enormous sculptures of Marx, Engels, Lenin, and Stalin, and the protagonist's ultimate physical obliteration in an underground tomb of a Great Old One mirrors his spiritual obliteration in the gulag.

Beyond the political overtones of Martian fiction, another possible reason for the lack of the planet in Lovecraft's work was that he was merely reflecting the science of his era, the 1930s being a time when astronomers were less attentive toward Mars and the planet was relatively insignificant to science (Huntington 80-85; Crossley, *Imagining Mars* 168-70). This was demonstrated in contemporary fiction by Martian tales increasingly focusing on the Red Planet as simply a setting for either 'sword and planet' swashbuckling tales or satires of such earthly issues as sexuality, racism, war, and colonialism (Caidin et al. 98-102; Lane 201-13). And as noted in his 1934 essay "Some Notes on Interplanetary Fiction," Lovecraft believed that "Social and political satire are always undesirable" in speculative fiction (CE 2.181).

As scientific interest in Mars revived after the 1930s doldrums, it became increasingly clear that there was no intelligent life, and perhaps no life at all, on the world. Martian fiction of this era tended to be set on a habitable, canal-ridden Mars based not on science but nostalgia of the Lowell era. The archetypal example of this postwar trope is Ray Bradbury's *The Martian Chronicles* (1950). Lovecraft is even mentioned in the story "Usher II," along with Edgar Allan Poe and Ambrose Bierce, as one of the authors whose works a character hopes to preserve on Mars from Earthly censors (Bradbury 105). In another story, "The Exiles," Lovecraft initially appeared, as the story depicted Mars as a sort of purgatory for authors whose works were being destroyed on Earth; Lovecraft eats ice cream and writes letters to L. Frank Baum, Samuel Johnson, and Charles Dickens. However, Bradbury removed Lovecraft's appearance from all subsequent reprints of the story (Perridas).

While Bradbury was representative of one authorial tendency, that of simply ignoring the modern consensus on Mars, others dealt by transferring the trope of the dying desert planet to different solar systems. Anthea from Walter Tevis's novel *The Man Who Fell to Earth* (1963) and Arrakis from Frank Herbert's novel *Dune* (1965) are early examples of this "Martian imposter syndrome" (Crossley, "Cultural Mirror" 166-68; Caidin et al. 110-36). Even in *Star Wars* (1977), in a scene on the desert world Tatooine, Greedo—the green-skinned, bug-eyed bounty hunter whom Han shoots first—was referred to by the production crew simply as "Martian" (Titelman 61). This trend was finalized by the arrival of the Space Age to

Mars: on July 15, 1965—two weeks prior to the publication of *Dune*—NASA's *Mariner 4* became the first spacecraft to return images from Mars. Showing a world that appeared completely desiccated and crater-blasted, it seemed to put the question of Martians to rest—although a few dissenters claimed the pictures were too grainy and few to fully dismiss the belief in canals (Caidin et al. 128–29).

The Lowell Influence

If other locations could symbolically step in for Mars after the start of the Space Age, why couldn't it have happened earlier, too? Lovecraft was, after all, a man ahead of his time in so many other genre innovations. As it was, his own view of Lowell's theory of intelligent canal-building Martians has a tumultuous history, as seen in a series of his early newspaper articles on astronomy. In 1903, he wrote that Lowell's claims were "perfectly ridiculous" (CE 3.15); in 1906, that they were "not only possible, but even probable" (CE 3.24–25); in 1915, 1917, and 1918, that the "true nature of the canals . . . is a matter of great dispute" but deserved consideration based on the fact that Lowell was the "leading authority on all matters relating to the planet Mars" (CE 3.291-94, 319-20, 251-54). In 1917, he penned an elegiac poem dedicated to Lowell after the astronomer's death the year before (AT 107). Yet amidst all this praise, Lovecraft stated in a 1916 letter that "I never had, have not, and never will have the slightest belief in Lowell's speculations" (SL 1.21-22).

However, nearly the whole of Lovecraft's output contains material and topics that he himself, the atheist materialist skeptic, did not personally believe in. While Lovecraft did argue that interplanetary fiction needed to adhere strictly to the latest scientific knowledge (CE 2.180), his one signif-icant entry in the genre, the 1936 short story "In the Walls of Eryx" (co-written with Kenneth Sterling), was set on a Venus depicted as swampy, despite that popular trope having been disproven by spectroscopic obser-vation as early as 1921 (St. John and Nicholson 208-9). S. T. Joshi has noted that the first science fiction story that probably Lovecraft wrote as a youth, now lost, was set on the far side of the moon using an astronomical theory that Lovecraft knew had been discredited decades earlier (IAP 87). It would therefore not be inconsistent that Lovecraft could draw inspira-tion from Lowell's Martian theories, even if he disagreed with them as un-scientific.

In particular, there are two aspects of Lowell's Martian canal theory that can be seen as influencing Lovecraft's fiction. The first is evident in his 1906 and 1915 articles on Mars, where Lovecraft referenced the nebular hypothesis of eighteenth-century French astronomer Pierre-Simon, marquis de Laplace. In this concept, largely discredited since the late 1800s, the solar system formed from an interstellar cloud cooling from the outside in, with planets progressively younger the closer they are to the sun. Therefore, to quote Lovecraft, "as Mars is an old planet, compared to the earth, the population might be vastly more civilised and advanced than that of our globe" (CE 3.25). At the end of his career, Lovecraft would again reference the nebular hypothesis in "The Shadow out of Time." From the viewpoint of Peaslee on modern-day Earth, the inhabitants of Jupiter's outer moon lived "six million years in the past" (CF 3.398), the inhabitants of Venus "would live incalculable epochs to come" (CF 3.398), and "as the earth's span closed" (CF 3.399) the Great Race would migrate to Mercury, as Earth will be a "cold planet," its survivors "burrowing to its horror-filled core" for heat (CF 3.400). Lovecraft's use of the nebular hypothesis is one of many aspects of "The Shadow out of Time" that August Derleth misinterpreted in his 1957 sequel, "The Shadow out of Space," which states that the Great Race "had fled outward into space, at first to the planet Jupiter, and then farther" (Derleth 238).

The second possible influence from the canal theory can be seen in Lovecraft's 1906, 1915, and 1917 Mars articles. In them, Lovecraft noted that to be seen from Earth, the Martian canals would have to be of an "immense scale, out of all proportion to the known works of mankind" (CE 3.292-93, 319) and that as "a thoughtful person will be apt to doubt the ability of humans to construct such great work" the canals would have to be made by beings "able to accomplish much more than our race in a mechanical way" (CE 3.25). A civilization far older than human history with the ability to engage in feats of Cyclopean construction, and yet for all its technology unable to prevent the slow death of their world: these are all hallmarks of Lovecraft—with R'lyeh and the Antarctic city of the Old Ones as the primary examples—which Lowell had previously claimed about Mars. Indeed, in Lovecraft's sole fictional reference to Mars in "Through the Gates of the Silver Key," the character Randolph Carter, his disembodied spirit travelling across space and time, "gazed at the Cyclopean ruins that sprawl over Mars' ruddy disc" (CF 3.315).

By the end of the nineteenth century, Lowell's Martian canal theory came under increasing derision in the astronomical community. In 1906, Lowell attempted to rehabilitate his scientific reputation by initiating a search for what he called "Planet X," a world whose gravity could explain apparent discrepancies in the orbits of Uranus and Neptune. Lowell died in 1916, but his project continued after his death, resulting in the discovery of Pluto at his observatory in 1930. Lovecraft would incorporate this into "The Whisperer in Darkness," where Pluto is actually the Mi-Go planet Yuggoth, and its discovery a result of the Mi-Go ending their psychic shrouding of the planet (CF 2.538). Lovecraft had developed Yuggoth in *Fungi from Yuggoth* (1929–30). It is therefore ironic that, prior to equating Yuggoth with the planet found as a result of Lowell's attempt to escape from his own canal legacy, Lovecraft would devote "The Canal" to describing an abandoned, lifeless canal in Yuggoth:

> A deep, black, narrow channel, reeking strong
> Of frightful things whence oily currents race.
> Lanes with old walls half meeting overhead
> Wind off to streets one may or may not know,
> And feeble moonlight sheds a spectral glow
> Over long rows of windows, dark and dead" (AT 74).

The Martian Connection to *At the Mountains of Madness*

It is in Lovecraft's novel *At the Mountains of Madness* (1931) that the most parallels to Lowell and the Martian fiction he inspired can be found. A small team of scientists use custom-built flying machines to establish a base in a distant, inhospitable frozen desert filled with mountains, valleys, and plateaus. There, the scientists find the ruins of an ancient alien civilization that, despite its advanced technology, was unable to halt the decline in its environment and the concomitant rise in attacks by barbarous lesser beings. Lovecraft himself was seemingly inspired to write the novel as a result of his plans to write interplanetary fiction. In a letter to Clark Ashton Smith (3 December 1929), Lovecraft stated how

> I shall sooner or later get around to the interplanetary field myself—& you may depend upon it that I shall not choose Edmond Hamilton, Ray Cummings, or Edgar Rice Burroughs as my model! I doubt if I shall have any living race upon the orb whereto I shall—either spiritually or corporeally—precipitate my hero. But there will be Cyclopean ruins—god! what ruins!—& certain presences that haunt the nether vaults. (DS 187)

Lovecraft never wrote such an interplanetary story, but did begin writing At the Mountains of Madness approximately a year later, so it seems clear that the basic outlines of his Antarctic story originated in the ideas shared with Smith for a story set on another planet. Lovecraft even mentions Smith in the novel; the professors recognize the Old Ones' remains because they are familiar with Smith's sculptures of them based on the Necronomicon (CF 3.40). This sudden transposition of setting from one world to another is not as odd when it is realized that in doing so, Lovecraft was simply doing the inverse of connections between polar and interplanetary—specifically Martian—exploration that prior authors had been making for decades.

From 1887 to 1893, a series of articles titled "Letters from the Planets" were published in Cassell's Magazine, portrayed as correspondence sent by the Venusian traveler Aleriel to the author via the power of Druid stone circles. In the first letter, Aleriel relays the discovery of the ruins of an ancient civilization on the moon; in the second, a visit to the south pole of Mars, where he chides his human correspondent on how "you actually know less of [your Antarctic regions] than of the Antarctic realms of Mars, for these you can see in your most powerful telescopes—you can at least discern the outlines of land and sea. But of the Antarctic realms of the earth no man can tell whether they are land or sea, whether the Antarctic continent is a fable or a fact" (Schroeder 103). In Gustavus W. Pope's 1894 novel Journey to Mars, the survivor of a doomed U.S. Navy expedition to Antarctica encounters a Martian expedition on the southern continent; after going with them to Mars, the sailor is eventually returned to the Antarctic sea (Pope 21-56, 515-31). Edwin Lester Arnold's Lieutenant Gullivar Jones: His Vacation (1905) sees the titular U.S. Navy officer transported to Mars by an "Oriental" magic carpet inscribed in suitably Lovecraftian form with a mix of symbols representing the solar system and "characters halfway in appearance between Runes and Cryptic-Sanskrit" (Arnold 6-7). On Mars, Jones has a prolonged adventure encountering unfriendly natives as he treks across the Martian Arctic (Arnold 157-82) and explores the "the ruins of a Hither [Arabesque Martian civilization] city, a haunted fairy town to which some travellers have been, but whence none ever returned alive" (Arnold 201).

While the missives from Aleriel were and remain extremely niche, Pope's and Arnold's novels are widely seen as influences of Edgar Rice Burroughs, whose own works had an impact of Lovecraft's writing, including *At the Mountains of Madness* (Fulwiler 60–65; Price, "Warlord" 66–68; Callaghan 77–78). Closer to home than the Mars of those authors, Chuck Hoffman suggested that a film adaptation be set on Earth's moon rather than Antarctica. Robert M. Price subsequently linked *At the Mountains of Madness* with another extraterrestrial ice sheet, that of Jupiter's moon Europa, suggesting that an adaption of it be set on that planetary body (Price, "Episode 20").

If finding alien artifacts on the moons of Earth and Jupiter sounds like Arthur C. Clarke's *2001: A Space Odyssey* and its sequels, Price has also discussed the belief that *At the Mountains of Madness* was an inspiration for *2001* (Price, "Episode 11"). This is perhaps not as outlandish as it may seem; Clarke was a fan of Lovecraft and one of his first published stories was a 1940 parody titled "At the Mountains of Murkiness." The Antarctic explorers in his parody even compare the scenery they traverse to that of the moon (Clarke, "At the Mountains" 96), the location where explorers found ancient alien monoliths in the more famous Clarke story.

Early drafts of the *2001* novel included scenes in which the astronauts discuss the idea of aliens contacting ancient human civilizations (Clarke, *2001* 112–13), and the crew being transported to an alien city whose architecture resembles that of Lovecraft's City of the Old Ones, including a statuary "line of cyclopean heads" (195) and buildings consisting of "hemispherical domes ... giant beehives ... [some] plain and angular, being based on a few simple elements, others were as complex as Gothic cathedrals or Cambodian temples" (207). Even the final *2001* novel names one of its early hominid characters contacted by the alien monolith as "the One Old" (Clarke, *2001* 3). And Clarke's three sequels to *2001—2010: Odyssey Two* (1982), *2061: Odyssey Three* (1987), *3001: The Final Odyssey* (1997)—each prominently feature the Europa that Price favored, with an enormous alien artifact appearing on the moon's ice-covered surface. *2010* even features a first expedition to Europa to explore its alien life, landing in a feature termed the "Grand Canal" and compared to Lowell's visions of Mars (Clarke, *2010* 55). The expedition ends in disaster, the last survivor broadcasting his testimony (59–69) before the HAL 9000 computer issues a Lovecraftian warning to humanity to "attempt no [further] landings there" (277).

In terms of real expeditions to terrestrial ice sheets, Lovecraft based his Miskatonic Antarctic Expedition on the U.S. Navy's 1928–30 Byrd Antarctic Expedition, led by Admiral Richard E. Byrd (Eckhardt 31–38; Callaghan 78). In 1948, rocket scientist Wernher von Braun developed the first technical outline of a Mars mission using available technology of the day; one of his influences for the structure of the Mars voyage was the U.S. Navy's subsequent 1946-47 Operation Highjump Antarctic expedition, also led by Byrd. Notably, von Braun's outline expedition landed at the Martian south pole, the ice cap providing an easy surface for his airplane-like "landing boats"; and just as with the Miskatonic Expedition and its transport ships, only some of von Braun's crew would make the final descent to Mars, the remainder staying on board the larger orbiting transfer spaceships. Although Lowell had long been discredited by the 1950s, von Braun remained inspired enough by his theories to discuss the potential of finding canals. *The Exploration of Mars*, co-written with Willy Ley—a prominent cryptozoologist, Atlantis advocate, advisor to science fiction films, and friend of Arthur C. Clarke—included an illustration of an ancient Martian temple ruin (Portree 1-2; Braun 65-66; Ley and Braun 66, 72, 158, 163; Clarke, *Lost Worlds* 127).

While this is not an indication that von Braun was inspired by Lovecraft, it is an indication that Lovecraft's Antarctic expedition and von Braun's Martian expedition—the prototype for all subsequent scientific plans for journeys to Mars—share a distant common ancestor in Byrd's Antarctic journeys. In its similarity to the later, more scientific postwar conceptions of expeditions to Mars, *At the Mountains of Madness* stands as a forerunner—despite its terrestrial setting—of the type of Martian tale to come, in contrast to those of Lovecraft's time. One Martian story that almost immediately reflected the shift embodied by the novel is "The Vaults of Yoh-Vombis," by Lovecraft's friend Clark Ashton Smith, to whom Lovecraft had written the initial idea of *At the Mountains of Madness* in 1929, when he still considered that it would be part of the "interplanetary field" (*DS* 187). Smith published his story in 1932, the year after Lovecraft finished his draft of the novel, but before the latter's 1936 publication. "The Vaults of Yoh-Vombis" also features the hospitalized last survivor of a scientific expedition to an abandoned city built by ancient aliens who cautions his peers not to return there, as apocalyptic creatures still exist in the ruins. The general plot parallels that of *At the Mountains of Madness*, with the location switched from the Antarctic to Mars (Gelatt et al.).

Burroughs and Wells

If even the scientific von Braun could reflect the lingering influence of Lowell into the 1950s, the canal theorist cast an even larger shadow among science fiction authors in the first half of the century. Perhaps the most notable example is Edgar Rice Burroughs in his tales of John Carter of Mars, of which Lovecraft had been a youthful fan. Carter was a Virginian gentleman and Confederate cavalry officer in the Civil War before being transported to Mars while prospecting in Arizona (the location of Lowell's observatory). There he marries into the Red Martian nobility, who fight to sustain their idealized slaveholder society against hordes of degenerate inhuman savages. The climax of the third book, *The Warlord of Mars*—serialized in 1913-14 in the *All-Story Weekly*, which Lovecraft read, and published in collected form in 1919—includes Carter leading an extended expedition to a lost city at the Martian north pole (Callaghan 71-72; Fulwiler 60; Burroughs 432-49).

Carter and his adoptive Red Martian society clearly parallel Lovecraft's own social and political views (AT 13, 473-74; Joshi, "Political and Economic Thought"). William Fulwiler and Robert M. Price argue that Burroughs's Barsoom series was an inspiration for Lovecraft's Dream Cycle; Alan Moore and Kevin O'Neill made the link explicit in their *League of Extraordinary Gentlemen* comic, establishing John Carter as Randolph Carter's grand-uncle (Fulwiler 64-65; Price, "Warlord" 66-68; Moore and O'Neill 160). Ironically, Lovecraft claimed that the name of Randolph Carter came from a real-life John Carter, a member of the Carter family of Virginia who relocated to Providence prior to the American Revolution, as the "transposition of a Virginia line to New England always affected my fancy strongly" (SL 2.351-53). And although Lovecraft criticized Burroughs for anthropomorphizing his Martians (CE 2.180-81), it is the Martians of Burroughs, far more than of H. G. Wells or G. P. Serviss, who reflect what Joshi identified as the three values of Lovecraft's own aliens: "pure intelligence, sound political organisation, and aesthetic sensibility" ("Alien Civilisations" 142).

The author most closely associated with Mars in Lovecraft's lifetime, aside from Burroughs, was H. G. Wells, with his *The War of the Worlds* (1897). Wells's Martian invasion can be interpreted as Lovecraft's quintessential "strange aeons": cosmic entities come to Earth to rule, reshaping the world and its ecology, with small bands of humans serving as collaborators. The Martian arrival in their cylindrical ships is originally believed to be a meteor impact—the chapter of the initial Martian landing is even titled "The Falling Star" (WW 10). In other words, the Martian arrival is quite literally when the "stars are right." During his flight from the Martians, Wells's narrator takes refuge in a farmhouse and witnesses the countryside become overrun by alien "red weed," a precursor to Lovecraft's "The Colour out of Space" (WW 128). The narrator even ruminates on how the Martian invasion "has robbed us of that serene confidence in the future which is the most fruitful source of decadence" (WW 181), which he characterized at the novel's start as the "infinite complacency [by which] men went to and fro over this globe about their little affairs, serene in their assurance of their empire over matter" (WW 3). These ruminations on the Martian shattering of human importance and confidence are reminiscent of the cosmicism expressed by Lovecraft in the famous opening lines of "The Call of Cthulhu" (CF 2.21-22).

And with their octopus-like appearance and their "intellects vast and cool and unsympathetic" (WW 3-4), Wells's Martians have obvious parallels with Lovecraft's cosmic entities. Lovecraft himself may even have drawn visual inspiration for Cthulhu from the original *War of the Worlds* illustrations of the Martians by Warwick Goble (WW 19-20; Price, "Episode 9"). The narrator's ending comments on the Martians are even evocative of the Great Race's temporal abilities: "To them, and not to us, perhaps, is the future ordained" (WW 182). Conversely, the narrator opens the novel by reminding the reader that "before we judge of them too harshly," the similarity of the Martians to human behavior should be remembered (WW 5). This conflates with Dyer's remark about the Old Ones: "whatever they had been, they were men!" (CF 3.143).

The events of Wells's novel also provide for mirroring of other Mythos aspects. The ironclad ship *Thunder Child* ramming a Martian tripod to destroy it parallels the yacht *Alert* ramming Cthulhu to defeat it in "The Call of Cthulhu" (WW 109-11; CF 2.54). Just as Cthulhu re-forms itself after the attack, the Martians themselves are impervious to human attempts to defeat them, succumbing instead to bacteria, "slain, after all man's devices had failed, by the humblest things that God" had created (WW 169-70)—in other words, by a fellow divinity. Even so, the Martians are not truly defeated, as the narrator fears they may yet attempt a second invasion, in addition to the subsequent invasion of Venus they undertake at the end of the novel (WW 180-81).

Both Lovecraft's and Wells's cosmic entities are therefore shown to be beyond creation or destruction. This is not the case in the unauthorized 1898 sequel *Edison's Conquest of Mars* by G. P. Serviss. The novel recounts a counter-invasion of Mars by a space fleet built by Thomas Alva Edison. Landing at the south pole of the Red Planet, Edison learns that the Martians were responsible for the creation of ancient religions and megalithic statuary in Earth's past. This is a clear predecessor to both the "ancient alien theory" and the Cthulhu Mythos, especially as Lovecraft was a fan of Serviss, even quoting from one of his nonfiction texts in "Beyond the Wall of Sleep" (Callaghan 72-73; CF 1.85; SL 5.412). Among the more notably Lovecraftian passages of the book are Edison's fleet passing by "an ancient watch tower [on the moon] composed of Cyclopean blocks larger than any that I had ever seen even among the ruins of Greece, Egypt and Asia Minor" (45) and the realization that the Great Pyramid of Cheops "was not the work of puny man, as many an engineer had declared that it could not be, but the work of these giants of Mars" (146)—language strikingly similar to that used by Lovecraft to describe the Martian canals in his 1915 and 1917 articles (CE 3.292-93, 319). Notably, while Lowell's canals are not mentioned by Wells, they are prominent features of the Mars of Serviss and Burroughs (and later Bradbury).

While there is only circumstantial evidence that Lovecraft read *Edison's Conquest of Mars*, other authors have illustrated the ease by which Martian invasion created by Wells and the Cthulhu Mythos created by Lovecraft can be integrated. Perhaps the first was Brian Aldiss's 1965 *The Saliva Tree*, explicitly a crossover of *The War of the Worlds* and "The Colour out of Space" in its depiction of the effects of a Victorian alien invasion on the life of a rural farm in East Anglia (Baxter, "Metaphor" 10-11; Nicholls vi-viii). Dave Wolverton's 1996 short story "After a Lean Winter" tells Wells's Martian invasion from the viewpoint of Jack London. The fictional London discovers that some Martians survived in the more Mars-like climate of the Arctic after succumbing elsewhere on Earth, and may have built an underwater settlement beneath the Arctic ice cap to survive even longer—just as Dyer hypothesizes about Old Ones surviving in an underwater city beneath the Antarctic ice cap in *At the Mountains of Madness* (Wolverton 322-24; CF 3.116).

Stephen Baxter's 2017 sequel novel to Wells, *The Massacre of Mankind*, incorporates the idea from Wolverton and takes the Lovecraftian similarity closer by including a 1937 expedition by airship into the Arctic to locate the last redoubt of the Martian survivors (456–73, 486). The elderly narrator of Wells has been hospitalized due to his obsession with the symbols of the Martians—"more images I find it hard to get out of my mind"—and has come to believe that the ultimate Martian plan was to eventually establish themselves in the Antarctic (151–52). Baxter even has a character muse, Dyer-like, "Some say the Martians were like us—once" (310). The Martian headquarters, dominated by the enormous cylindrical forms of their spacecraft sticking out of the ground, is even compared to suitably Lovecraftian ancient megaliths by the narrator, who sees it as a "Martian Stonehenge" (312). Notably, Baxter followed *The Massacre of Mankind* with an entry in the 2018 Lovecraft pastiche anthology *The Lovecraft Squad: Dreaming*.

But the most explicit link of Lovecraft and *The War of the Worlds* is Don Webb's 1996 short story "To Mars and Providence," published in the same anthology as Wolverton's story. This tale depicts a young Lovecraft witnessing the Martian invasion, at the end learning in the manner of "The Shadow out of Time" that he is an advance psychic scout of the Martians inhabiting a human body, taking the real Lovecraft's sense of alienation to a literal extreme (Webb 261). Baxter himself read Webb's story (along with Serviss's novel and Moore and O'Neill's comic) prior to writing *The Massacre of Mankind* (Baxter, *Massacre* 486; Baxter, "Metaphor" 7–8, 11–12).

While not as explicit as Webb's crossover, the most thematically Lovecraftian follow-up to *The War of the Worlds*, one also involving a covert hybridization of Martian and human, was appropriately written by Wells himself: his final science fiction novel, *Star Begotten* (1937). Its protagonist, historian Joseph Davis, conceives of a conspiracy by which Martians use cosmic rays to guide the evolution of select humans, with the goal of causing their descendants to evolve both physically and mentally toward the superior Martian form. Davis begins to suspect that he himself is one of those whom the Martians have selected for their influence. One of his confidants, the right-wing media baron Lord Thunderclap, transfers his anti-Semitism and anti-communism onto those who unknowingly carry the Martian blood, calling for "a vast sanitary concentration of all these people" with the Martian hybrids to be "arrested and secluded in protective isolation" to ensure "human race-purity" (Wells, *Star Begotten* 103–4). Ultimately, however, *Star Begotten* is ambiguous as to whether Davis is correct, let alone whether Martians even exist; in this way, it is closer to Lovecraft and R. H. Barlow's collaboration "The Night Ocean" (1936).

Conclusion

Star Begotten by H. G. Wells has clear echoes of "The Shadow over Innsmouth," "The Whisperer in Darkness," and "The Shadow out of Time." His previous novel, *The Croquet Player* (1936), has also been called Lovecraftian, due to its theme of an evil pall coming to an English countryside village after the discovery of a cave of Neanderthal remains causes the town's inhabitants to suffer from the psychic anguish of contemplating the vast span of human history (Macdonald). Wells died in 1946, and it was only three years after *Star Begotten* that Arthur C. Clarke, Wells enthusiast and future vice president of the H. G. Wells Society (a position that Baxter would also hold), wrote his Lovecraft parody. There is no evidence, however, that Wells was influenced by Lovecraft or indeed ever knew of him. Lovecraft certainly never had the chance to read *Star Begotten*, since it was published three months after his death in March 1937; he also may not have enjoyed it, given his low opinion of Wells's later works (*DS* 669–71).

It was only by a few additional years that Lovecraft missed Clarke and Bradbury's homages. Nevertheless, while he was not able to read those early works bridging his literary themes with Mars, and while he avoided Mars in his fiction, Lovecraft's interest in Mars was great and was the basis for some of his earliest writings. The influence of certain Mars-related authors—Serviss, Wells, Burroughs—is inarguable. The theories of Lowell, which influenced those authors, themselves show strong similarities to key aspects of Lovecraft's mythos: non-anthropological life, the unavoidable encroaching of a hostile environment, massive works of construction in lost cities, and a worldview where humanity is nothing more than a youthful upstart among the plurality of worlds.

And while *At the Mountains of Madness* was not set on Mars, Lovecraft's details of its expedition anticipated the type of expedition authors after him would conceptualize to voyage to Mars, even while its theme of a lost alien civilization was more common among the Martian fiction of his own time. And while the Miskatonic Expedition was the predecessor of the types of realistic Mars missions that scientific advocates from Wernher von Braun to Robert Zubrin and Andy Weir would develop, the Lovecraftian concepts of alien civilizations, as well as the individual alienation of such expeditions, would influence his later adherents in their own Mars fiction. While Don Webb might have been exaggerating in making Lovecraft into an actual Martian, Lovecraft himself undoubtedly had an interest in the Red Planet that caused his influence to sprawl over Mars' ruddy disc as much as any Cyclopean ruin witnessed by Randolph Carter.

Works Cited

Aldiss, Brian W. *The Saliva Tree and Other Strange Growths.* 1966. Boston: Gregg Press, 1981.

Arnold, Edwin Lester. *Lieut. Gullivar Jones: His Vacation.* 1905. New York: Arno Press, 1975.

Baxter, Stephen. "H. G. Wells's *The War of the Worlds* as a Controlling Metaphor for the Twentieth Century." *The Wellsian: Journal of the H. G. Wells Society* 32 (2009): 3-16.

———. *The Massacre of Mankind.* New York: Crown, 2017.

Bogdanov, Alexander. *Red Star: The First Bolshevik Utopia.* Bloomington: Indiana University Press, 1984.

Bradbury, Ray. *The Martian Chronicles.* 1950. New York: Bantam Spectra, 1979.

Braun, Wernher von. *The Mars Project.* Urbana: University of Illinois Press, 1953.

Burroughs, Edgar Rice. *John Carter of Mars: A Princess of Mars, The Gods of Mars, The Warlord of Mars.* New York: Fall River Press, 2009.

Caidin, Martin; Jay Barbree; and Susan Wright. *Destination Mars: In Art, Myth, and Science.* New York: Penguin Studio, 1997.

Callaghan, Gavin. "A Reprehensible Habit: H. P. Lovecraft and the Munsey Magazines." In *Lovecraft and Influence: His Predecessors and Successors,* ed. Robert H. Waugh. Lanham, MD: Scarecrow Press, 2013. 69-82.

Clarke, Arthur C. "At the Mountains of Murkiness." In *At the Mountains of Murkiness and Other Parodies.* Ed. George Locke. London: Ferret Fantasy, 1973. 94-111.

———. *The Lost Worlds of 2001.* New York: Signet, 1972.

———. *2001: A Space Odyssey.* 1968. New York: New American Library, 1999.

———. *2010: Odyssey Two.* New York: Ballantine Books, 1982.

Crossley, Robert. *Imagining Mars: A Literary History*. Middletown, CT: Wesleyan University Press, 2011.

———. "Mars as Cultural Mirror: Martian Fictions in the Early Space Age." In *Visions of Mars: Essays on the Red Planet in Fiction and Science*. Ed. Howard V. Hendrix, George Slusser, and Eric S. Rabkin. Jefferson, NC: McFarland & Company, 2011. 165-74.

———. "Percival Lowell and the History of Mars." *The Massachusetts Review*, 41, No. 3 (2000): 297-318.

Derleth, August. *The Watchers Out of Time and Others*. Sauk City, WI: Arkham House, 1974.

Eckhardt, Jason C. "Behind the Mountains of Madness: Lovecraft and the Antarctic in 1930." *Lovecraft Studies* No. 14 (Spring 1987): 31-38.

Fulwiler, William. "E. R. B. and H. P. L." In *Black Forbidden Things: Cryptical Secrets from the "Crypt of Cthulhu,"* ed. Robert M. Price. San Bernardino, CA: Borgo Press, 1992. 60-65.

Gelatt, Philip, Ruth, and Tim Mucci. "Episode #39: "The Vaults of Yoh-Vombis." *The Double Shadow*, 11 March 2014. player.fm/series/the-double-shadow/episode-39-the-vaults-of-yoh-vombis

Harpold, Terry. "Where Is Verne's Mars?" In *Visions of Mars: Essays on the Red Planet in Fiction and Science*, ed. Howard V. Hendrix, George Slusser, and Eric S. Rabkin. Jefferson, NC: McFarland, 2011. 29-35.

Huntington, John W. "The (In)Significance of Mars in the 1930s." In *Visions of Mars: Essays on the Red Planet in Fiction and Science*, ed. Howard V. Hendrix, George Slusser, and Eric S. Rabkin. Jefferson, NC: McFarland, 2011. 80-85.

Jones, Stephen, ed. *The Lovecraft Squad: Dreaming*. New York: Pegasus Books, 2018.

Joshi, S. T. "Lovecraft's Alien Civilizations: A Political Interpretation." 1985. In *Lovecraft and a World in Transition*. New York: Hippocampus Press, 2014. 122-43.

———. "The Political and Economic Thought of H. P. Lovecraft." 1979. In *Lovecraft and a World in Transition*. New York: Hippocampus Press, 2014. 99-104.

Lane, K. Maria D. *Geographies of Mars: Seeing and Knowing the Red Planet*. Chicago: University of Chicago Press, 2011.

Ley, Willy, and Wernher von Braun. *The Exploration of Mars*. New York: Viking Press, 1956.

Ligner, Meddy. "Trajectory of a Cursed Spirit." In *Future Lovecraft*, ed. Silvia Moreno-Garcia and Paula R. Stiles. Germantown, MD: Prime Books, 2012. 207–20.

Macdonald, Kate. "H. G. Wells does Lovecraft." *Kate Macdonald*, 24 July 2017. katemacdonald.net/2017/07/24/h-g-wells-does-lovecraft/

Moore, Alan and Kevin O'Neill. *The League of Extraordinary Gentlemen, Volume I*. La Jolla, CA: America's Best Comics, 2000.

Nicholls, Peter. "Introduction." In *The Saliva Tree and Other Strange Growths*. Boston: Gregg Press, 1981. vi–xii.

Perridas, Chris. "Ray Bradbury's circa 1950 Parody of HP Lovecraft." *H. P. Lovecraft And His Legacy*, 1 February 2008. chrisperridas.blogspot.com/2008/02/ray-bradburys-circa-1950-parody-of-hp.html

Pope, Gustavus W. *Journey to Mars. The Wonderful World: Its Beauty and Splendor; Its Mighty Races and Kingdoms; Its Final Doom*. New York: G. W. Dillingham, 1894.

Portree, David S. F. *Humans to Mars: Fifty Years of Mission Planning, 1950–2000*. Washington, D.C.: NASA History Division, 2001.

Price, Robert M. "Randolph Carter, Warlord of Mars." In *Black Forbidden Things: Cryptical Secrets from the "Crypt of Cthulhu,"* ed. Robert M. Price. San Bernardino, CA: Borgo Press, 1992. 66–68.

———. "Episode 9." *The Lovecraft Geek*, 17 March 2014. www.talkshoe.com/episode/4887700

———. "Episode 11." *The Lovecraft Geek*, 25 April 2014. www.talkshoe.com/episode/4887757

———. "Episode 20." *The Lovecraft Geek*, 16 October 2015. www.talkshoe.com/episode/4731995

Schroeder, David. "A Message from Mars: Astronomy and Late-Victorian Culture." Ph.D. diss.: Indiana University, 2002.

Serviss, Garrett P. *Edison's Conquest of Mars*. 1898. Burlington, ON: Collector's Guide Publishing, 2010.

Smith, Clark Ashton. "The Vaults of Yoh-Vombis." 1932. In *The Dark Eidolon and Other Fantasies*, ed. S. T. Joshi. London: Penguin Classics, 2014. 91–111.

St. John, Charles E., and Seth B. Nicholson. "On the Absence of Selective Absorption in the Atmosphere of Venus." *Publications of the Astronomical Society of the Pacific* 33, No. 194 (1921): 208-9.

Tostoy, Alexei. *Aelita*. 1923. Amsterdam: Fredonia Books, 2001.

Webb, Don. "To Mars and Providence." In *War of the Worlds: Global Dispatches*, ed. Kevin J. Anderson. New York: Bantam Spectra, 1996. 251-61.

Wells, H. G. *The Croquet Player*. 1936. Lincoln, NE: Bison Books, 2004.

———. *Star Begotten: A Biological Fantasia*. 1937. Middletown, CT: Wesleyan University Press, 2006.

———. *The War of the Worlds*. 1897. New York: Modern Library, 2002. [Abbreviated in the text as *WW*.]

Wolverton, Dave. "After a Lean Winter." In *War of the Worlds: Global Dispatches*, ed. Kevin J. Anderson. New York: Bantam Spectra, 1996. 299-324.

Yudina, Ekaterina. "Dibs on the Red Planet: The Bolsheviks and Mars in the Russian Literature of the Early Twentieth Century." In *Visions of Mars: Essays on the Red Planet in Fiction and Science*, ed. Howard V. Hendrix, George Slusser, and Eric S. Rabkin. Jefferson, NC: McFarland, 2011. 51-55.

Fascism Eternal Lies: H. P. Lovecraft, Georges Bataille, and the Destiny of the Fascists

Ray Huling
Ph.D. candidate, University of Massachusetts, Amherst

Introduction: Red-Hot Fascism versus the Anti-Fascist Tide

Had they met in the summer of 1936 and had each known the other's reputation, Georges Bataille would have refused to shake H. P. Lovecraft's hand—and Lovecraft might have refused Bataille's. This hypothetical is important, not only because of the recent comparative readings of Bataille and Lovecraft, but also because of the new concern for rising fascism, globally and in the United States.[1] Both Bataille and Lovecraft wrote insightfully about fascism, because they both saw that the centrality of disgust in fascist movements reflected and intensified the centrality of disgust in the formation of all human communities. For both of them, fascism succeeded because it acted as a warped mirror, showing a deep human truth in which the masses saw themselves. This reflection of an anamorphic human essence gave fascists the power to deliver sacred experiences, through formal ritual and through propaganda disseminated into the informality of daily life, a revolutionary movement that both explained their political victories (important to Lovecraft) and told how to defeat them (important to Bataille). Indeed, Lovecraft's and Bataille's positions on opposite sides of a phenomenon they perceived in almost the same way are what make their insights about fascism so clear and potent. This paper glosses the comparative scholarship recently done on Lovecraft and Bataille, explains Bataille's theory of fascism, considers Lovecraft's

---

1. Concerning the U.S., see Jason Stanley's *How Fascism Works* (2018) and Henry Giroux's *American Nightmare* (2018).

encomia to fascism in the light of that theory, and begins to distill from this consideration a way forward for contemporary anti-fascism. First, however, a return to the handshake both would have refused.

Their mutual disgust would have had its roots in their common interests, especially on the matter of cults: they differed on cults in general and on the biggest cult of their day, Nazism, in particular. Lovecraft and Bataille shared a sense of the meaning of the term "cult," as have scholars of fascism. A cult in Lovecraft's fiction is a religious group whose practices deviate from or even defy the orthodoxy of a given society's dominant religion, morals, and reason.[2] Bataille used the term in the same way, and both their conceptions conform to the general shape of Greek mystery cults.[3] Both also recognized the possibility that a cult may come to dominate society, as, in their view, the messianic cult of Jesus of Nazareth had done. Important for this sense of cultic efflorescence into the mainstream, a threat for Lovecraft and a promise for Bataille, is the recognition that cults deliver powerful experiences, a fact that has explanatory force in the scholarship of fascism—and of Lovecraft.[4]

Lovecraft sneered at the cultish practices of those peoples for whom he felt disgust, but he looked on the rituals and myths of the Nazis with an only slightly qualified admiration. He decried the violence of the former and exulted in his violent fantasies about the latter: "So far, Hitler is wrong," Lovecraft wrote to his friend, James F. Morton, an anarchist, on 12 June 1933, "But—when a clique of sharp, pushing Yids get hold of the professional & cultural life of a nation . . . then, by god, it's time to forget the fancy principles & do something to restore control & expression to the real population of the nation concern'd! On that point I'm a red-hot Nazi . . ." (JFM 323).

The well-known passage from "The Call of Cthulhu" (1926) that describes the age that the cult of the Great Old Ones hopes to bring about, which would render human life "free and wild and beyond good and evil,

---

2. See Waugh (1994) and Callaghan (2013).

3. In 1926, Bataille, André Masson, Michel Leiris, and Nikolai Bakhtin considered founding an Orphic secret society that they would have named "Judas" and that would have held its rites in a brothel. See Bataille, *Sacred Conspiracy* (169) and Kendall (44).

4. The seminal work of contemporary scholarship that considers the cultish aspects of fascism is Emilio Gentile's "Fascism as Political Religion"; Roger Griffin's "Fascist Temporalities as Remedies for Liquid Modernity" (2015) is a fine current exemplar.

with laws and morals thrown aside and all men shouting and killing and revelling in joy" (CF 2.39–40), evinces Lovecraft's antipathy toward excessive practices, especially religious ones, but a line from his letter to Robert E. Howard of 12 January 1933 brings this image into sharper ideological focus:

> Decadent cults will arise, in which weary worldlings will preach that the complex industrial order is not worth the labour and self-sacrifice necessary for its maintenance, and this feeling will subconsciously penetrate even those who do not consciously cherish it. There will be a steady letdown and return to the primitive—with the social disorders naturally accompanying such readjustment. (MF 519)

A movement from guardianship of the West and its high pleasures downward to apathy and down further still to the delights and horrors of barbarism was what Lovecraft feared cultish thought would bring about—and so he turned hopeful eyes to fascism, itself a cult, as a bulwark against the forces that would erode or overwhelm civilization.

Here, Bataille deviates from Lovecraft. Bataille undertook not just scholastic but practical studies of cults of every kind, and he saw fascism as a modern cultic practice; yet he hated the fascists and advocated for violence against them. His distinction from Lovecraft is philosophical and affective. Indeed, "the mad cacophony of the orgy" (CF 236) was just what Bataille recommended and sought in practice as a defense of human life, in order to bring the masses into conflict with Nazism:

> Many men love their country [*patrie*], sacrifice themselves for it, die for it. A Nazi can love the Reich to the point of delirium. We too, we can love to the point of fanaticism, but what we love, although we are French by origin, is not at all the French community, but the human community; it's in no way France, but rather the Earth. (Bataille and Kaan)

The philosophical divide between Lovecraft and Bataille would also have occasioned a personal breach, because of Bataille's own cultic oaths.

In 1936, three groups began to coalesce around Bataille: 1) the College of Sociology, an intellectual circle devoted to the study of sacredness, with a special interest in secret societies; 2) the journal *Acéphale*, devoted to literary exploration of the sacred, with several articles aimed at discrediting the Nazi appropriation of the work of Friedrich Nietzsche; 3) a secret society, also called Acéphale, a cult meant to enact the wisdom of the previous two efforts. Acéphale is most important here: the *acéphaliens* would meet before a great lightning-split oak in the forest of Marly, where, according to Patrick Waldberg, a participant, they practiced "every excess, including those that meant promiscuity" (595). Excesses, yes, but there were rules, too, and goals: Bataille meant, first, to found a religion to counter fascism, which he understood, as Lovecraft did, as a sacralization of politics, and, second, to avoid the coming war, which Lovecraft also saw on the horizon. As a cult, Acéphale had "periods of tension and periods of licentiousness," ritual orgies, as well as restrictions and asceticisms—taboos, in the observance of which, Waldberg says, "Bataille advised 'a Prussian stiffness of manners,' as well as 'British composure' in the face of the unexpected" (596).

Virtually all the values dear to Acéphale would have curled Lovecraft's lip, as the list of things he detested—"violence, ugliness, ignorance, sensuality, brutality, cruelty, abnormality, filth, cloddishness, rapacity, egotism, encroachment, violations of physical or spiritual integrity, and everything that goes with a dull acquiescence in the animal patterns of the lower part of creation" (MF 798)—all but matches the list of experiences the *acéphaliens* pursued: "the universal accomplishment of personal being in the irony of the animal world"; "perversion and crime, not as exclusive values, but as integrated within the human totality"; "the destruction of the existing world, with eyes open to the world to come" (Bataille, "Program" 78). Enough, perhaps, to keep Lovecraft's hand by his side, even at the urging of his sense of gentlemanly duty, had he met Bataille. What is certain is that, according to Michel Surya, Bataille would have been honor-bound to reject Lovecraft: "one of the few customs we know to have been observed by the Acéphale secret society consisted of refusing to shake hands with anti-Semites [. . .] this practice was adhered to" (239).[5]

The opposition of Lovecraft and Bataille is remarkable not only for its granularity but also for its intensity. Each had a heated emotional connection with fascism. Here is Lovecraft writing to Morton:

A hideous example of what Hitler is honestly—if crudely—trying to prevent is the stinking Manhattan pest zone. Faugh! Everything gone Yiddish—. . . hell!

---

5. Bataille distributed the "Program" in early April 1936 to the *Contre-Attaquistes* in his camp (*Sacred Conspiracy* 109). The proto-Acéphale "Sociological Group" had its first formal meeting on 4 June 1936. (ibid. 111) But the core group who would become the *acéphaliens* had been enjoying orgies of some kind with each other since at least 29 December 1934, "the soirée de Saint-Cloud," which was shut down by the police (*Sacred Conspiracy* 98).

There's an Augean stable for the future Nazis of America! . . . I'd like to see Hitler wipe Greater New York clean with poison gas—giving masks to the few remaining people of Aryan culture (even if of Semitic ancestry). The place needs fumigation and a fresh start. (If Harlem didn't get any masks, I'd shed no tears . . . . . & the same goes for the dago slums!). (JFM 324)

So Lovecraft wrote on 12 June 1933. In November of that year, Bataille published "The Psychological Structure of Fascism," an analysis that blended Bataille's peculiar approach to phenomenology with his first forays into the human sciences and that would lead him to endorse violence in the struggle against fascism. In late 1935, Bataille joined with André Breton to form Counter-Attack, a group of anti-fascist intellectuals and artists. One of their calls to violent action, juxtaposed here with Lovecraft's Hitlerist fantasy, gives a clear picture of Bataille's and Lovecraft's respective relationships to fascism.

This is Bataille, writing in May 1936. For over a year, the French have fought in the streets at the instigation of the fascists. Dozens of people have been killed. The Popular Front has formed, and Bataille reaches out to this coalition, with a manifesto titled "Popular Front in the Street":

The Popular Front in its present form is not, nor does it present itself, as an organized force within sight of taking power. It must thus be transformed, according to the plan of the socialist revolutionary Left, into a Popular Front of combat.

As for us, we say that this presupposes a renewal of political forms, a renewal possible in the present circumstances, when it seems that all revolutionary forces are called upon to fuse in an incandescent crucible. We are assured that insurrection is impossible for our adversaries. We believe that of the two hostile forces that will engage in the struggle for power, the fascists and the people, the force that gets the upper hand will be the one that shows itself most capable of dominating events and imposing an implacable power on its adversaries. . . .

After February 16.

500,000 workers, defied by little cockroaches, invaded the streets and caused an immense uproar.

Comrades, who has the right to lay down the law?

This ALL-POWERFUL multitude, this HUMAN OCEAN . . .

Only this ocean of men in revolt can save the world from the nightmare of impotence and carnage in which it sinks! (168)

That image of a "human ocean" would have disgusted Lovecraft, as would have much else in this passage: the violence from below, the undifferentiated masses, the very notion of revolution. Thalassophobia aside, most of Bataille's peers found his provocations just as offensive as Lovecraft would have. Breton himself split from Counter-Attack and denounced Bataille as a "surfascist," and the charge would stick down the years.

In "Truman's Apotheosis," a defense of Bataille against the indictment of fascism, Allan Stoekl relates an alarming anecdote: "Surya, Bataille's biographer, told me he was surprised to find, when he started work on his book, that quite a few people with whom he discussed his project, including some members of Bataille's generation, assumed that Bataille 'was a fascist'" (181). What could Bataille do but shrug? In "Psychological Structure," he had been quite upfront about the necessity of taking up fascism's sophisticated and methodical use of the experiences of disgust and sacredness "as a weapon" against fascism itself (159), a move that many intellectuals could only interpret psychologically as Bataille giving in to his lust for violence.

Yet we should see in Lovecraft's not-quite-jocular fantasy of scourging Manhattan with poison gas a vaticination of the threat that drove Bataille to action: it is stunning to read a reverie from 1933 that imagines Hitler exterminating non-Aryans with poison gas—especially one using the language of cleansing. Both Lovecraft and Bataille grasped the essence of fascism with astonishing immediacy: it is an ideology bound to radicalize to the point of unlimited violence. In continuation of a long debate on fascism, Lovecraft wrote to Howard on 27 July 1934, to explain how one would implement a Lovecraftian brand of it, "If the elements on the other side are given a chance to coöperate in such solutions, and then refuse, it is naturally quite all right to go ahead in as forceful a way as possible" (MF 794-95). Of course these "elements," the excluded peoples—and there would be many of them—would refuse Lovecraft's solutions and so become criminals; they would stand "outside the system of obligations prevailing among honest men" (MF 795), and thus deserve any violence done to them. What is more, this process of exclusion would never end.

Unlike capitalism and communism, both of which both Lovecraft and Bataille rejected and both of which are necessarily violent systems, even unspeakably so, fascism must come to war, and that war must become absolute; it must go to the point where its instigators turn against themselves. The peculiar cross-class, mass-movement nationalism of fascism, its uniting of the nation with the person of the absolute dictator, demand that it end in a generalized sadism, a violence actually without limits, meaning that it will come to encompass both the nation itself and the dictator himself: "he who weakens the grasp of a people upon their inheritance is most nefariously a traitor to the human species," declares Lovecraft, inventing a new and deadly sin (6 November 1930; JFM 242). And who does not sin so, under the most rigorous inspection? Fascism is an arc that bends through murder and ends in suicide, and, across the whole course of its curving path into universal disgust, the fascists themselves experience the sacred; they knot themselves together with powerful communications that form a death-bound community. This is the analysis of Bataille and the fury of Lovecraft on the matter of fascism, and why it is so fruitful and important to put them into conversation about it.

It is important, too, to keep in mind that they could have pressed flesh. In his only televised interview, speaking on the subject of his book *Literature and Evil*, Bataille avers that "literature doesn't permit us to live without perceiving human affairs in the most violent perspective," and that the value of this point of view imposed on us when we read literature is this: "By the same token, literature allows us to see the worst, to know how to live facing it and to know how to overcome it. In sum, the man who plays finds in the game the strength to overcome the horror the game entails." By cleaving to the sense of Lovecraft and Bataille as the real people they were, scholars of their work cleave through the resistance of scholarship to understanding itself as real, as having real effects, as answering to real issues. The most fundamental assumption of this paper is that the more evil the game of a particular literature—the taste for fascism in the fiction of H. P. Lovecraft, say—the more it helps to overturn evil in the flesh; the taste for fascism in the tongues of people living now, for example.

In this respect, the present study swims with the current of the main stream of Lovecraft scholarship. Though S. T. Joshi might disagree, his *H. P. Lovecraft: The Decline of the West* is one of the giants this paper stands on. Joshi investigates Lovecraft's philosophy and politics, including Lovecraft's racism and "somewhat unfortunate" (meaning both "disappointing" and "inaccurate") advocacy for fascism, as a way of deepening and enriching the experience of reading Lovecraft's fiction. What does such an intensification of the experience of this literature do for the reader's philosophy? For the reader's politics? What does reading Lovecraft do, in the world? This study seeks, in part, to answer these quite traditional questions.

From First Contact to Redemption

Over the past decade, several scholars have remarked upon the similarities between Lovecraft's writings and Bataille's. Before reviewing their research, the question of whether these similarities result from a direct exchange merits attention: did Lovecraft and Bataille read each other? If so, did this reading have an impact on either of them?

It is possible that Lovecraft read Bataille and likely that Bataille read Lovecraft; there is no evidence that either influenced the other. Michel Meurger's article "'Retrograde Anticipation'" sets out the history of Lovecraft's reception in France, which Meurger found to be wrong-headed, insofar as Lovecraft's first French admirers interpreted him as reflections of themselves, i.e., as a kind of primitivist myth-maker interested in promulgating occult practices.[6] Meurger's thesis aside, two of his citations need consideration: first, he marks Gérard Legrand and Robert Benayoun's 1953 article in the Surrealist journal Médium as the first to introduce Lovecraft to France; second, in order to establish a French intellectual tradition that connected primitivism to occultism, he cites the 1929 article by Michel Leiris that appeared "in Documents, Georges Bataille's journal devoted to dissident Surrealists" (8).

Lovecraft's entrée to France actually came a couple of years earlier, but first, there is the matter of the importance of Documents, yet another publication that could make some legitimate claim to being the first cultural studies journal. Bataille was its general secretary, not its editor, but he ran the magazine and made virtually all its major editorial decisions—much to the chagrin of its publishers. Documents lasted only fifteen issues, from 1929 to 1930. It covered an impressive variety of subjects: avant-garde and indigenous art, jazz, experimental theatre, film, philosophy, ethnography, even the covers of cheap crime novels. And it brought them all together under a unifying sensibility that explicitly abjured any thought of authenticity or purity. Lovecraft would have found Documents fascinating and disgusting, and

---

6. One could say that they welcomed HPL as if he had been Bataille. Meurger also offers a critique of Maurice Lévy's "Fascisme ou fantastique, ou le cas Lovecraft." Lévy's article establishes HPL's fascist sympathies; Lévy's "Lovecraft: Entre fascisme et socialisme" traces HPL's turn toward socialism. I agree with the conclusions of Lévy's articles, as HPL would have: "For my part, I believe I am both a fascist & what I would have contemptuously called a 'damn socialist' in my younger & middle-aged days" (25 July 1934; AG 205).

he could have read at least part of it: each issue featured an English-language supplement, and Bataille's work was translated there. It is possible that Georges Wildenstein, publisher of *Documents*, had the English-language supplements included because he wished to distribute the journal in New York, where he had contacts.[7] Lovecraft could have read Bataille.

Bataille could have read Lovecraft as early as the late 1920s, as part of his researches for *Documents*, which included some investigation into American pulp magazines; he had almost certainly come across Lovecraft by the mid-1950s. The reason for this certainty lies with Bataille's friend Raymond Queneau. Queneau met Bataille on the fringes of the Surrealist movement in the late 1920s, but Bataille's taking up of fascist sensibilities as a cudgel against fascism strained their friendship. By the time they reconnected, after the war, Queneau had become a fan of Lovecraft. In 1951, for the French journal *Critique*, Queneau wrote a review of two American science fiction anthologies, one edited by August Derleth, and, in this brief text, he refers twice to Lovecraft, as a founder of the genre and as a friend of Derleth. This marks the first mention of Lovecraft in a French journal. Bataille founded *Critique* and served as its editor. Queneau's review went through Bataille.

In the same period, Bataille published several pieces by Roland Barthes, whose work also appeared in *Les Lettres Nouvelles*, alongside the first translations of Lovecraft's fiction into French. Lastly, Gavin Parkinson has made the claim that Lovecraft's work influenced "André Breton's frequently bemoaned 'new myth' of 'The Great Invisibles'" (105): Breton's idea first saw light in *VVV*, a bilingual Surrealist exile journal published in New York during the war. The issue of *VVV* following the one featuring Breton's myth presented an article discussing Lovecraft, and the subsequent issue featured strong critiques of Bataille and Acéphale, one of them by Waldberg. Bataille would have attended to all these publications.

Lovecraft was in the postwar French air, especially among the avant-garde, and Bataille played a minor role in elevating him. Further, it is interesting to note that Bataille would have recognized and taken a poignant interest in "Breton's attempt to conjure a myth out of nothing" (106), as this was the very task at which Bataille and Acéphale had failed. One of the persistent rumors about Acéphale is that they practiced human sacrifice or, at least, wanted to, and there is a truth to it, according to Waldberg:

7. I am grateful to Denis Hollier for this suggestion.

The war having been sparked, Acéphale wavered, undermined by internal dissension, appalled by consciousness of its own incongruity in the bosom of worldwide disaster. At the last meeting, in the heart of the forest, there were only four of us, and Bataille asked us other three to please put him to death, in order that the sacrifice, by founding a myth, might guarantee the survival of the community. (596-97)

Bataille's attempt to conjure a myth through blood sacrifice, inspired by the fascist success at doing these very things, failed, and, if Parkinson is right, Breton then discursively tried his own hand at inventing myth, under the influence of Lovecraft. If Lovecraft and Bataille had read each other, then they would have recognized immediately that they were, to put it in terms employed by Bataille, attracted and repulsed by the same things, that they had the same understanding of the importance of attraction and repulsion to human experience, and that they differed only in what they wished to convince others to be attracted to and repulsed by and in how they went about the task of convincing.[8] Let me turn now to some of those others who have read both and found each attractive and repulsive.

For a long time, scholars and artists have brought Lovecraft and Bataille together in a quiet mode, as separate influences or objects of study, perhaps making their interest explicit but without coupling them. To this chaste group belong certain Surrealists, some contributors to Oulipo, some contributors to the Argentine journal *Sur*, as well as Gilles Deleuze and Félix Guattari, and John Zorn, the saxophonist. More recent scholarship—Nick Land, Benjamin Noys, Reza Negarestani, Eugene Thacker—gets us closer to where we are now: Bataille and Lovecraft facing each other, in communication. This meeting, out in the open, each one with his thought exposed to the other's, has been going on for at least a decade, perhaps most prominently in work associated with accelerationism and speculative realism.

This line of research sharpens the viewpoints shared by Lovecraft and Bataille and intensifies the stark picture of human life that they bring into focus, in order to see more clearly the way out of any number of contemporary predicaments, from capitalism to climate change. Very briefly, both Lovecraft and Bataille developed an epistemology—and a quasi-metaphysics—that identified terrible constraints on human experience, while suggesting practices that strike at those constraints, practices that amount to an ethics

---

8. See Bataille, "Attraction and Repulsion, I & II."

of a sort, but one organized around experiences of horror and terror, that is: organized by sacred experience. Thus, scholars compare Lovecraft's cosmicism or "cynical materialism" to Bataille's notions of the formless and base materialism. Ben Woodard, for example, brought Lovecraft and Bataille together to draw the outlines of what he calls "Shoggothic Materialism," a materialism of perpetual becoming that brings us into view of the "weirdness of the non-human" (8).

Scott Cutler Shershow and Scott Michaelsen, in *The Love of Ruins: Letters on Lovecraft*, consisting of thirty four letters that the authors exchanged over a period of a year or so, make a more substantive comparison of Lovecraft and Bataille (along with numerous other figures). One of the observations they make is crucial for a proper understanding of how Lovecraft and Bataille relate to fascism:

> Lovecraft is decidedly and identifiably a writer of prayers, a psychonautic seeker, a lover of apophasis and the unnameable, a trembler before sacrifice, an author of narratives of terrible conversion and revelation. Lovecraft, in short, always cuts the figure of the modern mystic. Because of this we should try to keep thinking about him side by side with, say, Crowley or Bataille. (135)

This is an accurate portrait of Lovecraft, and juxtaposing him with Aleister Crowley, as well as Bataille, is suggestive. S. T. Joshi has characterized Lovecraft as a kind of mystic in similar but less extravagant terms and for good reason, given that Lovecraft often declared that he did not understand his own encounters with sublimity, nor why he was motivated to have them.[9]

Bataille's contemporaries certainly understood him in just this way: Sartre's only substantive engagement with Bataille's work was a review of

---

9. Joshi cites HPL writing to Derleth, in 1930, in a long passage containing the following lines: "Just what those delights and freedoms are, or even what they approximately resemble, I could not concretely imagine to save my life; save that they seem to concern some ethereal quality of indefinite expansion and mobility, and of a heightened perception which shall make all forms and combinations of beauty simultaneously visible to me, and realisable by me." Joshi then comments: "Much as I admire the logician in Lovecraft—the fierce foe of religious obscurantism, the rationalist and materialist who absorbed Einstein and retained a lifelong belief in the validity of scientific evidence—I think a passage like this, personal and even mystical in its way gets closer to what Lovecraft was all about" (*IAP* 934).

Inner Experience titled "A New Mystic." Walter Benjamin and Simone Weil, both of whom knew Bataille personally, found him dangerously given to an irrationalism bordering on mystical fanaticism.[10] Lovecraft and Bataille's taste for mystical experience would place them on common ground, across which one might advance to meet Lovecraft's racist texts with a Bataillean gaze, especially when one keeps in mind the well-known mystical predilections of the fascists.

Shershow and Michaelsen also have an exchange over how to interpret "The Shadow over Innsmouth" (1931), a difficult text for them, given that their book is an explicitly anti-racist project:

> [For] my part, this story will always remain a ruin and an open wound. I cannot for the life of me find any way to exonerate it of its fundamental complicity with the historical discourses of racist pseudoscience. Nor can I quite forgive the sheer efficiency with which, in this text, Lovecraft transforms small bodily characteristics into vivid signifiers of disgust and menace . . . . (112)

"The Shadow over Innsmouth" is perhaps Lovecraft's most fascistic tale, even more so than "The Horror at Red Hook" (1925). It opens with the hybrid people of Innsmouth in concentration camps after a huge federal raid. As ever, the allegory is not subtle. But Michaelsen offers a valiant counter-reading:

> Surely what commands our fascination above all in this story, & leaves open at least the possibility of a redemptive reading, is this pervasive tension or oscillation of blindness and sight, of seeing and not-seeing; correspondingly, the evident fact, indicated in such tension, that the narrator's aversion is actually self-hatred, an unconscious act of recognition. (115)

They are doing their level best to redeem Lovecraft of his own racism and perhaps exculpate their own affection for his tales, and they leave Bataille out of it, because once Bataille comes on the scene there will be no redemption. Bataille's understanding of community explains the thick, gnarled roots that strangle Michaelsen's attempt to redeem Lovecraft.

In a lecture titled "Society of Collective Psychology" (1938), Bataille provides a brief account of the genesis of community. Bataille is trying to account for how human community—not groups of primates but communities of people conscious of their community as a community—first came

---

10. See Surya for both and Jean-Maurice Monnoyer, *Le peintre et son demon,* for Benjamin.

into being, and he suggests attitudes and taboos concerning the dead as their wellspring:

> To the extent that it is true that society formed around the dead, it is necessary to implicate a common repulsion, disgust, and terror in the coming together of men in primitive times. No doubt, it is paradoxical to suggest that society is founded on disgust and terror; one must recognize, nonetheless, that if we do not speak of this powerful feeling we run the risk that many things will remain unintelligible. In fact, originary disgust may be the only violently *active* force that could account for the characteristic of clear-cut exteriority peculiar to social phenomena. (285)

Disgust is communal, always. It is not racism that lies at the heart of everything Lovecraft did, but disgust. Lovecraft often remarked on his own propensity to write about that which disgusted him, a habit Christian Roy noted in his comparison of Lovecraft and Bataille in *Lovecraftian Proceedings 2*:

> Clearly, Lovecraft's sympathies were not, like Bataille's, on the side of the upheaval of shapeless underground powers boiling beneath the surface, but of civilization's desperate attempts either to repress or to channel them as long as possible before its own inevitable entropic downfall.—Or were they? Not wholly or consistently, one could argue, given the obvious relish with which he explored and described just what he consciously feared the most. (200)

Disgust is always the mark of the sacred, therefore of community.[11] An anti-racist project, one that would abjure racism through a subversive reading, precludes facing up to this aspect of Lovecraft's work: the reader's disgust for Lovecraft's disgust demands a turning away from the text or a twisting of the text until its penitential contortions redeem it of its racism. An anti-fascist project, one devoted to overcoming racism and sadism as social practices, requires following the flow of Lovecraft's disgust as it radicalizes and turns back on itself, without ever asking it to be something other than what it is. One must wade into what Bataille calls "the cesspool of the heart" (Bataille, "The 'Old Mole'" 1985, 41), to meet Lovecraft where he lies. It is at this point that we must consider Bataille's theory of fascism in some detail.

---

11. This approach is only one of several Bataille took with regard to thinking through community. For an overview, see Mitchell and Winfree.

Taboo *Über Alles*

In Bataille's analysis, fascism both evaded the failures and defied the profanations of capitalism and communism, and it did so and thereby achieved its status as an innovative ordering of society through the novelty of its reaction: a mass movement from below restored the king to sovereignty above, in the form of the fascist leader; that is what made fascism new—and dangerous. The sovereignty of the king had always meant the power to enact limitless violence, a circumstance Bataille felt was best described as sadism, the exalted sadism of the sacred figure of the king, who justified his rule over the productive and stabilizing capacities of the state through the exclusion of those who were taboo, the disgusting masses:

> In opposition to the impoverished existence of the oppressed, political sovereignty initially presents itself as a clearly differentiated sadistic activity [. . .] the exclusion of the filthy forms that serve as the object of the cruel act is not accompanied by the positing of these forms as a value and, consequently, no erotic activity can be associated with the cruelty . . . within the heterogeneous domain, the imperative royal form has historically effected an exclusion of impoverished and filthy forms, sufficient to permit a connection with homogeneous forms . . . . (146)

This passage contains many terms of art, but in brief we should understand that: 1) the king and the masses subject to his cruelty both belong to the heterogeneous realm, the realm of the sacred and the taboo, whereas the state and the productive capacity of society belong to the homogeneous one, the profane; and 2) the cruelty of the king toward, say, a beggar would give no erotic charge, no sacred experience, but the killing of a king by a beggar would. Fascism restores the sadistic power and sacred potential of monarchy, but it does so by elevating one of the disgusting, oppressed masses through the force of those masses. This movement explains both the sense of identification between the masses and the fascist leader and the necessity of fascism's radicalization in generalized sadistic violence: a great mass of the wretched seize power, captivate their society, and instigate widespread cruelty. As Robert Paxton characterizes it: "A fascist regime could imprison, despoil, and even kill its inhabitants at will and without limitation. All else pales before that radical transformation in the relation of citizens to public power" (142).

Paxton's fine book on fascism makes no mention of Bataille, and the mainstream of the scholarship of fascism pays little more attention to him.

Bataille's investigations would fall under the rubrics of cultural and psychohistorical approaches to the study of fascism, of which Paxton, despite his own definition of fascism as a cult, is skeptical, but even sympathetic surveys of them, such as Robert Griffin's find few scholars drawing from Bataille (218). For example, Simonetta Falasca-Zamponi, who has written extensively on Bataille, in regard to both the College of Sociology and environmentalism, relegates him to a footnote in her *Fascist Spectacle*.[12] Perhaps the only extended consideration of fascism through a Bataillean lens is Claudio Fogu's *The Historic Imaginary*, which merely opens and closes with reflections on Bataille, ignoring him in between (though Fogu's reflections are positive and important).

Yet certain assessments of fascism suggest the benefits of Bataille's perspective: "Fascism was an affair of the gut more than of the brain," writes Paxton (42). To study it properly, one must focus on its "most important register: subterranean passions and emotions" (41). Paxton notes that fascism distinguished itself from "predemocratic dictatorships" by its "demonic energy" (217) and that, ultimately, it "rested not upon the truth of its doctrine, but upon the leader's mystical union with the historic destiny of his people" (17). Paxton characterizes the phenomenon of the fascist leader in suggestive terms:

> The *Führer* and the *Duce* could claim legitimacy neither by election nor conquest. It rested on *charisma*, a mysterious direct communication with the Volk or razza that needs no mediation by priests or party chieftains. Their charisma resembled media-era "stardom," raised to a higher power by its say over war and death. (127)

Seventy years earlier and several years before the war, Bataille observed that "Mussolini and Hitler immediately stand out as something *other*" (143; Bataille's emphasis), that "the *force* of a leader is analogous to that exerted in hypnosis" (144; Bataille's emphasis), and that:

> [The] religious value of the chief is really the fundamental (if not formal) value of fascism ... The chief as such is in fact only the emanation of a principle that is none other than that of the glorious existence of a nation raised to the value of a divine force (which, superseding every other conceivable consideration, demands not only passion but ecstasy from its participants). (154)

---

12. She refers to Bataille just as she begins discussing "Mussolini's supernatural qualities and his proximity to the sacred" (72).

Here the destiny of the fascists is written out, alongside an explanation of the power of their great rallies, monuments, and exhibitions: fascists experience sacredness. They know the sacred through their leader and through war. Further, because of "the common consciousness of increasingly violent and excessive energies and powers that accumulate in the person of the leader and through him become widely available" (144) and because the sadistic violence they bring to bear on those whom they have excluded does not deliver a sacred experience, they eventually must direct their sadism on that which they do value, namely, themselves. "In the end, radicalized Nazism lost even its nationalist moorings," writes Paxton. "Hitler wanted to pull the German nation down with him in a final frenzy," a suicidal frenzy that "had a basis within the nature of the regime" (164).

We have already noted these themes in Lovecraft—aristocratic disgust, unlimited violence, a suicidal turning on oneself—and it is of utmost value to follow his thinking as it winds through the fascism rooted in his own viscera, the bodily predispositions that make sacred experiences possible for him and justify political violence: "I am an Englishman, & for the sake of my ego's own comfort would fight like hell against any influence opposed to the dominance of English culture. It isn't that I 'owe' my race anything, but that my adrenal glands get hot at the idea of any damn enemy curbing the pattern which means myself" (18 January 1931, JFM 274). Such claims by Lovecraft—and there are many—are more than illustrative. What is special about Lovecraft's understanding of his own fierce and fascist passions is his recognition and even exultation of their fundamental falseness. For him, it is the weak-minded who are shocked by the contradiction "betwixt the pompous & grandiose pseudo-significance—& the intense poignancy—of certain emotions as *subjectively* experienced & the actual triviality & fortuitousness . . . of these emotions themselves considered *objectively* in relation to the immediate environment & to the cosmos in general" (20 January 1933, AG 172). This astonishing consciousness of Lovecraft's is what makes positioning his fascist enthusiasm within Bataille's analysis of fascism so valuable. A clarification of the analysis will provide a better view of that affect.

Bataille's analysis rests on two divisions, their structure and movements among them. First, he divides the social whole into two parts: homogeneity and heterogeneity. Then he divides heterogeneity into imperative and subversive elements. Under the rubric of homogeneity fall all the people and things that contribute to economic growth and knowledge: capital, the bourgeois and middle classes, science and technology, bureaucracies, institutions, and money itself. The distinctions here can be quite fine: the proletariat at work belongs to homogeneity, but in all other respects it does not; it is heterogeneous whenever it is not productive. Under heterogeneity, Bataille places the dispossessed and disenfranchised, sacred objects and practices, violence, madness, waste, and filth. It is easy to see, then, the second division, the dividing of heterogeneity into pure and impure forms, the divine and the sacrilegious, the imperative and the subversive. Homogeneity consists of the profane; heterogeneity consists of the sacred, split into right-hand and left-hand. With regard to the latter, it is important to keep in mind that the right sacred, the pure, determines the left, the impure: imperative heterogeneity establishes subversive heterogeneity, by way of exclusion.

In other words, Bataille sees the homogeneous as means and the heterogeneous as ends. Capital, the bourgeois, money, productivity, efficiency—they are all pointless; they waste nothing and bring about growth, but for no reason of their own. The king, the beggar, a wedding feast, an orgy in a brothel—they are reasons in themselves; we work for them; we police them; they give no return on our investments in them. What is useful has no meaning; what is meaningful has no use.

Fascism happens when heterogeneous elements seize the powers of homogeneity during a moment of crisis, a crisis of homogeneity, which neither capitalism, nor communism can resolve, because both belong to the homogeneous realm. They have no values of their own and provide no sacred experiences. "That's one reason I'm so red-hot for fascism," writes Lovecraft on Halloween 1933:

> Anything that can sto[m]p the sniveling, crawling profit-motive & calculative psychology out of a people, helps to raise that people in the scale of absolute human values. When people no longer waste themselves on "rugged individualism" in mere *industry*, they will be ripe for a truer individualism as rational & aesthetick beings. Viva Mussolini! God speed a planned, aristocratick state before things blow up into the planned proletarian state of Little Sonny's dreams! (JFM 342; Lovecraft's emphasis)

His elitism brings Lovecraft to regard the profane world of work with disgust: he disdains the bourgeois who "waste themselves" on profit, rather than higher, unproductive pursuits, and he despises "the brachycephalic longshoremen & coal-heavers" who, he believes, lack the capacity to become sensitive to such values (22 October 1927; *Mysteries of Time and Spirit* 174).

He reserves praise for that aristocracy which would itself esteem him and exclude both the profane and the disgusting: "only such a group can create standards and conditions calculated to make life enjoyable for high-grade individuals," the latter being a category into which he would place himself (JFM 276). In Lovecraft's view, say what one will about fascism, it establishes values; it is, at least, an ethos, which capitalism and communism are not. Moreover, fascism stalls off an uprising of the lower classes. While it may appear that Lovecraft's last-minute advocacy for socialist policies overseen by a fascist aristocracy amounts to a softening of his views, we ought to keep in mind that, for him, this change had only practicality to recommend it, not ethical value: "It might be quite all right to 'let the bastards starve' in the approved Hoover way if one could be sure they *would* starve instead of revolting. But one can't be sure" (25 July 1934; AG 205; Lovecraft's emphasis).

Lovecraft's tastes conform nicely to the divisions in Bataillean heterogeneity: the heterogeneous is, Bataille says, "everything resulting from *unproductive* expenditure," "everything rejected by bourgeois society as waste or as superior transcendental value" (142; Bataille's emphasis). The profane sets itself apart from the sacred, and the right-hand sacred rejects the left; the profane obeys the right-hand and oppresses the left. Thus is justified Bataille's characterization of the heterogeneous as either imperative or subversive. The former works as it sounds: the king, the sovereign, is "the possibility of and the requirement for collective unity" (148), the *Führer* and the *Duce*. The subversive forms are those the leader excludes, those whom he banishes, those whom he demands his followers subjugate and even destroy.

Thus, we witness Lovecraft's phenomenology of disgust: "for the cringing, broken, unctuous, subtle type we have a *genuine horror—a sense of outraged Nature*—which excites our deepest nerve-fibres of mental & physical repugnance" (18 January 1931; JFM 282; Lovecraft's emphases). It is important that he makes this exclusion "an affair of the gut," and it is important that he uses the first-person plural. Banishment into the realm of violence happens communally; it is done by and against communities, whence Lovecraft's anti-Semitism:

> What we can't forgive in the Jew is not the tone of his prayers or the size of his nose, but *the fact that he is willing to survive under the conditions he accepts.* Being *weak* may not have been his fault—but it *is* his fault *that he is alive & not free & dominant.* If we were as weak as he, & could not fight our way to self-respect, we would perish utterly—taunting our foes, virile & unbroken, as the

last man fell. *That unbrokenness is all that matters.* (12 January 1933; JFM 325; Lovecraft's emphases)

The imperative, sacred virtue is "unbrokenness;" by way of it, Lovecraft feels a visceral disgust for what he perceives to be brokenness; and he excludes absolutely all that disgusts him. This same process leads to the sadism of the particular imperative heterogeneous forces that have come to power in Germany and Italy and with which Lovecraft sympathizes. Weakness is subversive; it threatens what Lovecraft and the fascists know as sacred.

This division makes clear the problem that Lovecraft posed for Morton, an anti-racist activist, and the problem that white supremacist ideology continues to pose to this day, a complete disjunction of values: "They think that everyone holds *justice* the supreme good (& we egg them on by pretending to live up their notion), whereas we have the wholly different criterion of *freedom, unbrokenness, power,* & *war-joy*" (JFM 325). Lovecraft also brings violence into view, which the profane world places entirely on the side of heterogeneity. Imperative violence discriminates; the subversive brand does not: "the herd seems a bit disgusting because each member of it is always trying to hurt somebody else or gloating because somebody else is hurt" (8 March 1923; JFM 29). What would distinguish "the herd" whose "chief sport" is inflicting pain, from the lover of "war-joy"? The answer is sacredness: recall that Bataille says sovereign, imperative violence against the left-hand has no erotic value; subversive violence is erotic, however, and this difference explains how such low types as Hitler and Mussolini can become sacralized.

Bataille tells us that the fascist leader "derives his profound meaning from the fact of having shared the dejected and impoverished life of the proletariat," unlike the bourgeois functionaries who keep the State and, indeed, all homogeneous society humming and directly opposed to the sacred purity of the royal sovereign (154). Yet this meaning would have no force, if not for the community of fascists committed to violence. As Bataille recognizes, Napoleon restored sovereignty just as fascism did, but the latter differs insofar as it has "a character in a sense purified by the fact that paramilitary gangs substituted for the army in the constitution of power immediately have that power as an object" (149). The king, the Napoleonic Emperor stands apart from the Army; the *Führer* and the *Duce* belong to the militias. That is the very meaning of the *fasces*, the meaning into which Lovecraft bundles himself with the cord of sacredness.

Lovecraft marks and elucidates his sacred experiences with admirable precision; if Bataille wished to establish a science of heterogeneity, a heterology or agiology, then Lovecraft was such a scientist:

> I account that instant—about 4:05 to 4:10 p.m., Dec. 17, 1922—the most powerful simple emotional climax experienced during my nearly forty years of existence. In a flash all the past of New England—all the past of Old England—all the past of Anglo-Saxondom & the Western world—swept over me & identified me with the stupendous totality of all things in such a way as it never did before & never will again. (12 March 1930; *JFM* 222)

His first sighting of Marblehead formed a peak experience for Lovecraft, but not a singular one: he wrote often of feeling this way, of experiencing himself enmeshed in a bounded and totalizing community. Perhaps he never again attained this high-water mark, but he spent years and much of his little cash on travels to find more moments of that kind, and find them he did, in Charleston, New Orleans, Quebec, and elsewhere. And always he characterized these experiences as a surpassing of limitations that took place within severe limits: "The visible beauty & dignity of a settled aesthetically integrated region take on a fresh degree of poignancy & motivating stimulation when one can feel one's own hereditary blood-stream coursing through the scene as through the veins of some vast & exquisite organism" (19 November 1929; *JFM* 180). What a bold coloring of transgression and exclusion: a sacred joining of himself with something enormously large, a union felt in the depths of the body, and one that depends absolutely on the banishing of others, those whom he would hold in disgust, who have no part of this huge, blood-filled being and can never attach to it.

Lovecraft demonstrates the necessity of this connection, its status as a structure of sacred experience, in a letter to Morton in which he conveys the pleasures of his new apartment, "of coming home through a carved colonial doorway, & sitting beside a white Georgian mantel gazing out through small-paned windows over a sea of ancient roofs," then, a few lines later, assesses April's Aryan laws: "Just now Friend Adolph is overdoing the selective anthropology a bit, yet there's a damn sight of sense in a lot of his contentions" (12 June 1933; *JFM* 180). Lovecraft disagrees with Hitler that exclusion must be a matter of blood, as lines of culture would suffice, but he agrees that one must exclude—and exclude absolutely—anything less would leave the sacred under threat.

In this logic, we find the means by which Hitler becomes sacralized.

"Now, even if it seems that the connections permitting the association of political left and right with sacred left and right are disputable," writes Bataille, "it is a fact that sacred objects, in the same way as political figures, are never consistently transmuted except from left to right" ("Attraction and Repulsion II" 122). Thus Hitler, the wounded soldier, the failed painter, the prisoner, abject and weak, becomes the Führer, the principle of reality of Germany, at the time, the most scientifically advanced society in history, the pinnacle of homogeneity, and he made this movement by delivering sacred experiences to the militias, the Nazi Party, and the masses, by turning repulsion into attraction, by transforming subversive violence into imperative sadism.

Bataille explains thereby the "principle of contagion" observed in mass movements, as a "feeling of permeability experienced when confronted with an other/socius"; the repulsion of the other becomes attractive and there is produced "something analogous to the production of electric current uniting, in a more or less stable manner, individuals who come into contact almost by chance" ("Attraction and Repulsion I" 109).

Bataille makes three claims in his analysis of the movement of heterogeneous forces from subversive to imperative: 1) sacred experience is mediated; 2) this medium is essential to human life; 3) the experience of this medium is terrifying. These claims ground his critique of the fascist moment, in which he sees Italy and, especially, Germany uniting around a program of unlimited violence and both the liberal democracies and the Soviet Union failing to respond or even to recognize the threat: "union among human beings is not immediate union but is accomplished around a very strange reality, an incomparable obsessive force," he declares, and, further, he warns, "that if human relations stop passing through this middle term, this nucleus of violent silence, they are emptied of their human character" (114).

Both Bataille and Lovecraft agree that both capitalism and communism have indeed hollowed out the people who live under them, while fascism fills its adherents with sacred terror. It was because Bataille found that the Nazis accepted and responded to the fullness of their humanity that he so urgently and desperately called for their destruction: war was coming; the sadism instigated by the dissemination on a mass scale of imperative heterogeneity could lead to no other end. And, as Lovecraft had noted, the industrialization of war had changed its character: war had become "a sanguinary nightmare of wholesale mechanical extirpation affecting both military & civilian populations," "an expansive pestilence & calamity like the cyclone or the earthquake" (18 Ianuary, 1931; *JFM* 279).

Against these forces, Bataille sought to awaken the world to the need to bring subversive violence to bear against fascism, which meant a coming to consciousness of the sacred and the filthy: "I believe that nothing is more important for us than that we recognize that we are bound and sworn to that which horrifies us most, that which provokes our most intense disgust" (114). Lovecraft could hardly have disagreed with a principle and formulation so Lovecraftian; he would have demurred only at the prospect of choosing sides, as, in his view, they had already been chosen, even if arbitrarily, and it is in this last respect that Lovecraft's perspective takes on its true depth.

Conclusion: "The Absolute Lie"

Lovecraft was wont to shock his correspondents with his actual beliefs. In one passage, he communicates with almost childlike earnestness the wonder of what we can only call a spiritual experience. In another, he slavers over his delectation for his own violent hatreds, happier to know himself as racist than to see racism enacted. And then there comes, time and again, a great denial of any condition that could ground the previous sentiments in a philosophical way: "No emotion or principle is really 'sacred,'" he writes to Robert E. Howard, "for each of our instinctively cherished values is merely an outgrowth of some former stage of anthropological experience wherein the given quality actually possessed a strong survival-value" (21 January 1933; *MF* 518). It was chance that stitched Lovecraft's nerves to the old quilts of New England and parted him from the whole rest of the fabric of humanity, and even that stitch is coming undone. Lovecraft accepts that the medium of his own sacred experience is threadbare, the nucleus of his terror and disgust is worn out and must soon tear. The "red-hot" emotions that would kindle such horrific violence and terrifying wonder must cool and fade:

> Naturally, the relinquishment of traditional standards and conditions (which lend so many illusions of significance and purpose to the empty process of life) is a woefully painful process for members of the two or three transitional generations—but sometimes it has to be accomplished. (21 January 1933; *MF* 518)

Lovecraft had a commitment equal to that of fascism, in that his sadistic fantasies have a logic destined to radicalize in his own destruction, and, simultaneously, he embraced the void that would slowly drain away the possibility of fascist sacredness. This contradiction hangs in Lovecraft's great dark consciousness like a star: everything radiates from it—his letters, his stories, his refusal to work—and it poses a great defiance to Bataille, who sought to rouse the masses against fascism by advocating for precisely the conflict Lovecraft lived.

The College of Sociology responded to the Munich agreement with a fierce denunciation of the capitulation and weakness of the liberal democracies and a call for a violent response:

> [The College] urges those, for whom the only solution anguish disclosed is the creation of a vital bond between men, to join with it, with no other determining factor than the awareness of the *absolute lie* of current political forms and the necessity for reconstructing on this assumption a collective mode of existence that takes no geographical or social limitation into account and that allows one to behave oneself when death threatens. (Bataille et al., "Declaration" 46)

Bataille wanted a renunciation of the imperative sacred, on the grounds of the Lovecraftian insight that the medium that delivers it is pure falsehood, but he does not wish to lose heterogeneity itself: any replacement of one sort of right-hand sacredness by another returns imperative violence to its sovereign position, where it would control the new and devastating forces of modern war; but to descend to subversive violence would be to experience heterogeneous power and, therefore, the fullness of human reality, without sadism.

"Judged by any theoretical ideal," Lovecraft writes to Howard, "all life is evil" (28 March 1933; MF 574). This judgment would include Lovecraft's own ideals, as he knew, and yet that knowledge had no effect on the sacred possibilities imprinted upon him. What Bataille would beg Lovecraft to consider is that Lovecraft's experiences of disgust are, of course, no more false than his experience of sacredness, and if the latter has given him a sense of community, then so may the former. The community of the sacred is real—and so is the community of evil. The difference is that one comes to the community of evil by knowing and experiencing the failure and the falsehood, "the absolute lie" of the community of the sacred—and that failure, that horror and disgust, they are the human universal. The community of evil is the "universal community," Acéphale sought to bring into conscious experience. In every place where Lovecraft communicates disgust—in letter, fiction, or essay—he gives a taste of the dark mass of human evil that, Bataille thought, alone could allow humanity to overcome the crisis of fascism.

For us, now, Bataille might suggest we consider some of the practices he undertook, with a hope for better results: an oath-bound denial of social niceties to bigots, for example. In an age of easy accusation, it is unlikely anyone's hand would prove worthy of all—and would such an outcome not have meaning? Despite this possibility, it is unlikely that Bataille could have relaxed Lovecraft's grip on his prejudices—and, as we know, any gestures of politesse on Bataille's part would have been ruled out. The same might hold true for the neo-fascists of today. But if Bataille had invited Lovecraft to one of the orgies in the woods? Or a riot in the streets? The former would have proved impossible, for perhaps the most tragic reason. Acéphale began its rituals in the Marly forest only in March 1937, but no one knows when precisely. The July 1937 double issue of the journal Acéphale offers a hint. There, in the article "Nietzschean Chronicle," in a discussion of a production of Cervantes's The Siege of Numantia, Bataille assesses the political circumstances of Europe as follows:

> Among the various convulsive conflicts in history, the one currently sundering the totality of civilized countries—the conflict between anti-fascism and fascism—appears the most corrupt. The comedy which—under the pretense of democracy—opposes German Caesarism with Soviet Caesarism, shows what frauds are acceptable to a mob limited by misery, at the mercy of those who basely flatter it. (208)

Bataille saw socialism, Christianity, and fascism as the "tricephalous monster" (capitalistic democracy, he thought, would just get eaten) (516). It was against these heads of society that he fought; they would all become Caesars. And when does one kill Caesar? On the Ides of March, which, in 1937, was the day Lovecraft died. It is possible that Lovecraft's long, tortured illness came to an end as Bataille and his fellow cultists burned sulfur, drew blood, and initiated their orgiastic rites in the woods for the first time. So much for the orgy, what of the riot? Lovecraft wrote this:

> About Brown rioting—yes, I did take genuine pride in the virile energy & healthy antinomianism displayed on Memorial Day. [. . .] It makes me sad to reflect that I've grown too old & grey to mix into inspiring rough-&-tumbles like this. I'd love to crack skulls in the name of free individualism, & smash office-appliance-shop windows as a symbolic nose-thumbing at the age of commerce, machines, time-tables, & aeroplane-speeded cosmic tail-

chasing. [. . .] Here's hoping the boys do better next year—ploughing up the new airport, burning the Rotary Club, & ducking a score of mill-owners & efficiency experts in the most oil-polluted spot in the Providence river! (30 July 1929; JFM 175)

Lovecraft was a sizable fellow, but surely he would not have survived such an indulgence. Would that not have been better? Would it not have been better for Lovecraft to die in a riot against profit rather than in the ignominious way he did? Would it not have been better then? Would it not be better for our fascists now?

Works Cited

Bataille, Georges. "Attraction and Repulsion I: Tropisms, Sexuality, Laughter and Tears." In *The College of Sociology 1937–39*. Ed. Denis Hollier. Trans. Betsy Wing. Minneapolis: University of Minnesota Press, 1988. 103-12.

———. "Attraction and Repulsion II: Social Structure." In *The College of Sociology 1937–39*. Ed. Denis Hollier. Trans. Betsy Wing. Minneapolis: University of Minnesota Press, 1988. 113-24.

———. *Literature and Evil*. Interview with Pierre Dumayet. Archives INA, 1958. www.youtube.com/watch?v=5XCnGuK8CVc. Accessed 31 October 2018.

———. [*le monstre tricéphale*]. In *L'Apprenti Sorcier*. Ed. Marina Galletti. Paris: Éditions de la différance, 1999. 516-19.

———. "Nietzschean Chronicle." In *Visions of Excess: Selected Writings, 1927-1939*. Ed. Allan Stoekl. Trans. Carl R. Lovitt. Minneapolis: University of Minnesota Press, 1985. 202-12.

———. "The 'Old Mole' and the Prefix *Sur* in the Words *Surhomme* [Superman] and *Surrealist*." In *Visions of Excess: Selected Writings, 1927–1939*. Ed. Allan Stoekl. Trans. Donald M. Leslie, Jr. Minneapolis: University of Minnesota Press, 1985. 32-44.

———. "Popular Front in the Street." *Visions of Excess*. Ed. and trans. Allan Stoekl. Minneapolis: University of Minnesota Press, 1985. 161-70.

———. "Program (Relative to Acéphale)." Trans. Annette Michelson. *October* No. 39 (1986): 78-79.

———. "The Psychological Structure of Fascism." In *Visions of Excess: Selected Writings, 1927–1939*. Ed. Allan Stoekl. Trans. Carl R. Lovitt.

Minneapolis: University of Minnesota Press, 1985. 137-60.

―――. *The Sacred Conspiracy: The Internal Papers of the Secret Society of Acéphale and Lectures to the College of Sociology.* Ed. Marina Galletti and Alastair Brotchie. Trans. Natasha Lehrer, John Harman, and Meyer Barash. London: Atlas Press, 2018.

―――. "Société de psychologie collective." In *Oeuvres Complètes, volume II.* Ed. Denis Hollier. Paris: Gallimard, 1970. 281-87.

Bataille, Georges, and Pierre Kaan. "LA PATRIE OU LA TERRE." In *Oeuvres Complètes, Volume I.* Ed. Denis Hollier. Paris: Gallimard, 1970. 389.

Bataille, Georges, Michel Leiris, and Roger Callois. "Declaration of the College of Sociology on the International Crisis." In *The College of Sociology 1937-39.* Ed. Denis Hollier. Trans. Betsy Wing. Minneapolis: University of Minnesota Press, 1985. 43-46.

Callaghan, Gavin. *H. P. Lovecraft's Dark Arcadia: The Satire, Symbology and Contradiction.* Jefferson, NC: McFarland, 2013.

Derie, Bobby. *Sex and the Cthulhu Mythos.* New York: Hippocampus Press, 2014.

Falasca-Zamponi, Simonetta. *Fascist Spectacle: The Aesthetics of Power in Mussolini's Italy.* Berkeley: University of California Press, 1997.

Fogu, Claudio. *The Historic Imaginary: Politics of History in Fascist Italy.* Toronto: University of Toronto Press, 2003.

Gentile, Emilio. "Fascism as Political Religion." *Journal of Contemporary History* 25 (May-June 1990): 229-51.

Giroux, Henry A. *American Nightmare: Facing the Challenge of Fascism.* San Francisco: City Lights Books, 2018.

Griffin, Roger. "Fixing Solutions: Fascist Temporalities as Remedies for Liquid Modernity." *Journal of Modern European History* 13 (January 2015): 5-23.

Joshi, S. T. *H. P. Lovecraft: The Decline of the West.* Mercer Island, WA: Starmont House, 1990.

Kendall, Stuart. *Georges Bataille.* London: Reaktion Books, 2007.

Lévy, Maurice. "Fascisme et fantastique, ou le cas Lovecraft." *Caliban* No. 7 (1970): 67-78.

―――. "Lovecraft: Entre fascism et socialisme." *Europe* No. 707 (March 1988): 64-76.

Lovecraft, H. P., and Donald Wandrei. *Mysteries of Time and Spirit: The Letters of H. P. Lovecraft and Donald Wandrei.* Ed. S. T. Joshi and David E. Schultz. San Francisco: Night Shade Books, 2002.

Meurger, Michel. "'Retrograde Anticipation': Primitivism and Occultism in the French Response to Lovecraft 1953-1957." Trans. S. T. Joshi. *Lovecraft Studies* Nos. 19/20 (1989): 5-19.

Mitchell, Andrew J., and Jason Kemp Winfree, ed. *The Obsessions of Georges Bataille: Community and Communication.* Albany: State University of New York Press, 2009.

Monnoyer, Jean-Maurice. *Le Peintre et son demon: Entretiens avec Pierre Klossowski.* Paris: Flammarion, 1985.

Paxton, Robert O. *The Anatomy of Fascism.* New York: Vintage Books, 2005.

Parkinson, Gavin. "Surrealism, Science Fiction and UFOs in the 1950s: 'Myth' in France Before Roland Barthes." In *Surrealism, Science Fiction and Comics*, ed. Gavin Parkinson. Liverpool: Liverpool University Press, 2015.

Queneau, Raymond. "Un Nouveau Genre littéraire: Les science-fictions." *Critique.* No. 46 (1951): 195-98.

Roy, Christian. "H. P. Lovecraft, Georges Bataille, and the Fascination of the Formless: One Crawling Chaos Seen Emerging from Opposite Shores." In *Lovecraftian Proceedings 2*, ed. Dennis P. Quinn. New York: Hippocampus Press, 2017. 189-207.

Shershow, Scott Cutler, and Scott Michaelsen. *The Love of Ruins: Letters on Lovecraft.* Albany: State University of New York Press, 2017.

Stanley, Jason. *How Fascism Works: The Politics of Us and Them.* New York: Random House, 2018.

Stoekl, Allan. "Truman's Apotheosis: Bataille, 'Planisme,' and Headlessness." *Yale French Studies* 78 (1990): 181-205.

Surya, Michel. *Georges Bataille: An Intellectual Biography.* Trans. Krzysztof Fijalkowski and Michael Richardson. New York: Verso, 2002.

Waldberg, Patrick. "Acéphalogramme." In *L'Apprenti Sorcier.* Ed. Marina Galletti. Paris: Éditions de la différance, 1999. 584-98.

Waugh, Robert H. "Dr. Margaret Murray and H. P. Lovecraft: The Witch-Cult in New England." *Lovecraft Studies* No. 31 (1994): 2-10.

Woodard, Ben. "Mad Speculation and Absolute Inhumanism: Lovecraft, Ligotti, and the Weirding of Philosophy." *Continent* 1 (2011): 3-13.

Stages of the Spiral:
Lovecraft's Descent into the Maelstrom

Sean Moreland
University of Ottawa

The impetus for this essay came from a remark by renowned mangaka Junji Ito, whose magnum opus of comic-cosmic horror, *Uzumaki,* is among the most powerful late twentieth-century examples of Lovecraftian sequential art. Asked about the inspiration for the eponymous spirals of *Uzumaki,* Ito replied that the "different stages of the spiral" visualized by the book "were definitely inspired from the mysterious novels of H. P. Lovecraft" (n.p.). Ito appears to be the first commentator to have noted the importance of spirals in Lovecraft's writings; despite their prevalence, the spirals that thread through Lovecraft's writings have yet received no sustained critical attention. This essay briefly traces the development and significance of the spirals that appear in some of Lovecraft's earlier writings, while their evolution in his later writings, and their visual transformations in Ito's manga, will be examined elsewhere. Tracing the emergence and evolution of spirals in Lovecraft's writings prior to 1927 further illuminates Lovecraft's relationship with the literary Modernism of writers including Ezra Pound and T. S. Eliot, as well as his reception of two of his most important literary precursors, Edgar Allan Poe and Lucretius, whose work Lovecraft situated as part of a speculative materialist literary counter-tradition to the metaphysical tradition championed by Eliot and Pound.

Spirals: The Whirled Image

Nico Israel's expansive study, *Spirals: The Whirled Image in Twentieth-Century Literature* launches from the recognition that "spirals are a crucial means through which twentieth-century writers and visual artists think about the twentieth century" (2). Israel reads the spirals that shape so much of the period's philosophy, literature and art as "embodying tensions between teleology and cyclicality, repetition and difference, locality and globality" (2). While Israel never mentions Lovecraft, much of his analysis is applicable to Lovecraft's work, which responds to many of the same cultural and scientific forces as that of the artists and writers with whom with first half of *Spirals* is largely concerned. Israel writes:

> In the early-twentieth-century work of the Italian Futurists, British Vorticists, and Russian Constructivists, the spiral was often associated with modernity, energy, and spatiotemporal expansion, whereas with Joyce and Duchamp spirals began to serve as a sign for an energy-sapping anemia that challenged those early-century associations, and in the later-century work of Beckett and Smithson spirals expressed a recoiling entropy that calls into question the very foundation of the project of modernity and the colonial-imperial project and man-centered histories it subtended. (8–9)

While the spirals in Lovecraft's later writings could be productively compared with those of Joyce, Duchamp, or even the entropic embodiment of cosmic time that characterizes Robert Smithson's geological art-work "Spiral Jetty," this essay focuses on the spirals that appear in Lovecraft's writings from 1916 through to 1927, during which time he is very much in dialogue with the early Modernist texts that are the focus of the first phase of Israel's analysis in *Spirals*. This periodization reflects Lovecraft's completion of the first edition of "Supernatural Horror in Literature," the research for which led him to intensively revise his ideas of weird fiction and cosmic horror, revisions reflected in the more complexly textured uses of vortical and spiral imagery in his later fictions. While these will be anticipated in my conclusion, they will not be fully explored here.

From the Spencerian Spiral to the Vortical Spiral

Vorticism, a literary and artistic movement founded by Wyndham Lewis and Ezra Pound, who named and chiefly promulgated it, was most prominent in Britain from roughly 1912 until 1915. In what would become a manifesto for the movement, Pound declared that the poetic image, the aesthetic core of Vorticism, was "a radiant node or cluster," "a VORTEX from which, and through which, and into which, ideas are constantly rushing" (Kenner 146). Pound's desire to orient this movement around an energetic image stemmed from his insistence on the truth of a statement in Justinian's Institutes, *Nomina sunt consequentiae rerum*: "names are a consequence of things," and ideas are thereby best expressed by things. Lovecraft's spiralling vortexes emerged slightly later than those trumpeted by the Vorticists; they begin appearing in his writings during the course of World War I, which Lovecraft notably described as a "maelstrom." Unlike Pound, Lovecraft never formally presented the spiral vortexes in his writings as emblematic of his philosophy and aesthetics. However, Lovecraft's spirals during this period, like those of the Vorticists, are attempts to radically break from both Romantic vitalism and Victorian philosophical ideals.

The spiral as image of Romantic vitalism converged with Victorian evolutionary thought via an 1858 essay called "On Physical Morphology" by British biologist James E. Hinton. The essay describes at length the prominence of spiral structures in the growth patterns of various organisms. A particular passage in that study, focused on the spiral forms found throughout nature, circulated through subsequent Victorian scientific and philosophical literature with a reach and frequency Hinton could not have foreseen. The passage reads:

> Throughout almost the whole of organic nature the spiral form is more or less distinctly marked. Now, motion under resistance takes a spiral direction, as may be seen by the motion of a body rising or falling through water. A bubble rising rapidly in water describes a spiral closely resembling a corkscrew, and a body of moderate specific gravity dropped into water may be seen to fall in a curved direction, the spiral tendency of which may be distinctly observed. (487)

Following these remarks, Hinton describes how spirality structures not only botanical life, but many of the organs of complex animal life, explaining the frequency with which life develops along spiral patterns as dictated by growth along the path of least resistance. The excerpt cited above is quoted in its entirety by Herbert Spencer's *First Principles* (1860) and included with subsequent revisions and reprintings of Spencer's book, the most popular and influential philosophical text of the late Victorian period.

Spencer saw in Hinton's description (which built on observations by earlier scientists and writers, notably including Goethe) a powerful visualization of life's ordered progression through conflict, competition and environmental resistance toward a *telos* of adapted integration. This view was the bedrock of Spencer's cosmic philosophy, and he saw it as equally applicable to biological, social, and astronomical phenomena. Among Lovecraft's most important sources of evolutionary thought was the volume *Evolution in Modern Thought* (1917; see *Lovecraft's Library*, no. 323), in which H. Höffding criticizes Spencer's evolutionary thought by comparing it to Hegel's idealistic philosophy, with which it shares its unscientific character. Höffding notes: "In Spencer's hands the theory of evolution acquired a more decidedly optimistic character than in Darwin's" (206). For Spencer, the spiral was a figuration of cosmic optimism, a harmonious, teleological, and spiritualized vision of evolution. In developing his own sense of "cosmic pessimism," Lovecraft would radically transform the significance of this spiral.

The vortexes of both Pound and Lovecraft during this period disrupt the Spencerian spiral by returning to the atomist philosophical tradition that began with the pre-Socratic Greek philosophers Leucippus and Democritus, and was carried on by their post-Socratic descendent, Epicurus. While Pound's conception of Vorticism was shaped by late nineteenth- and early twentieth-century scientific concepts, it was primarily his readings in pre-Socratic Greek cosmology that inspired his imagistic concept of the vortex, derived from the δίνη (*dinē*), the cosmic vortex of atoms that according to Democritus gave rise to the manifold forms of the world.[1] This image pervades and shapes Pound's poetics from his Vorticist period onward, informing his subsequent articulation of Imagism and inspiring the fragmentary and involute form of the *Cantos* in his later career, from his opening revision of the Homeric *nekuia* (3–5) to the later image of the "Rose in the Steel Dust" (469).

Particularly important for Pound's early focus on the δίνη, was John Burnet's *Early Greek Philosophy* (first published in 1897, it would go through numerous revised editions until 1930). Attempting to disentangle the physical and cosmogonic theories of the pre-Socratic atomists from their Epicurean synthesis, Burnet conceded the difficulty in doing so based on the elliptical, partial records that remain of their writings, although he speculated that much of what was original in Epicurus's philos-

---

1. See, for example, Pound's gnomic gloss on Democritus, Lucretius, and atomism in *Guide to Kulchur*, "Sophists" (119). For a discussion of the meaning of the vortex in Pound more broadly, see "Vortex" in *Glossolalia* (39). For a more detailed discussion of some of its philosophical and scientific sources, see Pfannkuchen, "From Vortex to Vorticism." For a discussion of Pound's interpretation of Leucippus via neo-Platonism, see for example the second chapter of Peter Liebregts, *Ezra Pound and Neoplatonism*.

ophy resulted from an attempt to reconcile Aristotelian thought with that of Leucippus and Democritus: "It seems to me that the nightmare of Epicurean atomism can only be explained on the assumption that an Aristotelian doctrine was violently adapted to a theory which really excluded it. It is unlike anything we meet with in earlier days" (397).

The combination of antiquity and violent novelty foregrounded by Burnet's description appealed to Pound, and he adopted the vortex as the symbol for the artistic movement he and Lewis founded. For Pound, however, the δίνη, which had served Plato as a crucial metaphor for chora in *Timaeus*, was inextricably connected to Neoplatonic philosophy, which he would eventually try to reconcile with both philosophical materialism and Confucianism. It is an imagistic concept equally, although differently, crucial for Lovecraft, whose reception of the Democritean δίνη was part of a rejection of Plato, and idealistic and religious thought generally. Lovecraft situated himself within a materialistic and scientific philosophical tradition, declaring:

> The world and all its inhabitants impress me as immeasurably insignificant, so that I always crave intimations of larger and subtler symmetries than these which concern mankind. All this, however, is purely aesthetic and not at all intellectual. I have a parallel nature or phase devoted to science and logic, and do not believe in the supernatural at all—my philosophical position being that of a mechanistic materialist of the line of Leucippus, Democritus, Epicurus and Lucretius—and in modern times, Nietzsche and Haeckel. (*SL* 2.160)

Pound once quipped, "I suppose men still can read Lucretius. I prefer to respect him" (119). Lovecraft didn't just read Lucretius, however; he made him a literary-philosophical precursor. Until near the end of World War I, Lovecraft conceived of himself as an Epicurean, and of Epicurean philosophy as largely compatible with a modern scientific viewpoint. By 1918, however, this had changed.

At the core of Lucretius's poetic promulgation of Epicurean ethics and physics is his at least partially original refinement of Epicurean physics via the clinamen, or declination, of atoms, often translated into English as a "swerve." The clinamen was Lucretius' conception of a spontaneous and undirected deviation of atoms. As they fall through the endless void of space, rather than falling forever in a straight line, each atom periodically makes an imperceptibly minute swerve, making its descent a downward spiral that enables it to collide and combine with other atoms, giving rise to universes full of innumerable recombinative forms (2.216–93). While Israel recognizes the influence of Lucretius's swerve in shaping the spiral images in Enlightenment art and literature, he notes this influence only in passing, writing that

> despite the condensation that takes place in the translation from Greek *helix* to Latin *spiralis*, in the late Middle Ages the spiral form preserved a sense of its helical depth and extensity, drawing on its association in the classical period with the movement of the celestial spheres and of the soul's wandering (Plato) and with zoological ideas about natural life, as in Virgil's *Georgics* or indeed in Lucretius, who, in *De rerum natura*, uses the term *clinamen* to describe the "swerving" movement of atoms. (26)

The problem, for Lovecraft, is precisely with how Lucretius imagines the atoms coming together in their descent. Lucretius' clinamen presents an analogy between the indeterminacy of atomic movement and human free will, one that would lead the dogmatically determinist Lovecraft to reject Epicurean physics, a divorce retrospectively dramatized in his 1922 essay, "A Confession of Unfaith." Karl Marx's doctoral dissertation on Democritean and Epicurean natural philosophy anticipated, in certain respects, Burnet's attempt to disentangle various strands of Greek atomistic philosophy. Marx wrote admiringly of Lucretius' exposition of the clinamen, which he read as revealing the revolutionary potential inherent in matter itself: "Lucretius therefore is correct when he maintains that the declination breaks the fati foedera [bonds of fate] and, since he applies this immediately to consciousness, it can be said of the atom that the declination is that something in its breast that can fight back and resist" (Chapter 10, n.p.).

Marx saw revolutionary potential in Lucretius' materialist poetics; Lovecraft, however, rejected Lucretius' analogy as both unscientific and aesthetically distressing. Despite his otherwise intense self-identification with Lucretius and Epicurean philosophy, Lovecraft's response typifies the reaction to the clinamen described by Michel Serres in his 1977 study, *The Birth of Physics*. Serres writes,

> From Cicero to Marx and beyond, down to us, the declination of atoms has been treated as a weakness of the atomic theory. The clinamen is an absurdity. A logical absurdity, since it is introduced without justification, the cause of itself before being the cause of all things; a geometrical absurdity, in that the definition that Lucretius gives is incomprehensible and confused; a mechanical absurdity, since it is contrary to the principle of inertia, and

would result in perpetual motion; an absurdity of physics in general, since experimentation cannot possibly reveal its existence. (3)

However, Serres claims that the clinamen's crucial importance for philosophy begins with its banishment from the language of physics, for with this excommunication it "finds a haven in subjectivity, moving from the world to the soul, from physics to metaphysics, from the theory of inert bodies in free fall to the theory of the free movements of living beings" (3). Lovecraft's writings uniquely dramatize this transition, as once the clinamen is banished from his philosophy, it subsequently re-emerges as an animating force in his weird fiction. In Haeckelian language, Lovecraft's writings offer an exemplary ontogenic recapitulation of the phylogenic transition traced by Serres's *Birth of Physics*.

Lovecraft, however, went further than discarding the clinamen from the domain of positivistic philosophy. He also rejected the possibility of both free will and ontological indeterminacy, a rejection influenced by his reading of Hugh Elliot's *Modern Science and Materialism* (1919; see, for example, *IAP* 367-68). Indeed, Elliot frames his discussion of volition and purposiveness in language that Lovecraft would have recognized as invoking the Democritean δίνη, whose radical determinism is undermined by the Epicurean concept of undirected atomic movement. Elliot writes that we designate as "purposive" "the majority of those redistributions which issue from the little whirlpools of matter and energy called organisms, and those factors in particular by which the immediate continuance of such whirlpools is ensured" (164).[2]

Elliot's "whirlpools" in this passage are distinctly Democritean, rather than Epicurean, in that they are determinate, and in principle, entirely predictable. The atomic vortex as imagined by Lucretius, however, arises from a declination, an undirected, and therefore unpredictable, swerve, and it is precisely this that leads to its rejection by Lovecraft. Where writers including Marx, Bergson, Deleuze, and Serres are drawn to this aspect of *De Rerum Natura*, Lovecraft finds the concept of ontological indeterminacy distressing.

Serres influentially resituates the clinamen using the language of modern fluid mechanics, describing it as the minimal angle of deviation from a laminar flow required to create turbulence. He emphasizes that in Lucre-

---

2. See also Joshi's discussion in *Decline* 43.

tius' account it is this turbulence that is the condition for atoms to collide and combine, meaning that turbulence, which introduces disorder into a laminar atomic flow, is *also* the precondition for the emergence of order. Serres writes:

> The physical theory of turbulence contains a paradox. Laminar flow, the figure of chaos, is at first sight a model of order. The atoms pour out in parallel, without mixing or sticking to each other. These preliminary rows are already a taxonomy, as the word itself indicates. Turbulence seems to introduce a disorder into this arrangement. This is what the language means: *turbare* means a disorder, a confusion, a disruption or, as we say, a perturbation. Disorder emerges from order. Yet it is precisely the reverse that is to be described and that occurs. Physics tries to explain how things and the world are formed naturally out of the atomic chaos, in other words how an order, or several orders, emerge from disorder. And it is turbulence that secures the transition. (28)

From the clinamen emerges the chaotic collisions of *turba*, the confused crashing together of atoms, and from this emerges the structure of *turbo*, the spiral, spinning cone or vortex, the image adopted as an emblem by Pound. In Lovecraft's writings from this period, spirals and vortices tend to figure either *turba*, disturbance, perturbation, chaos and disorder, or *turbo*, the emergence of patterns of force and organization from this disorder. Consider, for example, "From Beyond" (1920), in which the vortex becomes an image of disorder and unintelligibility: "in my terror my mind again opened to the impressions coming from what Tillinghast called 'beyond.' I was now in a vortex of sound and motion, with confused pictures before my eyes" (CF 1.198). Notably, the narrator's description of this chaotic vision corresponds with Lovecraft's criticism of the chaotic formlessness of Modernist literary experimentation, discussed below. In contrast, consider Lovecraft's use of the spiral staircase as a means of revealing previously hidden, timeless realities in both "Celephaïs" (1920) and "The Festival" (1923). In the former, "Kuranes walked up a damp stone spiral stairway endlessly" (CF 1.189), and in the latter, the narrator descends "a narrow spiral staircase damp and peculiarly odorous, that wound endlessly down into the bowels of the hill past monotonous walls of dripping stone blocks" (CF 1.413). While one is a Dreamlands tale marked by ascent, the other a horror tale marked by descent, both use architectural spirality to expose their protagonists to a visionary world beyond time. The spiral leads to a transhistorical vision here, much as it does for Pound (even if, in the case of "The Festival," this vision is horrifying). Both tales also anticipate the way spirals effect a "violation of the galling limitations" of time and space in Lovecraft's later fiction.[3]

"The Festival," which tells of a man's return to the horrific half-forgotten rites of his ancient family, makes a particularly useful portal into Lovecraft's return to a predominant literary precursor, whose work shaped his evolving spirality along lines markedly different from those pursued by Poundian Vorticism. This is, of course, Edgar Allan Poe, whose work is rife with Gothic staircases winding into dank cellars, as well as vortexes spiralling down into oceanic depths or astral bodies whirling up and out through the unfolding universe of stars. Indeed, the spiral, in the dynamic form of the vortex, is the most pervasive and important motif in Poe's writings, and engenders his aesthetics of the grotesque and arabesque, as Patricia Smith observes:

> The arabesque as Poe sees it is an attempt to suggest something kinetic—the motion toward unity—in a static medium; symbolically, it is always moving in the direction of the form-obliterating spiral. The man whirling about on Aetna resolves all he sees into a radical blur by means of his spin; the universe itself, in *Eureka*, collapses ultimately into a state of nihility. As in the Maelstrom, where all things "meet together at the bottom," the final vision toward which the arabesque points is one in which unity is perceived, and it is impossible to distinguish one thing from another.[4] (42)

Poe's vortexes reflect his materialist metaphysics, which in turn derive from his own transformative reception of the classical atomist influences he shares with Lovecraft. The intersection of these influences in Lovecraft's imagination is suggested by their inter-whirling in the poem that first expresses his own developing cosmic materialist vision, "Aletheia Phrikodes," first published as part of "The Poe-et's Nightmare" in 1918.[5]

---

3. For a meditation on this relationship Juan L. Perez-de-Luque, "Descending Spirits" 89–106.

4. For a discussion of HPL's rhetorical positioning of Poe via Epicurus, see Sean Moreland, "Beyond the Flaming Walls of the World." For a detailed analysis of HPL's multifaceted reception of Lucretius, see Moreland, "The Poet's Nightmare" and "The Birth of Cosmic Horror." For more on Poe's own complex relationship with Lucretius and Epicurean atomism, see Moreland, "Beyond 'De Rerum Naturâ, Esqr.'"

5. For a detailed analysis of how HPL's poetry builds suggestively on Poe's poetics, see Studniarz, "Lovecraft's Poetry and Poe's Poetics," and for a fuller consideration of

A blank verse Lucretian imitation, "The Poe-et's Nightmare" is Lovecraft's mock-epic love-letter to his Augustan idol Alexander Pope, once called the "English Lucretius." This cosmic-comic stew is peppered with allusions to Poe, beginning with the title itself. However, the "Aletheia Phrikodes" section shows Lovecraft moving beyond the woodenly parodic format of the framing poem, providing a hallucinatory description of the cosmos's emergence from a turbulent flux, reimagining the Democritean δίνη through both Lucretian and Poe-esque spectacles. Lovecraft owned and consulted Cornelis Schrevel's 1814 Greek *Lexicon*, which defines δίνη as "a whirlpool, eddy, gulf, whirlwind" (154), phrases that recur throughout the poem, which is rife with vortical imagery. The poem's vortices are memorably captured by John Arfstrom's illustrations, which accompanied its posthumous reprinting, minus the comic frame, in the June 1952 issue of *Weird Tales*.

"Aletheia Phrikodes" offers an extended improvisation on both Lucretius's cosmogonic and meteorological passages, all of which emphasize various forms of turbulence as macrocosmic extensions of the microcosmic clinamen. These are combined with vivid descriptions of the soul's perishable materiality, a concept also derived from Lucretius, but bracketed by Lucullus' psychogenic indigestion as unreal. As the poem outgrows its own parody, it takes on the cosmic visionary style of Poe's angelic narratives, from the versiform "Al Aaraaf" to the prose-poetic "Conversation of Eiros and Charmion":

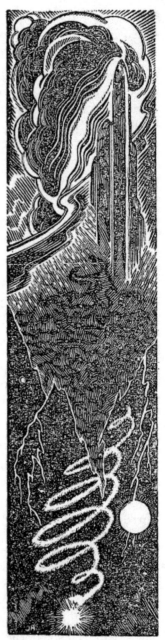

Weird Tales 44, No. 5 (July 1952): 46.

"The Poe-et's Nightmare" see Tittle, "Rarebit Dreamers."

> Whilst *whirling* ether bore in *eddying* streams
> The hot, unfinish'd stuff of nascent worlds
> Hither and thither through infinity
> Of light and darkness, strangely intermix'd;
> Wherein all entity had consciousness,
> Without th' accustom'd outward shape of life.
> Of these swift circling currents was my soul,
> Free from the flesh, a true constituent part;
> Nor felt I less myself, for want of form. (AT 41–42; my emphasis)

This passage illustrates how Lovecraft uses the δίνη to twine Lucretius and "Eddy" Poe together. Like the narrator of "The Festival," through the poem Lovecraft ritualistically invokes his literary ancestors, an ironic parallel to the *nekuia* that begins Pound's *Cantos*, which, in Leon Surette's words, "involves the adoption of the Eleusinian ritual of spiritual death and rebirth in the form of a journey to the Underworld" (55).

In describing these fluctuating vortexes of metamorphic materiality as "eddying" streams in this Poe-etic homage, Lovecraft underlines Poe's importance as part of a materialist literary and philosophical tradition.[6]

Lovecraft's implicit delineation of a counter-Modernist tradition of speculative poetics in which Lucretius and Poe are key figures finds a curious parallel in William Ellery Leonard's contemporaneous translation of Lucretius. Lucretius' first American English translator, Leonard retrojected Poe into a number of passages of his 1916 translation. Leonard's translation of the sixth book's description of a whirlpool reads:

> And when the force of wind
> Hath rived this cloud, from out the cloud it rushes
> Down on the seas, and starts among the waves
> A wondrous seething, for the *eddying whirl*
> Descends and downward draws along with it
> That cloud of ductile body. (VI.267)

Leonard's phrasing reinforces the resemblance between this passage in

---

6. This view of Poe, even more evident in "Supernatural Horror in Literature" (1927), resembles that propounded by James A. Harrison in his 1902 edition of Poe's collected works. Harrison declared that "Both, in their poems, were passionate iconoclasts, idealists, dreamers of the speculative philosophies that looked into the causes of things; both set aside what they considered the degrading superstitions," and were "refined materialists of an almost spiritual type," which could as well be an aspirational self-designation by HPL. See Harrison 279.

De Rerum Natura and Poe's description of the whirlpool in "A Descent into the Maelström," a tale that signals its own atomistic underpinnings by
both its epigraphic reference to the Democritean δίνη and its deliberate
echo of Lucretius's most famous passage, the *suave mari magno* description
of a shipwreck that opens *De Rerum Natura II*. Leonard makes his Poe-tical
homage even more evident a few pages later. Lucretius provides a natural-
istic explanation for the absence of birds at Greek oracular sites including
Cumae, an absence traditionally attributed to the awful supernatural influence of the gods. Instead, Lucretius explains that noxious gases that
leak forth from the earth keep the birds away from such sites, which
Leonard renders as "birdless tarns," echoing Poe's use of this antiquated
term in describing the miasmic body of water into which the House of
Usher falls. Leonard's translation reads:

> And such a spot there is
> Within the walls of Athens, even there
> On summit of Acropolis, beside
> Fane of Tritonian Pallas bountiful,
> Where never cawing crows can wing their course,
> Not even when smoke the altars with good gifts,—
> But evermore they flee—yet not from wrath
> Of Pallas. (VI.280)

This echo of "The Raven" suggests, much as "The Poe-et's Nightmare"
does, Poe's concatenation with Lucretius. Whether Lovecraft knew Leonard's translation is unclear, but it is telling that both writers, *soi-disant* op-
ponents of Poundian Modernism, returned to the Democritean δίνη via
such parallel descents.

Dizzying Vortex: The Spiral Nebulae

Lovecraft's intense admiration for Poe's version of vorticism also informed
his enthusiasm for Harry Clarke's Poe illustrations, which powerfully
visualize Poe's aesthetics of the grotesque and arabesque. Lovecraft
claimed that "Clarke seems to be about the only illustrator who has fully
caught the spirit of Poe & done him justice on a large scale. In years to
come, he may be traditionally associated with Poe as Sime is with Dunsany
& Dore with Milton, Dante, & the Ancient Mariner" (*O Fortunate
Floridian* 203). Significantly, among the handful of Clarke's illustrations
Lovecraft particularly praises the "dizzying vortex in the 'Maelstrom'

picture" (204). In Clarke's illustration, the darkly whirling waters draw the tiny vessel and the viewer's eyes alike down into the blackness beneath and below the limits of the page. However, with its white-speckled black vortex, Clarke's "Maelström" looks more astronomical than nautical, emphasizing the resemblance between Poe's vortices and early twentieth-century photographic images of spiral nebulae, calling attention to the cosmological context of "The Poe-et's Nightmare." The year before publishing the poem, Lovecraft wrote in an amateur astronomical essay called "June Skies":

> A recent discovery of immense importance to our knowledge of the structure of the universe is that of the incredibly rapid rotation of certain large spiral nebulae. It has been found that many of these vast objects, whose distance is virtually inconceivable, revolve on their axes at rates as high as 200 miles per second; a condition which necessitates the revision of many long-accepted theories regarding their nature. Each fresh advance of celestial science demonstrates with new force how little and how rudimentary is our present information regarding the larger outlines of the visible creation wherein we dwell. (CE 3.225)

These early photographic images of the spiral nebulae provided the visual context for Lovecraft's earliest literary expression of cosmic horror in "Aletheia Phrikodes," and this phrasing anticipates his most famous later expression of it with "The Call of Cthulhu." These images figured an epistemic shock, evoking in Lovecraft mingled awe and horror at "how rudimentary" human epistemological advances remained. This reaction would recur, more intensely, the year after "The Poe-et's Nightmare" was published. Einstein had predicted that the sun's gravity would bend light, an aspect of his general theory of relativity, and one confirmed by observations conducted during the solar eclipse of 19 May 1919. Lovecraft's melodramatic, and oft-cited, reaction follows:

> My cynicism & skepticism are increasing, & from an entirely new cause—the Einstein theory. The latest eclipse observations seem to place this system among the facts which cannot be dismissed, & assumedly it removes the last hold which reality or the universe can have on the independent mind. All is chance, accident, & ephemeral illusion—a fly may be greater than Arcturus, & Durfee Hill may surpass Mount Everest—assuming them to be removed from the present planet & differently environed in the continuum of space-time. There are no values in all infinity—the least idea that there are is the supreme mockery of all. (JFM 45)

The progressive, teleological universe of Herbert Spencer that had ordered

Lovecraft's youth was by this point long gone. This new revelation seemed to threaten even the mechanistic, deterministic view of the universe he had since developed. The resulting epistemic shock is clear from an early letter to Frank Belknap Long, which is also among Lovecraft's most incisive responses to the poetics of Pound and Eliot:

> In art there is no use in heeding the chaos of the universe . . . I can conceive of no true image of the pattern of life and cosmic force, unless it be a jumble of mean dots arrang'd in directionless spirals. And so far are real dots and actual curves from depicting the utter formlessness and emptiness of life and force, that they stand confest as artificial as Mr. Pope's couplets when view'd against the bland and nebulous reality they struggle to depict.[7] (SL 1.261)

As Norman R. Gayford's essay "The Artist as Antaeus" persuasively argues, this passage does not signal a wholesale rejection of literary Modernism so much as it "testifies to Lovecraft's immersion in the modernist argument" (289). In it, Lovecraft repudiates "neither Pope nor Eliot"; indeed, Lovecraft goes on to characterize Eliot's approach as "very well meant, but quite ironically futile," since the universe is an "infinite chaos where the very conception of a value is a local and transient accident" (SL 1.262). As Gayford puts it, at this point Lovecraft "articulates a position that separates art and scientific philosophy. No artistic pattern can represent reality" (289).

Lovecraft also expounds this view in a critical response to Eliot's *The Waste Land* published in his amateur journal, the *Conservative*, in 1923. Lovecraft characterizes the "poem" as "disjointed and incoherent," a

> practically meaningless collection of phrases, learned allusions, quotations, slang, and scraps in general; offered to the public (whether or not as a hoax) as something justified by our modern mind with its recent comprehension of its own chaotic triviality and disorganisation. (CE 2.64)

Lovecraft links his critical condemnation of Eliot's poem explicitly to the need for a preservation of traditional modes of artistic expression in the face of cataclysmic epistemic changes wrought by scientific discovery:

---

7. Christian Roy uses this letter to align HPL's cosmic horror with the excremental thought of Georges Bataille in "H. P. Lovecraft, Georges Bataille, and the Fascination of the Formless." It also supports Vivian Ralickas's argument that cosmic horror "converts the sublime turn into a dynamics of descent" synonymous with Julia Kristeva's account of abjection, a theory itself described in terms of a downward spiral. Ralickas, "Cosmic Horror," 387.

To reduce the situation to its baldest terms, man has suddenly discovered that all his high sentiments, values, and aspirations are mere illusions caused by physiological processes within himself, and of no significance whatsoever in an infinite and purposeless cosmos . . .[. . .] having made these discoveries, he does not know what to do about it; but compromises on a literature of analysis, chaos, and ironic contrast. (CE 2.64)[8]

This illuminates the philosophical grounds that differentiate Lovecraft's spiral vortexes from Pound's. For Pound, the vortex, for all its flux, reflects of a kind of transcendent order that the artist makes visible through such analysis, chaos, and ironic contrast. The published version of *The Waste Land*, which cut much of the context from Eliot's earlier, more expository draft, relied heavily on Pound's doctrine of the "Luminous Detail," a technique that depended on a belief in the natural emergence of order from chaos, *turbo* from *turba* in Serres's Lucretian terminology. Moving past his early articulation of Vorticism, Pound would develop this idea through an increasingly Neoplatonic and Confucian worldview, one that led to his later emblem of "The Rose in the Steel Dust." The artist does not place each iron filing by hand, but allows them to be drawn into a rose by the force of the magnet, demonstrating the deeper order at work in nature. In short, Pound's aesthetics increasingly depended on a particular metaphysical stance for their intelligibility, contributing to the infrequency with which the *Cantos* are read today outside of university literature departments.

Lovecraft would return to and adapt the sharp distinction between scientific philosophy and literary aesthetics he received from Poe, whose poetry and fiction he would intensively revisit during his preparatory research for the writing of "Supernatural Horror in Literature." The essay was published in 1927, and a couple of months later, Lucretius swerved back into Lovecraft's consciousness, putting a different spin on his spiral obsession. This Lucretian return occurred in a form both the Roman poet and Sigmund Freud would have appreciated—a vivid dream.[9] This dream, detailed in several of his letters, offered Lovecraft a longed-for break from

---

8. See also Joshi, *Decline* 174.

9. Lucretius developed a detailed theory of dreams, to which Freud returned while researching *On the Interpretation of Dreams*, as Bram Stoker had done several years earlier while researching *Dracula*. In addition, HPL's edition of *De Rerum Natura* was that of Freud's father-in-law, Jacob Bernays.

the "intolerable bondage" of "time, space and natural law,"[10] one that would inspire more complex and contradictory forms of spirality in his subsequent fiction. In this dream, *De Rerum Natura* effectively became *Back to the Future*'s Delorean, or even better, *Doctor Who*'s TARDIS: a textual time machine allowing Lovecraft to swerve free of time's arrow, even if only for the space of a dream.[11]

This dream would signal a drastically different phase of spirality in Lovecraft's later writings. For example, in *At the Mountains of Madness*, Lovecraft spirals back to "the Epicurean nightmare" of the clinamen with his description of the shoggoth as "driving before it a spiral, re-thickening cloud of the pallid abyss-vapour" (CF 3.150). The shoggoth is *turba* embodied in a racially and politically inflected form, the very incarnation of undirected, animate matter, embodying all those things that Marx found so inspiring, and Lovecraft found so disturbing, in the Lucretian clinamen. Conversely, in stories including "The Dreams in the Witch House" and "The Shadow out of Time," Lovecraft imagines space-time as a turbulent flux, in which nonlinear eddying whirls occur and can be exploited, for example by the Great Race of the latter story, who use such non-linear turbulence to transmit consciousness bidirectionally through "the seething vortex of time" (CF 3.363). While these vortices are more original inventions than those that appear in Lovecraft's fiction of the 1910s and early 1920s, their prototypes can be discerned in the downward spiral into Poe and Lucretius Lovecraft had effected with the vortical *nekuia* of "Aletheia Phrikodes."

Works Cited

Burnet, John. *Early Greek Philosophy*. London: Adam & Charles Black, 1908.

Elliot, Hugh. *Modern Science and Materialism*. London: Longmans, Green, 1919.

Gayford, Norman R. "The Artist as Antaeus: Lovecraft and Modernism." In *An Epicure in the Terrible: A Centennial Anthology of Essays in Honor of H. P. Lovecraft*, ed. David E. Schultz and S. T. Joshi. 1991. New York: Hippocampus Press, 2011. 286–312.

---

10. For a detailed description of this dream, its variants and significance to HPL's literary imagination, see Byron Nakamura, "Dreams of Antiquity."

11. See further HPL to August Derleth, 21 November 1930 (*Essential Solitude* 288).

Haeckel, Ernst, et al. *Evolution in Modern Thought*. New York: Boni & Liveright (Modern Library), 1917.

Harrison, James A. *Complete Works of Edgar Allan Poe, Volume 1: Biography*. New York: Thomas Y. Crowell, 1902.

Hinton, James E. "On Physical Morphology." *British and Foreign Medico-chirurgical Review* 22 (July–October 1858): 366–76.

Israel, Nico. *Spirals: The Whirled Image in Twentieth-Century Literature and Art*. New York: Columbia University Press, 2015.

Ito, Junji. "Interview with Mira Bai Winsby." *78 Magazine*. Trans. Miyako Takano, www.78magazine.com/issues/03-01/arts/junji.shtml

Joshi, S. T. *H. P. Lovecraft: The Decline of the West*. Mercer Island, WA: Starmont House, 1990.

———, and David E. Schultz. *Lovecraft's Library: A Catalogue*. 4th ed. New York: Hippocampus Press, 2017.

Kenner, Hugh. *The Pound Era*. 1971. London: Pimlico, 1991.

Leonard, William Ellery. *Lucretius: Of the Nature of Things*. London: J. M. Dent; New York: E. P. Dutton, 1916.

Liebregts, Peter. *Ezra Pound and Neoplatonism*. Rutherford, NJ: Fairleigh Dickinson University Press, 2004.

Lovecraft, H. P. *O Fortunate Floridian: H. P. Lovecraft's Letters to R. H. Barlow*. Ed. S. T. Joshi and David E. Schultz. Tampa, FL: University of Tampa Press, 2007.

———, and August Derleth. *Essential Solitude: The Letters of H. P. Lovecraft and August Derleth*. Ed. David E. Schultz and S. T. Joshi. New York: Hippocampus Press, 2008.

Marx, Karl. *The Difference Between the Democritean and Epicurean Philosophy of Nature*. marxists.catbull.com/archive/marx/works/1841/dr-theses/ch04.htm

Moreland, Sean. "Beyond 'De Rerum Naturâ, Esqr.': Lucretius, Poe, and John Mason Good." *Edgar Allan Poe Review* 17, No. 1 (2016): 6–40.

———. "Beyond the Flaming Walls of the World: Poe After Lovecraft." In *The Lovecraftian Poe*, ed. Sean Moreland. Bethlehem, PA: Lehigh University Press, 2017. xv–xxiv.

———. "The Birth of Cosmic Horror from the S(ub)lime of Lucretius." In *New Directions in Supernatural Horror: The Critical Legacy of H. P. Lovecraft*, ed. Sean Moreland. New York: Palgrave, 2018. 13–42.

————. "The Poet's Nightmare: The Nature of Things According to Lovecraft." In *Lovecraftian Proceedings 2*, ed. Dennis P. Quinn. New York: Hippocampus Press, 2017. 31–46.

Nakamura, Byron. "Dreams of Antiquity: H. P. Lovecraft's Great Roman Dream of 1927." In *Lovecraftian Proceedings 2*, ed. Dennis P. Quinn. New York: Hippocampus Press, 2017. 13–30.

Perez-de-Luque, Juan L. "Descending Spirits: Ideological Implications of the Vertical Movements in Poe and Lovecraft." In *The Lovecraftian Poe*, ed. Sean Moreland. Bethlehem, PA: Lehigh University Press, 2017. 89–106.

Pfannkuchen, Antje. "From Vortex to Vorticism: Ezra Pound's Art and Science." *Intertexts* 9, No. 1 (Spring 2005): 61–76.

Pound, Ezra. *Guide to Kulchur*. New York: New Directions, 1968.

Ralickas, Vivian. "'Cosmic Horror' and the Question of the Sublime in Lovecraft." *Journal of the Fantastic in the Arts* 18, No. 3 (71) (2007): 364–98.

Roy, Christian. "H. P. Lovecraft, Georges Bataille, and the Fascination of the Formless." In *Lovecraftian Proceedings 2*, ed. Dennis P. Quinn. New York: Hippocampus Press, 2017. 189–207.

Serres, Michel. *The Birth of Physics*. Trans. David Webb and William Ross. New York: Rowman & Littlefield, 2018.

Smith, Patricia C. "Poe's Arabesque." *Poe Studies* 7, No 2 (December 1974): 42–45.

Spencer, Herbert. *First Principles*. 1861. New York: Appleton, 1898.

Studniarz, Sławomir. "Lovecraft's Poetry and Poe's Poetics." In *The Lovecraftian Poe*, ed. Sean Moreland. Bethlehem, PA: Lehigh University Press, 2017. 123–40.

Surette, Leon. *The Birth of Modernism*. Kingston, ON: McGill-Queens University Press, 1994.

Tittle, Miles. "Rarebit Dreamers: The Poetics of Poe, Lovecraft, and Winsor McCay." In *The Lovecraftian Poe*, ed. Sean Moreland. Bethlehem, PA: Lehigh University Press, 2017. 141–62.

Wolfreys, Julian, ed. *Glossolalia: An Alphabet of Critical Keywords*. New York: Routledge, 2003.

H. P. Lovecraft and the Dynamics of Detective Fiction

Heather Poirier
Independent Scholar

> Assuming that I was sane and awake, my experience on that night was such as has befallen no man before. [. . .] Mercifully there is no proof, for in my fright I lost the awesome object which would—if real and brought out of that noxious abyss—have formed irrefutable evidence.

H. P. Lovecraft, "The Shadow out of Time" (CF 3.363)

As a man struggling to discover the truth about his past, Nathaniel Wingate Peaslee in "The Shadow out of Time" becomes a detective on his own trail. His returning memories, which he relives during his exploration of the city of the Great Race of Yith beneath the Australian desert, bolster the evidence he has collected from his readings on amnesiac episodes. That investigation of the underground city leads him to a library shelf there containing conclusive, damning evidence: his own handwriting on the pages of an impossibly old book. Intending to take the book to his son at their above-ground camp, Peaslee is discovered and pursued by one of the creatures the Yithians most feared. During his escape, Peaslee loses the only evidence proving his mental journeys with the Yithians—and is relieved by the loss. In the quotation above, we see key elements of detective fiction—investigation, collection of evidence, and explanation of events—turned by Lovecraft to his own purposes.

Scholars frequently treat H. P. Lovecraft's narrators as doorways to the study of cosmic horror, an approach that is entirely reasonable. However, they less frequently study narrators as investigators, and the critical literature does not offer extensive analysis of Lovecraft's use of detective fiction tropes and conventions. This gap in knowledge prevents us from understanding the energy these elements bring to Lovecraft's fiction. Rather than simply patterning his stories after those of detective fiction writers, Lovecraft's use of the genre's tropes energizes his stories and helps amplify the form and structure of his brand of weird fiction. Rather than merely being influenced by this or that author, Lovecraft's use of detective fiction tropes and dynamics suggests his more adaptive approach. This study looks at how those tropes and dynamics work in Lovecraft's weird fiction.

Detective fiction's roots include such diverse narratives as the biblical story of Bel and the Dragon (Daniel 14:1–22) and the story of Oedipus in *Oedipus the King*. In the story of Bel and the Dragon, Daniel reveals the deceptive methods of the false priests of Bel and, in so doing, reinforces the cultural position of those following YHWH. With a similar cultural end in play, Oedipus brings about his own downfall through his determination to find the murderer of Laius and end the plague in Thebes. Once the crime has been solved, Oedipus' incest with Jocasta must be punished, an act that reinforces the norms of Theban and Western culture (Sophocles 1499–1504). Even as far back as these examples, the function of detection in culture has largely been to reinforce social norms and affirm social conventions, whether the inciting incident is a mystery or a crime.[1]

The first consciously crafted detective story is, of course, Edgar Allan Poe's "The Murders in the Rue Morgue" (published April 1841). Between the biblical and Greek examples above and the better-known works of late Victorian and early twentieth-century detective fiction lie works by authors such as Wilkie Collins, whose novel *The Moonstone* (1868) is widely cited as the first English detective novel. Its roots in Gothic horror make it a significant influence on numerous writers, and its plot involving a mystery, rather than a crime, is highly influential.[2] Lovecraft would have been well aware of these late Victorian writers who produced detective fiction; for example, Sir Arthur Conan Doyle published his Sherlock Holmes stories during Lovecraft's lifetime.[3] Lovecraft discusses some works by Al-

---

1. Authors and critics of detective fiction debate the use of the terms "mystery" versus "crime" in the genre and whether detective fiction properly fits either. Larry Landrum and Christopher Pittard address this from different points of view.

2. Landrum and Dorothy L. Sayers, the latter a popular and highly respected writer of detective fiction herself, are just two among many who cite the importance of Collins's novel within the genre. *The Moonstone* is a common jumping-off point for a discussion of the history of detective fiction; given the length and depth of the genre, an extensive history of it would take more space than this work allows.

3. *A Study in Scarlet* was published when HPL was a tender seven years old, the final

gernon Blackwood and William Hope Hodgson, mentioning Sheridan Le Fanu in passing, in his essay "Supernatural Horror in Literature," evaluating in a general way the effectiveness of detective fiction elements. Occasional works before Poe's time have some of, but not all, the elements of detective fiction; Poe brings the elements together.

The ground laid by these early authors and others made possible the works of Sir Arthur Conan Doyle (1859–1930), whose novel *A Study in Scarlet* (1887) introduced Sherlock Holmes to the world. Although Holmes himself began as something of a degenerate in *A Study in Scarlet*, his reformation and subsequent investigations reinforce the norms and values of Victorian England in numerous stories such as "The Man with the Twisted Lip," in which Holmes agrees to conceal the truth about Neville St. Clair—that he earned a gentleman's income posing as a beggar—in order to preserve the social mores and class constraints of the British Empire. Concealment of untidy truths is a key element of preserving social mores and class constraints, and in Lovecraft, it becomes an important prop to the existing social, scientific, governmental, and cultural orders.[4]

Another important influence on nineteenth-century detective novels is the relationship of Gothic horror to race. As Keen notes, the Gothic has its roots in racial insecurity:

Holmes story in 1927 when HPL was thirty-seven.

4. The revelation of what was concealed is part of the thrill of the genre, with its origins in Gothic fiction. As Suzanne Keen notes in *Romances of the Archive*, "The intense feeling with which characters respond to revelations about the past carries over from eighteenth- and nineteenth-century Gothic and sensation fiction into contemporary mystery thrillers and the Lovecraftian sub-genre called gothic horror [. . .] secrets of hidden messages in boxes, chests, and cabinets (or other pieces of furniture with concealed compartments) [. . . and finding them] may endanger the life or sanity of the quester. The unspeakable contents or occult power of the letters, diaries, scraps, recipes, maps, or suggestive lists contained in gothic hiding-places unleash hazardous knowledge about the past that is often better off contained, sealed, buried, or cast in a crevasse" (70–71). For HPL's purposes, the location of the hidden secrets is less significant—sometimes only slightly so—than the contents themselves. The thrill of the discovery is primary; location is secondary to message. The revelation of the contents does indeed endanger life and sanity in HPL; the contents unleash hazardous knowledge as in Gothic fiction, but of the present and the future as well as of the past. Human history as a construct is shaken by the discoveries made by HPL's narrators.

[C]ritics, particularly those focusing on the later nineteenth-century gothic revival, see in it a convenient imaginative space in which to work out guilt about mistreating other races and appropriating their lands (while allowing the continuance of the profitable British adventure) [. . .] In accordance with the Manichaean logic now strongly associated with Orientalism as described by Edward Said, an English self-understanding arises out of the characterization of exotic difference and depravity. (71)

English identity, and by extension the identity of white European writers, was in some ways defined by the other. Extending this to Lovecraft, the self as narrator sometimes worries about losing his humanity in the face, however obliquely presented, of the encountered horror. For example, in "The Horror at Red Hook," the detective Malone rejects the minorities he sees in the Red Hook neighborhood as he investigates the cult. Malone's struggle is not only with the cultists and their leaders; his own race-based distaste for the cult's practitioners, who are largely if not entirely minorities, is a significant part of the narrative.[5]

By the twentieth century, detective fiction changed again, this time in parallel with changes in philosophy and literature.[6] Agatha Christie may have refined the parlor-game subgenre of detective fiction during the Golden Age, but in *Curtain: Poirot's Last Case*, her final novel for Hercule Poirot, she makes him the murderer of a man who has committed no crimes himself—the detective becomes the criminal. Poirot leaves a full, written confession, stating that he killed a technically innocent man to protect society, then killed himself to right the wrong he committed, making both himself and his victim scapegoats whose deaths redeem the society-in-miniature reflected in Christie's plot. Poirot is both defiler and savior. As Christopher Pittard notes in his book *Purity and Contamination in Late Detective Fiction*:

---

5. Numerous authors address issues of race and ethnicity in HPL's works. This subject, like that of occult detectives, has become its own industry and cannot be adequately covered in this article.

6. Within Lovecraftiana, new developments expand on these changes. Occult detectives, like those in Sheridan Le Fanu and others, have experienced a revival and are now a minor industry within HPL studies. The number of books, stories, graphic novels, and the like that have occult detective protagonists has exploded during the past few years. A full discussion of them is a study in itself and is beyond the scope of this work; however, Darrell Schweitzer notes that HPL specifically has no recurring main characters and thus no occult detectives (24).

[T]he fictional detective [. . .] became an outcast, a link between crime and society who, by the nature of his task, had to work alone in order to protect his community from the taint of criminality. With the arrival of the detective, society was able to separate itself from the taint of criminality, but as a result the detective himself would be condemned to a life of crime. (146)

Even though investigators may be outliers—some through societal distrust, others self-imposed—many detectives do not work alone. The detective's sidekick, a figure such as Arthur Hastings for Poirot and John Watson for Holmes, functions as both an audience foil and a normative voice. In contrast to their sidekicks, detectives like Poirot and Holmes are both within and without society, liminal figures traversing the border between law and crime, a border repeatedly negotiated by those sidekicks (Pittard 20).[7]

These elements of influence are important to keep in mind when looking at Lovecraft and detective fiction. To arrive at Lovecraft's use of the genre's conventions, however, we must return to Poe. Not only is Poe a writer whom Lovecraft admired since boyhood (Moreland 238), he is also widely credited with the creation of the modern short story and the first detective fiction short story, "The Murders in the Rue Morgue."[8] Although most critics examine "Rue Morgue" in detail, for purposes of this analysis, the story "The Mystery of Marie Rogêt" is better suited.

---

7. This is especially true of the hard-boiled detective, a literary product very much of the twentieth century, but the shifting status of the detective long precedes it. Police forces were first established in the nineteenth century, and public objections to them were common, especially in England. As Pittard notes, "Before the founding of the Metropolitan Police in 1829 and the detective department in 1842, detection was seen doubly as both the intrusive power of the state and as foreign, un-English espionage [. . .] The detective, on the margins of respectable society, was a liminal figure [. . .] 'To have been at the margins is to have been in contact with danger, to have been at a source of power.' If detectives cleansed social dirt, then some of that mess moved onto them. [. . .] (20) In terms of "mess," HPL's investigators, if they are exceedingly lucky, escape encounters with cosmic horror with only the memory of their encounters and slip back into quiet lives, even though some, such as Francis Wayland Thurston in "The Call of Cthulhu," know that an unpleasant end awaits them. What matters to these investigators is that the truth has been revealed, if just once, and even if it is buried again to protect society.

8. Three of his tales of ratiocination were published during a three-year period: "The Murders in the Rue Morgue" in 1841, "The Mystery of Marie Rogêt" in 1842, and "The Purloined Letter" in 1844.

Poe's significance in Lovecraft's development cannot be overemphasized. Lovecraft sets aside Poe's tales of ratiocination in his essay "Supernatural Horror in Literature" before laying out Poe's influence on his own sense of weird fiction. The critical new element Poe offered, according to Lovecraft, is the use of psychological elements rather than moral ones as the core of the examination of the human psyche. Poe reoriented horror away from moral obligations to the reader and toward a psychological realism rarely employed as a primary method by earlier writers of horror and Gothic fiction. After analyzing some of Poe's works, Lovecraft concludes that "Poe's weird tales are *alive* in a manner that few others can ever hope to be" (CE 2.103; Lovecraft's emphasis).

The common ground between Poe and Lovecraft with respect to fiction is the idea of epistemological order and disorder (Cassuto 50). Epistemological order—that is, having an orderly understanding of how we know what we know—underpins social norms. Resolving epistemological disorder helps to restore social norms. Poe's tales of ratiocination, as with many detective fiction works, use the act of rational examination to restore epistemological order and social norms (Sayers 102; Landrum 52). This sense of order is a part of their popular attraction. After all, the comforts of middle-class life are enjoyed through the resolution of self-induced fear or tension. As Pittard notes, "the very structures of 'community' and 'family' are crucial to the construction of the criminal as a figure to be feared. Because these social units encourage and fetishise order, the appearance of disorder, no matter how localized, becomes a universal threat" (69–70). This engagement of disorder is central to Poe's story. Poe's detective C. Auguste Dupin, as part of his personal investigation into Marie Rogêt's death, goes into significant detail discussing the various newspaper articles covering and updating the police investigation (Poe 175–78, 182; 192–93). This need to examine and to reveal is part of the process of restoring social and epistemological order; without it, the risk of more murders and more disorder is high. As René Girard notes in his work on early social groups, the need to suppress violence so that it is not replicated is at the core of social order, and the figure who suppresses it can be traced to the detective.

For his story about Marie Rogêt, Poe takes the true crime event of Mary Rogers's death in New York as the basis for his narrative (169). Dupin is socially prominent and thus at a social arm's length from both the reader and the police force representatives. This distance moves him closer to the fringe, as do his dalliances with decadence. In addition, his investigative procedures and mental processes are opaque at best (Sharp 65–66). The victim in Poe's story is a shopgirl who would have been otherwise unknown but for her exceptional beauty. Her existence itself is not a violation of the social order, however. It is Rogêt's disappearance that causes the first episode of epistemological disorder; when questioned, her aunt states that she has not seen the girl even though Mlle. Rogêt told a male acquaintance that she was going to visit her aunt (Poe 173). The discovery of the girl's body in the Seine (Poe 174) throws Parisian society into full-blown epistemological disorder. Newspapers and their editors, all created by Poe but based on actual publications produced in New York during the Mary Rogers investigation, devote numerous column inches to speculation on methods and motives, and until Dupin becomes involved, the police suspect a gang of ruffians are responsible for Mlle. Rogêt's death. Dupin brings his considerable exegetic skills to the case and determines that a particular sailor is likely responsible for the girl's death (Poe 204-6). Much of Dupin's exegesis is devoted to these newspaper accounts and editorial commentaries. Poe concludes the story without showing the arrest of the sailor, thus dismissing the importance of the revelation of the criminal, confirmation of the criminal's guilt, and elucidation of the details of the case. Instead, the importance of this fictional account is the opportunity it provides Poe to lay out the structure of the detective fiction short story. Through footnotes inserted in the story text, Poe references the actual texts and events of Mary Rogers's death, illustrating his methodology. Like both a criminal and a detective, Poe reveals and explains his plot to the reader.

Unfortunately, a full return to normality many never be possible for Poe's Parisians. As Leonard Cassuto observes, "Dupin is Poe's agent for epistemological order. The sleuth's role in the detective stories is not so much to solve the crime as it is to save the entire category system, the reliability of which the crime has called into question" (50). The category system gives the investigation moral significance. For epistemological order to be restored, the criminal investigation must be on par with a scientific investigation, i.e., a truth-finding pursuit. It also must represent narrative, normative values so that it can attribute responsibility to the offender. Because of this need represented by the risk imposed to the category system, detectives wrestle with moral issues as well as criminal ones (Poirier 217). The nature of crime is such that it cannot be destroyed, only temporarily hidden. Crime transgresses boundaries by its very existence. If a central human desire for harmony and order exists, then crime violates that desire through its innate ugliness and disharmony.

A note here on the distinction between detective fiction and mysteries is appropriate. Larry Landrum, in his book *American Mystery and Detective Novels: A Reference Guide*, a critically important text for students of detective fiction, observes that

> [d]etective stories are more specific than mysteries. They focus the narrative more directly on the solution of a puzzle that the solution of a crime poses. Detective stories demand keen observation, superior reasoning, and the disciplined imagination of their protagonists. [. . .] [d]etective novels as a more specialized form of the mystery are constructed around the formal investigation [. . .] while mysteries more broadly address the solution to a generally threatening situation. (ix–1)

In terms of interest to the detective, though, these boundaries are not hard and fast, as Dr. Watson observes in "A Scandal in Bohemia." Watson, waiting for Holmes to return home, muses, "I was already deeply interested in his inquiry, for, though it was surrounded by none of the grim and strange features which were associated with the two crimes which I have already recorded, still, the nature of the case and the exalted station of his client gave it a character of its own" (167). Irene Adler's machinations are of as much interest to Holmes and Watson as crimes they recently investigated, even though she has not yet committed a crime against the King of Bavaria.

At first blush, it would seem that Lovecraft's stories are more mysteries than detective fiction, and they do indeed largely concern themselves with threatening situations. So did he write mysteries, or did he write detective fiction? Strictly speaking, he wrote weird fiction, so neither answer is correct. However, in his early stories his narrators are out to solve mysteries, such as in "The Statement of Randolph Carter," in which Carter and his companion Harley Warren try to find a mysterious passage to the underworld (albeit in Florida, an unlikely locale). Lovecraft's later stories, especially "The Call of Cthulhu" and some published after it, have narrators who become investigative in their attempts to understand events, some of which involve crimes.

For Lovecraft, the thrills of Gothic horror and the broad devices of detective fiction are trappings, not substance, and are an unsteady structure for weird fiction. For instance, Lovecraft discusses numerous works by William Hope Hodgson in "Supernatural Horror in Literature," and his opinion of *Carnacki, the Ghost-Finder* places that collection at the bottom of his list of Hodgson's works. For Lovecraft, the combination of a "conventional stock figure" with "an atmosphere of professional 'occultism'" is nearly fatal to the narrative (*CE* 2.115). Similarly, in his discussion of Algernon Blackwood, Lovecraft describes *John Science–Physician Extraordinary* as "marred only by traces of the popular and conventional detective-story atmosphere" (*CE* 2.121). Despite these traces, as well as the "professional occultism" in Blackwood's story "The Camp of the Dog" (in *John Silence*), Lovecraft notes that the stories are among Blackwood's best, producing "an illusion at once emphatic and lasting" (*CE* 2.121).

The elements of detective fiction in Lovecraft's own work go well beyond superficial application. In a letter to Alfred Galpin, Lovecraft notes that he read all the published Sherlock Holmes stories as a boy (*AG* 19). As Darrell Schweitzer notes in his study of Lovecraft and detective fiction, Lovecraft in his reading of pulp magazines would have read numerous detective stories in publications such as *Argosy* and *All-Story* (20). And although Schweitzer characterizes Lovecraft's maturation as a writer as involving "a philosophical parting of the ways" with detective fiction (21), Lovecraft does acknowledge Holmes's "brilliance and rationality and the deft artistry of the Doyle stories" (22). Of course, Lovecraft would not be attracted to crime alone, given his cosmicism, as Schweitzer notes (22). He also asserts that Lovecraft's lack of attraction goes beyond a mere rejection of the supernatural. And although Schweitzer agrees that "many Lovecraft stories resemble detective stories in their structure" (23), more attention to Lovecraft's stories reveals that the structure allows Lovecraft to first invoke, then invert the tropes of detective fiction. Schweitzer concludes by acknowledging that "what Lovecraft was doing, then, was applying the Holmesean method to the universe at large [. . .] his characters proceed with the same logical, step-by-step deduction that Holmes used for mundane matters" (24).

In his landmark biography *I Am Providence: The Life and Times of H. P. Lovecraft*, S. T. Joshi adds details to the interplay of Lovecraft's works and detective fiction. Lovecraft was mindful of the market for detective fiction among readers of popular fiction. Joshi notes that in 1925, Lovecraft tried to sell "The Shunned House" to *Detective Tales* (*IAP* 592), but it was rejected. Later that year in August, Lovecraft spoke of writing a piece with a "detectivish" slant (*IAP* 592) but apparently did not. The same month, he spoke of sending "The Horror at Red Hook" to *Detective Tales*, given that the character Malone is "a much more orthodox detective than any charac-ter in previous tales of Lovecraft's" (*IAP* 592). And in fact, Lovecraft submit-ted "The Call of Cthulhu" to *Mystery Stories* in the spring of 1927, but the story was rejected, not because it did not involve a mystery, but because it was "too heavy" (*IAP* 675). Even though Lovecraft did not write detective fiction per se, he knew the genre and used its elements in selected works.

Just as Lovecraft used detective fiction elements in service of his larger cosmic views, detective fiction itself has a teleological purpose related to society. In most detective fiction, the revelation of the truth has a normal-izing effect on the social order. Through investigation and revelation, the detective restores order to the disorder created by the socially destructive actions of the criminal. Lovecraft's fiction contains these elements as well, but in Lovecraft, the impulse is described, then turned. Lovecraft estab-lishes the idea of social order, then inverts it, using it as a tool to expose the horror at the core of cosmicism. Although in detective fiction the normative effect of the detective's actions enables the resolution of the case, this approach, this desire for epistemological order, cannot hold in Lovecraft. With a figure such as Thurston in "The Call of Cthulhu," the investigation only seems to be a way to resolve matters.

The overall plot elements of "The Call of Cthulhu" are like those of garden-variety detective fiction, especially that published during the Gold-en Age.[9] The critical difference between Lovecraft and garden-variety de-tective fiction is Lovecraft's cosmicism and cosmic horror. Whereas the detective in mainstream detective fiction focuses on a relatively limited scope of items and events, Lovecraft's investigators have their awareness wrenched open by initial mundane experiences that, upon pursuit, lead them to cosmic revelations. In the case of Thurston, even the discovery of the cult in south Louisiana was only a tease. The narrative of the Norwe-gian seaman Gustaf Johansen and his account of the rising of R'lyeh re-veals to Thurston man's tenuous place in planetary history. As S. T. Joshi notes in *H. P. Lovecraft: The Decline of the West*, "What we are presented with in the tales beginning with 'The Call of Cthulhu' is a series of *counter-civilisations*—civilisations in many cases as fully evolved as our own but im-placably hostile or at least carelessly indifferent to ours" (142). For Thurston at the end of the story, the knowledge that he will die at the

---

9. The Golden Age of detective fiction occurred from roughly the 1920s through the first part of the 1950s and paralleled the appearance of the hard-boiled detective.

hands of the cult is diminished in significance, perhaps only slightly, by his new understanding of the larger cosmic ends the cult seeks to realize.

Thurston tells us that "there was one box which I found exceedingly puzzling, and which I felt much averse from shewing to other eyes. [. . .] I succeeded in opening it, but when I did so seemed only to be confronted by a greater and more closely locked barrier. For what could be the meaning of the queer clay bas-relief and the disjoined jottings, ramblings, and cuttings which I found?" (CF 2.23). Ordering the contents of the box leads to Thurston's eventual comprehension of their significance, which is typically a normative function, and in detective fiction, normative functions bring understanding and relief to the detective and to the community at large. However, the ordering of this box's contents begins an investigation that exposes Thurston to the experience of cosmic horror, which sets aside the normative functions of comprehension and understanding. Revelation leads to exposure and psychological damage, not resolution and restoration.

Thurston's discovery introduces epistemological disorder, i.e., the "greater and more closely locked barrier" to his understanding of the mysterious events. Rather than a physical barrier, Thurston experiences an inability to fully understand the significance of the items in the sealed box. The barrier is in his mind, and the more he discovers, the more disorder is revealed.

Epistemological disorder is one element introduced by the crime and the criminal, but it alone is not enough to power the plot of a given work of detective fiction. After all, a puzzle game stirs epistemological disorder until it is solved, and merely having certain elements in a plot is not sufficient to classify a literary work as detective fiction. Brooks Hefner notes that an "emphasis on semiotics appears in a variety of pulp genres, including both the weird tale and the detective story, each of which turns on questions of investigation and interpretation: in other words, the reading of signs" (656). Detective stories go far beyond the simple plot structure of crime, investigation, capture, and punishment. The genre of detective fiction has a tripartite dynamic at its core, that of the detective, the criminal, and society. This notion is derived from the work of sociologist René Girard on ritual violence and social order as necessary aspects of the sacred.

In his seminal work *Violence and the Sacred*, Girard discusses the critical relationship between ritual and sacrifice in early societies. As a sociologist, Girard is primarily interested in the social origins and consequences of ritual violence (4). The fear of violence is based in the fear of mimesis, i.e., the fear that violence once begun will spread uncontrollably. Mimesis, as a specific understanding of a sign or signs, is both cause and motivation for ritual violence: in order to prevent mimetic violence within a group, the priests of that group perform acts of violence on chosen victims. This ritualized violence is an act of community reconciliation (Girard 8) because the act of violence, when performed by a priest, cleanses and redeems the community. Because vengeance is a never-ending process, ritualized violence must be used to end it. And because all members of society are susceptible to the physiology of violence, all are affected by it. Girard observes that "recent studies suggest that the physiology of violence varies little from one individual to another, even from one culture to another. According to Anthony Storr, nothing resembles an angry cat or man so much as another angry cat or man" (2). Mimesis is independent of cultural variables, so the risk of the spread of violence is also independent of those variables. The "menace of chain reactions" becomes the greatest risk (39).

The priest steps in as the mediator between the sacrifice and the community. The risk of the spread of violence can be abetted through ritual sacrifice, and accordingly, the priest sacrifices the victim in a ritual designed to bring the violence to an end (Girard 144). This sacrifice protects the community and restores peace by eliminating the source of violence, whether that source is the actual perpetrator or an agreed-upon scapegoat (42).

Given the mediating relationship of the priest to the community through the act of ritual violence, we can begin to see the relationship of the priest/sacrifice/community to that of the detective/criminal/society. The detective performs the parallel function of the priest by responding to the crime and discovering the identity of the murderer. The criminal, once at large but now identified (if not captured), must be sacrificed in a cultural context and manner that will redeem society. Should the criminal not be caught, the risk of mimetic violence increases. With each unsolved crime, that risk increases. It is critical that the detective catch, or at least identify, the criminal so that society is not increasingly implicated in its own violence. In the act of identifying and capturing the criminal, the detective restores the norms and stability needed for social functioning.

As part of a larger discussion of ritual violence in literature, Girard examines several Greek tragedies. He notes that the tragedy *Medea* "reminds us of a fundamental truth about violence: if left unappeased, violence will accumulate until it overflows its confines and floods the surrounding area. The role of sacrifice is to stem this rising tide of indiscriminate substitutions and redirect violence into 'proper' channels" (10). Similarly, the violence in *Oedipus the King* first raises Oedipus to the throne, then causes his downfall. Oedipus is both an investigator/priest and a criminal/sacrifice. His drive to discover the killer of Laius, his own father and the previous king of Thebes, leads to the revelation that Oedipus himself is the murderer. In this cultural context, Oedipus's banishment lifts the plague from Thebes, redeems the community, and restores the social order.

The threat at the core of *Medea* and *Oedipus the King*, the threat of violence and destruction, is the same threat recognized by Lovecraft's narrators. The alien, sometimes extradimensional creatures the narrators encounter pose an existential threat to human society. Sometimes, the unfortunate narrator himself becomes the sacrifice in the tripartite dynamic, even if only a psychological sacrifice. As Peter Counter notes,

> The detective, when placed in the tradition of cosmic horror, is heroic for holding on to humanity in the face of forbidden knowledge that which would drive weaker-willed individuals mad. They are the explorers and prospectors of existential frontiers, a testament to our unshakeable human condition. They [. . .] are able to look into the darkness for meaning and upon finding the incomprehensible, accepting the challenge of living as a human in the abyss.

The consequence of being that "human in the abyss" is that the narrator lives in both worlds, in a sense—not fully in one because of his knowledge of the other. This parallels the detective's liminal state between the criminal world and society at large. As Pittard reminds us, if crime is "matter out of place," then the person investigating that crime is contaminated by that disorder (3). Similarly, as Peter Cannon observes, "an isolated environment can drive people, especially unenlightened ones cut off from the civilizing influence of the outside world, to commit horrible crimes with no fear or concern for the possible consequences" (5). Both Doyle's and Lovecraft's narrators are at risk of the consequences of too much knowledge. Instead of the Enlightenment ideal of broadening and deepening ourselves and our worlds, knowledge brings about isolation. Even Lovecraft's Great Old Ones in Antarctica, the secondary protagonists of that tale, are brought down by their knowledge of the horrors in the old city.

Yet Lovecraft's narrators are not deterred by the prospect of disorder, whether personal or social. These men, and they are men, from various walks of life possess the curiosity, courage, and determination that are key to the development of investigative sensibilities. Lovecraft observed that "the sensitive are always with us, and sometimes a curious streak of fancy invades an obscure corner of the very hardest head; so that no amount of rationalism, reform, or Freudian analysis can quite annul the thrill of the chimney-corner whisper or the lonely wood" (CE 2.83). Consider, for instance, Nathaniel Wingate Peaslee's determination to find the source of his dreams, and his harrowing trip through the Australian desert only to discover his own handwritten record in the archives of the Great Race. Similarly, in At the Mountains of Madness, William Dyer follows the history of the Great Old Ones through their icy Antarctic city, tracing figures in bas-reliefs lit by his and Danforth's flashlights, and learning the scope and depth of the Old Ones' civilization. Dyer's scientific training helps him become, at first, a detective on the trail of the killers of his crew members. These killers, as quasi-criminals, then become victims of horrors much worse. The disturbing experiments on Dyer's crew—a matter of disorder that becomes understandable as Dyer learns more about the Old Ones, to the extent that he refers to them as "men"—shrinks in comparison to the horrors that wait for both Old Ones and humans in the Antarctic city.

In Girard, we have the priest/sacrifice/community. In detective fiction, we have the detective/criminal/society. And in Lovecraft, we have the narrator/cosmic horror/society. But these tripartite dynamics alone are not enough to energize a story. From these dynamics come the power for numerous tropes that energize both detective fiction and Lovecraft's weird fiction. A short list includes such elements as

- Tropes of vision: revelation/concealment, light/darkness, and clarity/obscurity, which Lovecraft uses deftly in the first paragraph of "The Statement of Randolph Carter" as well as in numerous other stories
- Masking/unmasking, most deliberately used in "The Whisperer in the Darkness"
- Sin/atonement, which is referenced obliquely in the earlier stories, usually matched with a character's twisted sense of aesthetics
- Private/public, seen in the raid on Innsmouth, a raid conducted in private and later made public, as well as any of the stories involving concealment of actual events[10]

---

10. The classic film noir Chinatown, which is also a work of detective fiction, uses this trope to heartbreaking effect.

- Guilt/confession, such as the opening of "The Thing on the Doorstep"
- Amateur/professional, given that most but not all of Lovecraft's narrators are amateurs at investigation
- Truth/deceit, where Lovecraft's narrators cannot reveal the truth without being accused of some form of deceit, including self-deceit
- The critically important trope of the palimpsest

In detective fiction, the umbrella trope is revelation and concealment. Out of its simplest form, where the detective reveals what the criminal has attempted to conceal, we find tropes of vision, identity, guilt, privacy, truth, and capability. Ideally, the detective reveals the truth by bringing to light clues and information about the crime, making clear what is important and unmasking the criminal. In early detective fiction, as well as in more mainstream detective works, the criminal confesses his crime, and the entire story of the crime is made public to a degree suitable within the story's context. Darkness is dispelled, masks discarded, and sins atoned, and in so doing, the community is redeemed by having the criminal removed from its midst. Whether the detective is a professional or an amateur, all is resolved.

These dynamics are a critical aspect of Lovecraft's works, though employed to different ends. He uses, then subverts, the genre's conventions. In most detective fiction, a detective investigates a crime or mystery, then presents a clear-cut case with facts to support the conclusions. The offender is caught, and justice is served. In contrast to these conventions, Lovecraft's investigators are sometimes unreliable, yet the reader comes to trust them during the course of a given narrative. Investigations lead to the dire clarity of cosmic horror, which must then be concealed. Truth and deceit are meaningless in the face of cosmic horror, yet that terror lends strange energy to the investigator's pursuit of the truth. Evidence and facts are collected yet have uncertain status. Confessions are disregarded, crimes are concealed, and investigators face incarceration, while perpetrators cannot be caught. Justice cannot be served because no redemption is possible.

An example of Lovecraft's inversion of the revelation and concealment trope occurs when Dyer sets down his account of the Antarctic expedition, not to exhort the authorities to act, but to implore them not to. Humanity cannot defeat the shoggoths inhabiting the Old Ones' city without facing mass insanity, and the knowledge of the Old Ones' history would be too disturbing for modern-day people to accept. Should humanity learn that it was created by the Old Ones as an experiment turned joke, rather than by the hand of an omnipotent, omniscient deity, civilization and social order would be shattered. This trope of concealment for the good of society reaches back through numerous works by other authors. As Gavin Callaghan has noted, "much like Lovecraft's Dyer and Danforth, who 'had to adopt an actual rule of strict censorship' in what they told, in the interest of 'the public's general peace of mind,' so too will Holmes and Watson conceal far more than they reveal with regard to events of both public importance and personal privacy" (226). Rather than revelation, Dyer begs for concealment, not for the protection of Danforth and himself but for the greater good of the social order.

Similarly, "The Dreams in the Witch House" offers many examples of these inverted tropes. Walter Gilman becomes the detective who is both victim and investigator. His dreams lead him to a better understanding of higher mathematics, but at the cost of his physical well-being and sanity. He becomes increasingly unreliable, yet because the reader accompanies him in his dreams, and because of his bent of mind as a mathematician, we see the truth in his experiences. The more Gilman investigates, the closer he comes to cosmic horror, until he finds himself at the attempted sacrifice of a child. There is no evidence, no set of facts that Gilman can present about his dream-world activities; a confession would be useless because it could not be corroborated. Justice cannot be served because Keziah Mason and Brown Jenkin exist in extradimensional space. Learning the truth brings about no resolution. The only concrete evidence that the authorities can consider is the mystery of Gilman's death and the pile of human bones later found on the site of the Witch House.

Other tropes are used more directly. Masking is perhaps most famously employed in "The Whisperer in Darkness," where Albert N. Wilmarth learns from Henry Akeley that Vermont is teeming with extraterrestrials. As evidence sent from Akeley mounts, Wilmarth becomes convinced that an investigation would be worthwhile. His interview with Akeley is nothing short of bizarre, and after he discovers the nature of the alien machines, he sees lying on a chair the mask and hands used by one of the Mi-Go to impersonate Akeley. Rather than being unmasked by Wilmarth as in a conventional story, the Mi-Go eventually unmasks itself, unconcerned with any consequences that mankind is able to muster. This unmasking occurs without revelation; Wilmarth does not see the creature behind the mask, only the mask and hands themselves.

The trope of the palimpsest runs throughout both detective fiction and Lovecraft's works. In its original definition, a palimpsest is a manuscript page, usually vellum, on which the original writing has been scraped off so that the parchment may be reused, but on which traces of the earlier writing remain. These traces can be perceived, even if only partially. Medieval monks reused parchment in this way, and traces of previous words and letters potentially affected translations and thus exegesis. In detective fiction, this idea becomes the layering of terrain, activity, time, and significance. For instance, in detective fiction, a crime scene has multiple layers when understood as a palimpsest:

- The original site before the crime
- The scene during the commission of the crime
- The scene between the commission of the crime and the discovery of the crime
- The discovery of the crime at the scene
- The arrival of the police to the scene
- The establishment of the official crime scene by the police, usually defined by tools such as yellow tape and tent cards
- The arrival of the detective to the scene
- The collection of evidence at the scene
- Potentially the return of the criminal to the scene
- Potentially the presentation by the detective of the solution to the crime at the scene itself

The palimpsest, both here and in medieval documents, functions both temporally and physically. That is, the physical space takes on significance through layers of meaning assigned over time. Whereas the crime scene may have been an otherwise unremarkable place, the conduct of first the crime, then the investigation, adds significance at each step. Pittard also notes the importance of the palimpsest to the genre:

> Referencing this idea of layering, the literary critic Tzvetan Todorov argues that the detective novel "contains not one but two stories: the story of the crime and the story of the investigation" [. . .] the distinction between the story and the plot [is that] "the story is what happened in life, the plot is the way the author presents it to us." The plot of the investigation forms the body of the detective story and it is read by the actual reader; this includes the story of the crime, as read by the detective. (23)

This is the core structure of the palimpsest as presented in detective fiction, and Lovecraft's use of science and cosmic horror brought new elements into the mix.

In Lovecraft, the palimpsest melds itself within the "cosmic" aspect of cosmic horror. Earth itself has been the scene of rising and falling alien civilizations; no place is spared. R'lyeh waits to rise again; Y'ha-nthlei houses the Deep Ones below Devil's Reef; Elder Things once inhabited their city in the warm forests of Antarctica; and flying polyps lived in the underground caverns of the Australian desert as recently as the 1930s. Each of these layers, and more from other stories, have been discovered by inquisitive and sometimes terrified investigators, and their respective significance reckoned accordingly.

Lovecraft even uses the idea of the palimpsest in spoken language. Delapoer, the unfortunate main character of "The Rats in the Walls," devolves after learning the truth about his cannibalistic witch-cult forebears, to the extent that he speaks in languages that, layer by layer, recede backward in time: "archaic English, Middle English, Latin, Gaelic, and primitive ape-cries" (Joshi and Schultz 222). The sheer force of Delapoer's family history overwrites him, as it were, a consequence of his determined investigation. The identity he believed was authentic is consumed by his family history; the man himself is lost but for his physical self.

In an interesting chronological reversal of the palimpsest idea, Peaslee in "The Shadow out of Time" discovers in his own modern-day time the existence of his handwriting from eons ago, locked away in the archive of the Great Race. Rather than finding traces of the Great Race's writing in his own time, Peaslee finds the opposite. Because he drops the evidence in his desperate escape from the underground tunnels in Australia, he cannot prove that his experiences have been authentic. Instead, he retains the dreams and memories, isolated in what he has learned.

Detective fiction as a popular genre has its roots both in stories with ancient origins and in core impulses in early societies; the impulse to structure and order our world so that we are kept safe is a constant. Lovecraft's fiction takes the impulses of modern man, as passed through millennia from early societies to the present day, and reshapes them to address cosmicism and cosmic horror. Even as detective fiction presents the ongoing struggle to restore social norms in a chaotic, violent world, Lovecraft takes those structures and norms as tools to demonstrate the impossibility of any kind of permanent social order. Although it is not obvious that numerous links exist between Lovecraft's work and structures used in detective fiction, a close, informed examination shows that they are numerous and substantial. This little-recognized intersection of writer and genre has much to offer scholars and casual readers alike. More work in this area should offer many fruitful rewards.

Works Cited

Callaghan, Gavin. "Elementary, My Dear Lovecraft: H. P. Lovecraft and Sherlock Holmes." *Lovecraft Annual* 6 (2012): 199–229.

Cannon, Peter. "Parallel Passages in 'The Adventure of the Copper Beeches' and 'The Picture in the House.'" *Lovecraft Studies* No. 1 (Fall 1979): 3–6.

Cassuto, Leonard. 'Poe's Force of Disorder: The Grotesque in Cultural Context.' In *Masques, Mysteries, and Mastodons: A Poe Miscellany*, ed. Benjamin F. Fisher. Baltimore: Edgar Allan Poe Society, 2006. 45–62.

Collins, Wilkie. *The Moonstone*. 1868. New York: Century, 1903.

Counter, Peter. 'The Strange Game: When Sherlock Holmes Meets H. P. Lovecraft.' *Everything Is Scary*, 13 July 2015. www.everythingisscary.com/page/sherlock-holmes-meets-hp-lovecraft.

Doyle, Arthur Conan. "The Man with the Twisted Lip." In *The Classic Illustrated Sherlock Holmes*. Stamford, CT: Longmeadow Press, 1987. 80–94.

———. "A Scandal in Bohemia." In *The Complete Sherlock Holmes, Volume 1*. Garden City, NY: Doubleday, 1960.

———. *A Study in Scarlet*. In *Sherlock Holmes: The Novels*. Ed. Michael Dirda. New York: Penguin, 2015. 15–91.

Girard, René. *Violence and the Sacred*. Stanford: Stanford University Press, 1978.

Hefner, Brooks. "Weird Investigations and Nativist Semiotics in H. P. Lovecraft and Dashiell Hammett." *Modern Fiction Studies* 60 (Winter 2014): 651–76.

Joshi, S. T. *H. P. Lovecraft: The Decline of the West*. Mercer Island, WA: Starmont House, 1990.

———, and David E. Schultz. *An H. P. Lovecraft Encyclopedia*. Westport, CT: Greenwood Press, 2001.

Keen, Suzanne. *Romances of the Archive in Contemporary British Fiction.* Toronto: University of Toronto Press, 2005.

Landrum, Larry N. *American Mystery and Detective Novels: A Reference Guide.* Ed. M. Thomas Inge. Westport, CT: Greenwood Press, 1999.

Moreland, Sean, ed. *The Lovecraftian Poe: Essays on Influence, Reception, Interpretation and Transformation.* Bethlehem, PA: Lehigh University Press, 2017.

The New Oxford Annotated Bible: New Revised Standard Version with the Apocrypha. Ed. Michael D. Coogan et al. New York: Oxford University Press, 2018.

Pittard, Christopher. *Purity and Contamination in Late Victorian Detective Fiction.* Farnham, UK: Ashgate Publishing, 2011.

Poe, Edgar Allan. *The Complete Tales and Poems of Edgar Allan Poe.* New York: Vintage, 1975.

Polanski, Roman, dir. *Chinatown.* Paramount, 1974.

Poirier, Heather. "Ripples from Carcosa: H. P. Lovecraft, *True Detective,* and the Artist-Investigator." In *Lovecraftian Proceedings 2,* ed. Dennis P. Quinn. Hippocampus Press, 2017. 208-24.

Sayers, Dorothy L. "Introduction." In *The Omnibus of Crime,* ed. Dorothy L. Sayers. 1928. Garden City, NY: Garden City Publishing Co., 1929. 9-47.

Schweitzer, Darrell. "Eldritch, My Dear Watson." *Sherlock Holmes Mystery Magazine* 4, No. 2 (2018): 19-25.

Sharp, Roberta. "Poe's Duplicitous Dupin." In *Masques, Mysteries, and Mastodons: A Poe Miscellany,* ed. Benjamin F. Fisher. Baltimore: Edgar Allan Poe Society, 2006. 63-76.

Sophocles. *Oedipus the King.* In *The Norton Anthology of World Masterpieces: Volume 1,* ed. Maynard Mack et al. New York: W. W. Norton, 1985. 651-700.

Lovecraft out of Space: Echoes of American Weird Fiction on Brazilian Literature and Cinema

Lúcio Reis Filho

I. Lovecraft's Reception in Brazil

H. P. Lovecraft was first published in Brazil in 1966, translated into Portuguese by George Gurjan from *The Dunwich Horror and Others* (Arkham House, 1963). The collection *O que sussurava nas trevas* (*The Whisperer in Darkness*) presented three short stories to Brazilian readers: the title story (1930), "The Call of Cthulhu" (1926), and "The Colour out of Space" (1927). This venture was part of the plan by the publishing house Edições GRD (GRD Editions) to revolutionize the Brazilian publishing market with works that renewed the literature. The introduction by editor Gumercindo Rocha Dórea opens the volume:

> Howard Phillips Lovecraft (1890-1937) is arguably one of the greatest authors of all time in the fantasy genre, whether represented by science fiction, macabre, or horror. Here [. . .] the stories [. . .] show the grandeur of his creative capacity and the scope of his imagination, ensuring his placement in the universal history of literature next to a Poe, a Bierce, a Potocki. When H. P. Lovecraft died, almost thirty years ago, he was unknown in his own homeland. The world did not know him, except for the small circle of his admirers. Today, the world—including the United States of America—honors him, placing him in his rightful place, where he belongs since he published his first stories. Brazil, logically and naturally—considering the delay in which we live regarding culture—does not know H. P. Lovecraft.[1] (1)

Lovecraft was not known in Brazil before the mid-1960s. The reason for such unfamiliarity, as implied, is the "delay in which we live regarding

---

1. Translated by the author.

culture." Brazil is always a few steps behind the latest trends in Europe and the United States. However, this delay coincides with the history of Lovecraft's popularity worldwide. As Lachman corroborates, Lovecraft was relatively unknown when he died in 1937, except to devotees of *Weird Tales*. Three decades later, he was one of the best-selling authors in the United States, his name mentioned in the same breath as Borges, Kafka, and Beckett (39). In the 1960s, translated versions of his writings had reached countries outside the Anglo-Saxon world, such as France and Brazil.

Lachman highlights the collective effort of several authors in giving Lovecraft recognition, guaranteeing his posthumous popularity. Among them, August Derleth stands out. In 1937, Derleth and Donald Wandrei founded Arkham House, a publishing venture aimed to preserve Lovecraft's work. In 1939, they released the first compilation of his stories, *The Outsider and Others*, followed by *Beyond the Wall of Sleep* (1943), *Marginalia* (1944), and *Something about Cats and Other Pieces* (1949).

Known for its conservative, proselytizing literature, as defined by Christofoletti in his study on the science fiction literature in Brazil (212), GRD has specialized, since the 1960s, in publishing books of fantastic fiction and Catholic content. Science fiction was growing in the Brazilian editorial market since that decade, influenced by the "First Wave" of the genre in our literature. Cited by Christofoletti, Laurence Hallawell states that the GRD editions were of substantial importance in the country's editorial transformation. Like most small Brazilian publishers, GRD relied on the support of the United States Information Agency (USIS). The publishing house released many works of national literature, and some new editions of remarkable foreign books (Christofoletti 213, 215). The initiative of GRD is worthy of recognition, considering that Lovecraft's renaissance in the late 1960s and early 1970s is, in part, due to the flood of paperbacks issued by mass-market publishers worldwide.

Cinema also played an important role. During the 1960s, Lovecraft was adapted to the screen for the first time in Roger Corman's *The Haunted Palace* (1963), which borrows its title from a poem by Edgar Allan Poe. This film was followed by American and British productions such as *Die, Monster, Die!* (Daniel Haller, 1965), *The Shuttered Room* (David Greene, 1967), *Curse of the Crimson Altar* (Vernon Sewell, 1968), and *The Dunwich Horror* (Daniel Haller, 1970). In the Brazilian cinema, we could not identify any Lovecraft adaptations before the 2000s; in fact, they would only emerge in the second decade of the twenty-first century. This is the case of

Nervo craniano zero (*Cranial Nerve Zero*, Paulo Biscaia Filho, 2012) and *Mar negro* (*Black Sea*, Rodrigo Aragão, 2013), both having Lovecraftian themes, though not related to any of his works; and even adaptations per se, as *A cor que caiu do espaço* (*The Colour out of Space*, Petter Baiestorf, 2016). This "delay"—paraphrasing Dórea's introduction to the GRD edition—can be explained by some idiosyncrasies of the Brazilian literary field that reflect cultural, social and historical values.

First, as Roberto Schwarz observes, in the early 1960s both producers and the audience did not consider Brazilian films "true cinema." Brazilian films had a large and enthusiastic audience, but only foreign films were appreciated—in particular those coming from the United States or Europe. A remarkable shift in that regard was gaining ground—for that was a moment of contemporary national and class awareness—but the democratizing dimension of the process ended with a coup d'état in 1964. Secondly, the intrinsic "myopia of the Brazilian publishing market," as suggested by Alfredo Suppia, had historically affected genres such as science fiction and horror. As Suppia highlights, "Brazilian criticism is predominantly of a romantic-conservative nature, worshiper of the authorial genius and of the styles most adherent to realism-naturalism, with eventual elements of *avant-garde*, whether in literature or in cinema." According to Brazilian pulp writer Rubens Francisco Luchetti, the *Weird Tales* contributors suffered great prejudice in the Brazilian literary field. "For example, [critics] called August Derleth, who was greatly responsible for preserving Lovecraft's writings, a charlatan. Authors like Lovecraft were called illiterates," Luchetti said in an interview.

As we can observe, Lovecraft's recognition was not immediate in Brazil. This would only happen in the new millennium, with the writer gaining some popularity starting in the second decade of the 2000s. However, despite the absence of Lovecraft-inspired productions in Brazil, a horror film from the 1970s presents the rich themes of his early writings: Carlos Hugo Christensen's *A mulher do desejo: A casa das sombras* (*The Woman of Desire: House of Shadows*, 1975). This film appropriates Gothic themes and conventions present in Lovecraft's more Gothic stories, such as *The Case of Charles Dexter Ward* (1927) and "The Thing on the Doorstep" (1933). It also bears striking similarities to *The Haunted Palace*, a film that Christensen could have watched even if he had never read any of Lovecraft's stories. Through the analysis of this piece of the Brazilian horror cinema, and considering Lovecraft's reception in Brazil, I propose to examine this case of unacknowledged inspiration.

II. The Unfathomable and the Unholy in Carlos Hugo Christensen

Carlos Hugo Christensen (1914–1999), the son of Danes, was born in Santiago del Estero, a province of Argentina. According to Laura Cánepa, his career as a filmmaker began in the early 1940s, during the golden age of Argentine cinema. In the years to come, he circulated through other countries in Latin America, producing films in his homeland and in Chile, Peru, and Venezuela. In 1954, Christensen's violent crime drama *Mãos sangrentas* (*Bloody Hands*) debuted in Brazil, where the main phase of his work, produced between the 1950s and the 1980s (Cánepa 230).

As Cánepa observes, Christensen used to adapt famous or obscure texts, usually appealing to fantastic themes. This is apparent in several of his films, such as *La dama de la muerte* (*The Lady of Death*, Chile, 1947), adapted from Robert Louis Stevenson's *The Suicide Club* (1878); *La muerte camina con la lluvia* (*Death Walks with the Rain*, Argentina, 1949), based on the works of the Belgian André-Stanislas Steeman; *La balandra Isabel llego esta tarde* (*Corvette Isabel Arrived this Afternoon*, Venezuela, 1950), adapted from a short story by the award-winning Venezuelan writer Guillermo Menezes; *No abras nunca esta puerta* (*Never Open this Door*, Argentina, 1952) and *Si muero antes de despertar* (*If I Die Before I Wake*, Argentina, 1952), inspired in two fantastic stories by the American writer William Irish (Cornell Woolrich) (Cánepa 230–31).

In the early days, *La dama de la muerte* and *La muerte camina con la lluvia* were atmospheric and created suspenseful situations. From then on, as Andrea Ormond puts it, Christensen's work approached certain unfathomable and unholy themes. During the 1970s while already working in Brazil, his style might be found in the guise of a dark liturgy. This is how *Enigma para demônios* (*Riddle for Demons*, 1975), *The Woman of Desire*, and—according to its plot—the unfinished *A casa de açúcar* (*The Sugar House*) emerged. Even *A intrusa* (*The Intruder*, 1979) has a certain diabolical element, hidden in a hut lost in the pampas, as if the Nilsen brothers inhabited a den hanging in the air. Christensen made such houses a fundamental component of his stories—an element that is a product of a long film (and literary) tradition, in the genre of haunted houses.

During the 1970s, Christensen flirted with several genres. Horror fiction was the main influence of *Riddle for Demons* and *The Woman of Desire*. According to Ormond, both films "dealt with the dogmas of Lovecraft,

E. T. A. Hoffmann and the thousand aeons of eternity."[2] Cánepa observes that Christensen himself wrote the scripts, with dialogues by the Brazilian writer Orígenes Lessa, inspired by a note from Nathaniel Hawthorne, the works of Samuel Taylor Coleridge, and the Brazilian poet Carlos Drummond de Andrade (1902–1987) (230–32). As addressed in the epigraph of *The Woman of Desire*, the starting point of the narrative shows a flower based on an image drawn from a passage in Coleridge's unpublished notebooks that inspired the plot:

> If a man could pass through Paradise in a dream, and have a flower presented to him as a pledge that his soul had really been there, and if he found that flower in his hand when he awoke—Aye! and what then? (282)

The translation into Portuguese and the insertion of Coleridge's passage in the opening credits refers us to a correlate source, as S. T. Joshi reminds us that the English poet was the major literary influence in the early development of Lovecraft's taste for the weird (*IAP* 33). Apparently, Christensen was following the same path. Also, Cánepa suggests that his film took Lovecraft's famous novel *The Case of Charles Dexter Ward* as unacknowledged inspiration. It is also possible to identify echoes of "The Thing on the Doorstep," one of his later stories.

III. *The Woman of Desire:* A Gothic Story

The Woman of Desire is a story of haunting and possession that begins when the lawyer Domício (Ary Fontenelle) calls the young Marcelo (Jose Mayer) and his wife Sônia (Vera Fajardo), to inform them that they are the heirs of the young man's uncle, whom Marcelo barely knew. The late Uncle Osman, an eccentric, reclusive old man, left for his nephew a substantial amount of money and an old manor in the colonial town of Ouro Preto. The heirs receive the news with great surprise; however, the will is inflexible and requires that the couple move immediately into the mansion, keeping the place exactly as it is. The uncle "wanted the house to be maintained inhabited by family members," and their presence is mandatory even for the funeral.

The new residents are greeted by the sinister butler Nicolau (José Luiz Nunes), who reveals the obsession of Uncle Osman for Sonia, whom he

---

2. Despite this intriguing argument, more research is required to understand if elements of Lovecraftian cosmicism have informed Brazilian horror filmmaking.

knew only through the photos of his nephew's marriage ceremony. In his last days, the old man only talked about the woman and his desire that she move to the mansion after his death. In fact, Osman used to face death with a strange voluptuousness. Later, the couple discovers that he was in love with a woman identical to Sonia, an unrequited love with tragic consequences. The butler also shows the couple opening the coffin with the dead man's body inside, holding an orchid in his cold hands. The sinister servant warns the new tenants and introduces the theme of the haunted mansion: "Mr. Osman [. . .] *demands* that the house be kept exactly as he left it, and you'd better do it, sir. A house is like a person [. . .] It accepts or takes revenge. A house has a soul."

After a nightmare, in which Marcelo confronts the dying uncle who hands an orchid to Sonia, the young man increasingly starts to behave aggressively and violently. In the next day, dressed in his uncle's robe, he starts to investigate some old documents in his uncle's cabinet and discovers the identity of the mysterious woman in the picture. Her name was Ligia, and Osman had been in love with her for a long time. This part of the script clearly derives from Poe, not Lovecraft. As in Coleridge's phrase, the flower delivered in the dream is brought to the real world: the spirit of the deceased, represented by the orchid, uses the nephew's body to seduce his wife, who is identical to Ligia. Marcelo acquires the personality and mannerisms of his uncle, leaving his wife worried, until finally she panics and leaves for help.

Later, supernatural phenomena occur in the old house. A strange face lurks in darkness, the furniture and the wooden floor creak, and the effects on Marcelo are clear. The man he was before is now a personification of the evil uncle. He behaves in an anachronist fashion, with a pompous, aristocratic manner. Sexual intercourse with Sonia gets wild and violent as he tries to rape her. In the final stage of the transformation, Marcelo limps on one leg and his voice changes, shouting as a decrepit elder man. He is now Osman himself. Sonia accuses him of killing her spouse, to which he responds: "I am his *continuation* . . . and you are Ligia. I will possess your body." The woman appeals to Father Paulo (Neimar Fernandes), a young priest who performs an exorcism and expels the evil spirit, setting Marcelo free.

The Woman of Desire is a quintessential nineteenth-century horror story about possession and evil doppelgänger. For Carlos Primati, Christensen constructs with subtlety and mastery an oppressive, terrifying atmosphere, making the house alive, pulsating with doors and walls that crack, a haunting scene filled with animated shadows that move and absorb furniture and objects. It is horror with a classic atmosphere—including the sound-track, with music by Richard Wagner—in the tradition of American and European Gothic films. Just as in *Riddle for Demon*, as Cánepa observes, the Gothic manifests itself in style and narrative. The story about hapless female characters, who are exactly similar to their ancestors and end up thrown into a violent family plot, has been set in colonial locations that help build an atmosphere of fear through contrasted photography and Catholic symbols (Cánepa 232).

In the prologue to her book *Galería fantástica* (*Fantastic Gallery*, 2009), the Argentine critic and writer María Negroni observes that what has far been defined as fantastic literature in Latin America is, in fact, Gothic lit-erature (9). Sandra Casanova-Vizcaíno and Inés Ordiz assert that several Latin American works of fiction contain literary motifs associated with the Gothic.[3] However, Latin American Gothic fiction has remained a margin-alized form if compared to fantastical or magical realist fiction.

> Gothic in Latin America is very much rooted in local realities and histories, and often linked to different processes of modernization. These include the colonization and occupation of the region by Europe or the United States; the formation of the new nation-states following the wars of independence; and the collapse, failure, exhaustion, and absence of national projects that lead to violence, inequality, and exclusion. (22)

In the *The Woman of Desire*, as Cánepa points out, the buildings of Ouro Preto[4] pose as Gothic edifications. The interior of Osman's house, for example, is always dark, with locked windows and few lightening spots, filled with antique furniture and artifacts adorning the stone walls, and broad hollow spaces (Cánepa 235). These motifs inspired Christensen, who brought Gothic to an old Brazilian colonial town, merging the motifs of the genre to the singular idiosyncrasies of the traditional culture: the

---

3. Works of criticism that explore the Gothic in literature, film, and culture in Latin America have started a crucial dialogue that opens multiple readings of the region as a Gothic space. We can mention *Gender and Sexuality in Latin American Horror Cinema* (2016) by Gustavo Subero, and *Horrofílmico: Aproximaciones al cine de terror en Latino-américa y el Caribe* [*Horror Cinema: Approaches to Horror Film in Latin America and the Caribbean*] (2012) by Rosana Días-Zambrana and Patrícia Tomé.

4. The property is located in Ouro Preto, a place of economic importance in the nineteenth century during the gold rush of the colonial era.

authority of the rural oligarchy, the submission of its dependents, and the power of the Catholic religion. In the *Encyclopedia of Brazilian Cinema* (2012), Afrânio Catani addresses the apparent conservatism in all Christensen's stories. "Although his cinema was considered fairly transgressive [. . .] it ends up, paradoxically, reinforcing traditional morals" (cited in Cánepa 230).

IV. Christensen, Corman, and Lovecraft's Gothic/Poe-esque vein

During his time, Lovecraft was aware that the properties of the Gothic had lost all symbolic value, turning into banal and standardized tropes, more likely to produce laughs than chills (*IAP* 46). This perception led to the progressive reformulation of his literary style, although the writer never completely abandoned the Gothic vein. For Erik Davis, the early works of Lovecraft have some "pastiche" of this genre; but, with his tales of the 1920s and 1930s, he "crafted a new gothic, linking it with science fiction, releasing a raw power of despair and disgust" (James Goho, cited by Vox 11–12). However, what interests us in the present study are the "Poe-esque" stories of Lovecraft, Gothic in their scenarios, characters, and taste for death.

Many of Lovecraft's stories were set in the *locus horribilis* of the American Gothic, the old house—haunted, solitary and forgotten in a remote place, with its interior immersed in darkness, with lots of furniture and rustic decor, full of history and memories. In the nineteenth and twentieth centuries, the old house would become the most popular convention of the genre. According to Grunenberg, Edgar Allan Poe's masterful setting of the scene in the opening paragraph of "The Fall of the House of Usher" still stands as the pinnacle of the production of an uncanny atmosphere. Replacing the medieval castle, "the house functions as a matrix for memory and the exploration of hidden rooms, forbidden spaces, locked doors, closet, and cupboards . . . summons to consciousness displaced and undigested experiences and dreams" (176). In Lovecraft's stories such as "The Picture in the House" (1920), "The Lurking Fear" (1922), *The Case of Charles Dexter Ward*, and "The Dreams in the Witch House" (1932), the old houses are the perfect habitat for monstrous occurrences.

Significantly, many Lovecraft's villains and antiheroes adhere to the Gothic/Poe-esque archetype. For example, in *The Case of Charles Dexter*

Ward, Curwen is a social outcast, suspected of demonic alliances that cannot be named, understood, or proven. Such characters stand out for a number of characteristics: individualistic and egocentric behavior, prominent social standing within a closed parochial society, higher than average intelligence and charisma, and low moral standards. They have power to deal with evil, unnatural forces, avoiding the negative side effects of such activities. Furthermore, they do not mind affecting or wounding innocent people, even if they are relatives or associates. In *The Woman of Desire*, Uncle Osman follows the pattern of the Gothic villain: a mysterious, eccentric old man who does not care about society, from which he hides behind a wall of sardonic arrogance. The citizens of Ouro Preto fear him and the strange phenomena that take place in his manor. When Osman reveals his evil deeds, he shows himself as a despicable, domineering, and violent figure, capable of mistreating his own kind.

According to Darryl Jones, the best of Lovecraft's works resulted in some powerful regional Gothic (128). Regarding the reception of Lovecraft's writings in Brazil, *The Woman of Desire* can be seen as a piece of the Colonial Gothic, and the result of an unacknowledged inspiration in at least two of his "Gothic" stories: *The Case of Charles Dexter Ward* and "The Thing on the Doorstep." According to Joshi, both of them feature central themes to Lovecraft's Gothic (and to the Gothic in general): the "fragility of the human reason," the "influence of the past upon the present," and the "baleful call of ancestry" (*IAP* 460). These stories demonstrate, therefore, that Lovecraft never completely abandoned the Gothic.

Joshi considers *The Case of Charles Dexter Ward* "a story of textual and tonal richness" and "one of the most carefully wrought fictions in Lovecraft's entire corpus" (*IAP* 666). The protagonist is a young man from a distinguished Rhode Island family who flees from the asylum—he was admitted due to a prolonged state of madness, in which he suffered unexplained physical transformations. The story follows the investigation of his family doctor, Marinus Bicknell Willett, who tries to figure out the causes of Ward's insanity. Willett finally discovers that the young man spent the last years obsessed with a possible kinship with the occultist Joseph Curwen, a fact proved later. Ward was a perfect look-alike of his ancestor, and the replication of Curwen's alchemical and cabalistic deeds leads him to resuscitate the sorcerer. When Willett manages to track him down, something surprising has happened: although still of youthful appearance, Ward's speech is now eccentric and old-fashioned. Willett confronts him, only to realize that he is no other than Curwen. Taking advantage of his resemblance to the young man, the sorcerer kills and takes the place of his modern descendant, resuming his evil activities. Despite convincing everyone that he is Ward, Curwen's anachronistic mannerisms make the authorities consider him insane and lock him up in an asylum.

As Joshi argues, "The Thing on the Doorstep" is a "reprise" of *The Case of Charles Dexter Ward* (*IAP* 865). The story opens with a confession of the narrator Daniel Upton, who killed his best friend Edward Derby with six bullets in the head. Upton describes Derby's life and career, and the dramatic transformation of his mental faculties. Derby once claimed that the occultist Ephraim Waite, father of his classmate and future spouse Asenath Waite, was not dead. Later, Upton receives a call to rescue Derby, who was found wandering incoherently in a town in Maine. After his rescue, the man explains that Asenath was in control of his body, while Ephraim inhabited hers. Before concluding his version of the story, Derby suffers a convulsion, his personality changes, and he asks Upton to ignore everything he said. Later, he ends up locked up in an asylum. In a letter to Upton, Derby begs his friend to kill the person in the asylum—who in fact is Asenath, who has now permanently possessed his body.

In *The Woman of Desire*, Marcelo suffers from acute monomania and a state of mental degeneration caused by his new habits: the sudden interest in his uncle's artifacts and the inclination to keep the house as it has always been. A scholar devoted to ancient things, Charles Dexter Ward undergoes an analogous process. However, there is an important distinction: Ward (i.e., Curwen) ends up losing his interest in antiquities: "his final efforts were obviously inclined to dominate these common facts of the modern world which had been wholly and unmistakably expunged from his brain" (*CF* 2.218); Marcelo becomes more and more interested in them.

In Christensen's film, the search for the past leads the protagonist to investigate the mysterious woman in the portrait. Both cases exemplify the baleful call of ancestry and the influence of the past upon the present. In the film, however, Marcelo's anachronistic behavior proves to be the result of possession, just as it occurs in "The Thing on the Doorstep." On the other hand, as Joshi observes (*IAP* 865), there is no actual mind-exchange in *The Case of Charles Dexter Ward*, although Asenath's attempt to pass herself off as Derby is analogous to Curwen's.

The Woman of Desire bears striking similarities with *The Haunted Palace* (1963). In fact, both have the same structure. Inspired by *The Case of*

Charles Dexter Ward, Roger Corman's film is set in the fictional town of Arkham, New England. In the prologue, the sorcerer Joseph Curwen (Vincent Price) dies at the hands of the locals, burned alive in a re-enactment of the Salem witch trials. In 1875, a century after Curwen's death, his descendant Charles Dexter Ward (also played by Price) and his wife Annie (Debra Paget) arrive in the town as the heirs to the sorcerer's palace. The servant Simon (Lon Chaney) persuades them to stay and ignore the hostility of the locals. Ward knows the whole place as if he had already been there, and is surprised by the similarity of Curwen's portrait to himself. Later, the obsession with his ancestor causes his personality to change.

The plot is quite similar to the Christensen's film. In *The Woman of Desire*, as we have seen, Marcelo and his wife Sonia inherit from the late Uncle Osman a genuine "palace" in Ouro Preto, a colonial town located in one of the oldest Brazilian provinces. When they arrive in the new residence, they meet the sinister butler Nicolau, who persuades them to stay. The locals fear the house and its former owner. This is due to the widespread belief in the old man's alliances with the forces of evil. Soon Marcelo becomes obsessed with Ligia,[5] the woman in the portrait, because of her resemblance to Sonia. By unearthing his uncle's past, Marcelo's personality changes, and he ends up possessed by the spirit of his ancestor. Just like Vincent Price, the Brazilian actor José Mayer played both the Uncle Osman and his nephew Marcelo.

V. Conclusion: Echoes of Lovecraft

This essay relates Christensen's *The Woman of Desire* with two Lovecraft works: *The Case of Charles Dexter Ward* and "The Thing on the Doorstep." The main difference between these stories is the nature of the supernatural phenomena itself, merely suggested in the first, and evident in the latter, as well as in Christensen's film: the exchange of "soul" or minds performed by Uncle Osman follows the same path as Ephraim/Asenath Waite in Lovecraft's story. There are no references to Lovecraft in the film credits, nor is there any indication that Christensen

---

5. The character's name, Ligia, is phonetically similar to "Ligeia," a character in the story of that title by Poe and in one of the films of Corman's cinematographic cycle, *The Tomb of Ligeia* (1964).

has read the GRD edition or any of his stories. However, considering the filmmaker's interest in literature and the fact that Lovecraft was first published in Brazil ten years before the production of his motion picture, we cannot ignore the possibility of an unacknowledged inspiration. This may have occurred through parallel channels.[6]

The echoes of Lovecraft in *The Woman of Desire* are more likely a result of Poe being an influence on both the film and the stories cited. Christensen's plot is almost identical to the plot of *The Haunted Palace*—released ten years earlier, acclaimed by Brazilian critics, and regularly exhibited on the open TV grid[7] in the 1970s. Both films tell the story of the descendants of a wealthy lunatic who inherit his old house. The influence of Corman seems obvious, so we can perhaps conclude that *The Woman of Desire* is part of the history of the Lovecraftian films. In its own, perhaps unacknowledged way, the film merges Poe and Lovecraft, possibly inspired by the American production. Despite all mentioned echoes, Christensen created an original piece that moves the Gothic to an old Brazilian colonial town, blending the conventions of this genre, which are present in Lovecraft's stories, with the singular idiosyncrasies of Brazilian culture.

Works Cited

Cánepa, Laura Loguercio. "Medo de Quê? Uma História do Horror nos Filmes Brasileiros." Ph.D. diss.: State University of Campinas, 2008.

Casanova-Vizcaíno, Sandra, and Inés Ordiz, ed. *Latin American Gothic in Literature and Culture*. New York: Routledge, 2018.

Christofoletti, Rodrigo. "A controvertida trajetória das Edições GRD entre as publicações nacionalistas de direita e o pioneirismo da ficção científica no brasil." *Miscelânea: Revista de Pós-Graduação em Letras* 8 (July–December 2010): 208-25.

---

6. It should be noted that the first Portuguese translation of a Lovecraft work was *Os mortos podem voltar* (Lisbon: Livros do Brasil, [1955?]), a translation of *The Case of Charles Dexter Ward*.

7. The *Haunted Palace,* in Brazilian theaters in 1964, got positive reviews as "a work of pure and measured terror that at no moment loses its impact." The critics praised that the film had left behind the "surrealist grotesque and the caricature tone" of the previous *Tales of Terror* (1962) and *The Raven* (1963). A decade later, Corman's film productions aired on the Brazilian open TV grid, exhibited by TV Globo on the nights of 1973 and 1974, the years preceding the release of *The Woman of Desire.*

Coleridge, Samuel Taylor. *Anima Poetae: The Letters of Samuel Taylor Coleridge*. Ed. Ernest Hartley Coleridge. London: William Heinemann, 1895.

Davis, Erick. "Calling Cthulhu: H. P. Lovecraft's Magick Realism." *Erick Davis' Figments*. www.levity.com/figment/lovecraft.html Accessed 20 June 2017. Originally published in a condensed form in *Gnosis* (Fall 1999).

Grunenberg, Christoph. *Gothic: Transmutations of Horror in Late Twentieth Century Art*. Cambridge, MA: MIT Press, 1997.

Jones, Darryl. *Horror: A Thematic History in Fiction and Film*. London: Arnold Publishers, 2002.

Lachman, Gary. *Turn Off Your Mind: The Mystic Sixties and the Dark Side of the Age of Aquarius*. New York: Disinformation Books, 2001.

Lovecraft, H. P. *O que sussurrava nas trevas*. Rio de Janeiro: Edições GRD, 1966.

Luchetti, Rubens Francisco. Interview by the author. 27 July 2017.

Negroni, María. *Galería fantástica*. Siglo XXI, 2009.

Ormond, Andrea. "Carlos Hugo Christensen: desvendando o enigma in 'Ensaios'." In *Retrospectiva Carlos Hugo Christensen. Portal Brasileiro de Cinema Website*. Caixa Cultural; Heco Produções, 2015. www.portalbrasileiro decinema.com.br/christensen/ensaios-andrea-ormond.php?indice=ensaios. Accessed September 25, 2018.

"O Castelo Assombrado." *Jornal do Brasil* (13 December 1964).

"Os Filmes da TV." *Jornal do Brasil* (4 March 1973).

"Os Filmes da TV." *Jornal do Brasil* (2 August 1974).

Primati, Carlos. "A mulher do desejo (A casa das sombras)." In *"Análise de Filmes": In Retrospectiva Carlos Hugo Christensen. Portal Brasileiro de Cinema Website*. Caixa Cultural; Heco Produções, 2015. www.portalbrasileiro decinema.com.br/christensen/filme-a-mulher-do-desejo.php?indice=filmes Accessed 25 September 2018.

Ramos, Fernão Pessoa, and Luiz Felipe Miranda, ed. *Enciclopédia do cinema brasileiro*. São Paulo: Editora Senac São Paulo, 2012.

Schwarz, Roberto. *Sequências Brasileiras*. São Paulo: Cia. das Letras, 1999.

Suppia, Alfredo. "A miopia do mercado editorial atrapalha a ficção científica brasileira, diz professor de cinema." *Painel Acadêmico*. painelacademico.uol.com.br/espaco-alameda/8991-a-miopia-do-mercado-editorial-atrapalha-a-ficcao-cientifica-brasileira-diz-professor-de-cinema. Accessed 25 May 2017.

Vox, Lisa. *Existential Threats: American Apocalyptic Beliefs in the Technological Era*. Philadelphia: University of Pennsylvania Press, 2017.

Red Hand, Red Hook:
Machen, Lovecraft, and the Urban Uncanny

Karen Joan Kohoutek
Independent Scholar

From Thomas De Quincey and James Thomson to twentieth-century horror films such as *C.H.U.D.*, urban environments have been depicted as sites for the fantastic and the uncanny, settings appropriate for a state in which "an experience of disorientation, where the world in which we live suddenly seems strange, alienating, or threatening" can thrive (Collins and Jervis 1). Many artists and thinkers have contributed to the tropes found in urban fantasies, but Arthur Machen and H. P. Lovecraft can be seen to exemplify a pivotal period in the development of the urban uncanny. Machen's "The Red Hand" (1895) and Lovecraft's "The Horror at Red Hook" (1925) display a significant shift from an inward, psychological experience to one that focuses outward, projecting internal fears onto threatening populations within the city's boundaries.

Cities have existed since ancient times in all civilizations, and there is no predominant record of any particular angst associated with early forms of urban experience. In more recent recorded history, the city, metaphoric and literal, has been the site of diverse attitudes and symbolic meanings. As Julian Wolfreys has described it, the very existence of the city implies the presence of unfamiliar elements. What separates it from the village is its being a place where very different people, from different places, converge, so that the city itself can come to represent "the unfamiliar, the unhomely" (172). "Unhomely" is a literal translation of *unheimlich*, the word more generally translated as "uncanny," which connotes the opposite of one's literal home and all that is warm and familiar.

A quotation from Machen's story "The Red Hand" serves as an epigraph to Lovecraft's "The Horror at Red Hook," acknowledging the earlier story as an influence. While stylistically different, the two tales share a similar overriding storyline, in which a criminal investigation uncovers an ancient and sinister cult existing within a modern metropolis. The group in "The Red Hand" exists within in the backstory, functioning mostly as a red herring. An open discussion of whether "primitive men," possibly surviving troglodytes, are truly "lurking in our midst" or exist only as a metaphor for the surviving primitive instincts in modern humans brings the possibility of symbolism to the surface (2). The group in "The Horror at Red Hook" is more clearly literal: directly responsible for crimes, and actively working toward sinister ends.

Machen was a habitual wanderer of the city streets, experiencing its strangeness and the resultant personal unease. His personal experience of the urban as a site of the uncanny was translated through fiction into tales of crime and menace, in order to express impressions about life. As he describes the process in an introduction to his well-known story "The Great God Pan," "the emotions aroused by these external things reverberating in the heart, are indeed the story; or all that signifies in the story. But, our craft being that of letters, we must express what we feel through the medium of words [. . .] we are forced to devise incidents and circumstances and plots" (4). Given this, it is not improbable that his well-documented personal love of walking the streets of London, encountering what he perceived as mysteries within the mundane, is reflected in a story like "The Red Hand," in which his characters' actions lead them to strange "incidents and circumstances and plots," providing a symbolic means of expressing a sense of underlying mystery. In doing so, Machen ends up displacing his sense of the urban uncanny onto a minority population. In this case, it is a hidden group of people who have survived apart from the process of evolution: differentiated from the larger population by their position in time, not through any ethnic difference, or even one of social class.

The general tone and style of Machen's story fits into an earlier literary tradition that depicts the city—London, in his case—as a kind of panoramic backdrop for the writer's imagination. In its vastness, it contains the theater of humanity, which includes the negative aspects of human frailty, cruelty, and crime; but while the city was sometimes depicted as a site of threat, mostly from human vice and folly, its more uncanny elements were often seen to rise out of the narrator's own imagination. In this, Machen's work relates to that of writers like Thomas De Quincey (1785-1859) and James Thomson (1834-1882). In their essays and poems, the mysteries of the city tend to appear as symbolic reflections of internal struggles and existential awareness. De Quincey's poetic, opium-inspired reveries are grounded in his experience of poverty and homelessness in London as a young man, when he was "of necessity a peripatetic, or a walker of the streets." "The Red Hand" in particular has a direct link to De Quincey, as a quotation from his most famous work provides a clue to the mystery, operating as a secret code that referrs to a specific street, "for you remember how the opium eater dwells on his wearying promenades along that thoroughfare" (26).

Thomson's bleak tour de force, *The City of Dreadful Night*, uses its similarly evocative atmosphere to create a mood of proto-existential despair. The narrator walks, contemplating the futility of existence, in the streets of Edinburgh, where he has "seen phantoms there that were as men / And men that were as phantoms flit and roam," and where "Some say that phantoms haunt those shadowy streets, / And mingle freely there with sparse mankind; / And tell of ancient woes and black defeats, / And murmur mysteries in the grave enshrined." These descriptions, tinged with the supernatural, represent the darker aspects of existence in a work explicitly written for an audience of readers "whose faith and hopes are dead, and who would die."

Likewise, an early essay by Charles Dickens, "Night Walks" (1861), describes the kind of urban squalor that troubled Victorian reformers, but as with De Quincey and Thomson, his perspective centers on the city as a reflection of his psychological state. Unable to sleep and beset with philosophical questions, he imagines London's inanimate elements coming to uncanny life: "it tumbles and tosses before it can get to sleep" (127). He continues to muse, "What enormous hosts of dead belong to one old great city [. . .] if they were raised while the living slept, there would not be the space of a pin's point in all the streets and ways for the living to come out into" (133).

All these writers use their urban imagery to describe universal fears— death, fate, God, the potential meaninglessness of existence—and Machen uses it in much the same way, as a means to illuminate larger themes. Although he had a sideline as a newspaper writer and wrote essays on real-life crimes, realistic fears play little part in his fiction. The murderer in "The Red Hand" is treated as a figure of pity, not one of terror. The story's focus is not on the crime, or even on the discovery of a primitive race and their unnerving artifacts, but on the revelation of how little we can ever know about the world around us, and the unknown ways that the past, and the dark side of human history, continue to affect the present: "we live and move to my belief in an unknown world, a place where there are caves and shadows and dwellers in twilight" (11), as his character says in the quotation at the beginning of "The Horror at Red Hook."

Lovecraft uses some of the meditative mood familiar from Machen here, including some passages that read as fairly overt homage: "To Malone the sense of latent mystery in existence was always present. In youth he had felt the hidden beauty and ecstasy of things, and had been a poet; but poverty and sorrow and exile had turned his gaze in darker directions" (CF 1.483). In his work, however, the city's uncanny elements are directly displaced onto marginalized groups, a sinister demographic who are depicted as uncanny and threatening to the larger (presumably Anglo-Saxon) society and its values.

In "The Horror at Red Hook," a cult similar to that described in "The Red Hand" has migrated to New York with waves of immigrants (albeit facilitated by a wealthy white patron), and the ancient evil is explicitly linked to real-life populations of immigrants, people of color, and the economically disadvantaged, whose very existence is seen as sinister, regardless of their behavior. Young men standing on street corners are perceived as "leering vigils," and, in the description of them "in stupefied dozes or indecent dialogues around cafeteria tables" he appears to be threatened by the sight of them eating lunch (CF 1.485). In one telling description, the group condemned for their difference is equally condemned for attempts to assimilate, "grotesquely" wearing "flashy American clothing" (CF 1.489).

There is a distinct shift in Machen's representations of uncanny elements in urban life. The city's symbolic value as a site for existential and philosophical musing has become literalized, as the human fears previously explored there are displaced to a perceived underclass, ethnically and economically separated from the narrator, which has become a scapegoat, representing human evil. Although Lovecraft prided himself on his interest in the cosmic, the threats depicted in these horror stories are much more literal than is Machen's mostly theoretical race of primitive survivals. Such fears appear reflective of Lovecraft's personal discomfort with different ethnic groups and socioeconomic classes.

In January 1926, Lovecraft wrote to his aunt, Lillian D. Clark, in terms that show him grappling uncomfortably with the diverse population of New York City. He doesn't express much sense of these other ethnic groups as a personal threat, but his generalizations reveal that, were the groups to violently clash, it would be because of violence on the part of a "properly constituted" white majority (*Letters from New York* 269). He states that "on our side" there is such a "shuddering physical repugnance," that the Jewish people are likely to "be killed off in some sudden outburst of mad physical loathing" (ibid.), a sentence that disturbingly prefigures the Holocaust. If the races are unable coexist in an urban environment, Lovecraft literally states it is because of the violent impulses of the white race and an instinctive hatred he assumes they feel for anyone different from themselves. As he says, "it is not a matter of being orderly citizens" (ibid.), based on the immigrants' actual behavior, or any perceived "savagery in their daily life" (CF 1.485), so any critique based on their habits or degree of civilization seems beside the point.

Such critical, even phobic comments about the urban residents are consistently framed by Lovecraft in terms of ethnic and racial difference from the perceived norm of New England's white settlers. These attitudes appear in other stories; for example, in "The Street" (1920), he describes an area that is laudable so long as "the blood and soul of the people were as the blood and soul of their ancestors who had fashioned The Street" (CF 1.115), but that degenerates into crime and anarchy when residents who have "swarthy, sinister faces" and speak "unfamiliar words" move in (CF 1.116). Similarly, in "He" (1925), another story informed by Lovecraft's time in New York, he recoils from "squat, swarthy strangers" who are "without kinship to the scenes about them, who could never mean aught to a blue-eyed man of the old folk, with the love of fair green lanes and white New England village steeples in his heart" (CF 1.507).

In the common sense of the homelike and the un-homelike, "the weird is that *which does not belong*" (Fisher 10). This notion presupposes that what is thought to constitute the weird depends on one's perspective, specifically on one's position as an insider or an outsider, and the given context of that status. By this token, Lovecraft could have made use of his personal point of view, with the sense that immigrants and people of color do not belong in New England, rendering them uncanny to him, in order to create an atmosphere of the weird and uncanny. That has, in fact, been argued: "while abominable in ethical and political terms, Lovecraft's racism is undeniably effective in purely literary ones" (Harman 60) and "in certain rare cases reactionary views might improve the power of an imaginative writer" (59). Similar symbolic fears of an urban underclass continue to be seen in contemporary popular culture, where it frequently embodies a (presumably white) individual's fears of the city's unknown elements, especially when they occur in groups, such as gatherings of homeless persons or youth street gangs. In this, Lovecraft was unfortunately ahead of his time.

Whether the shift between Machen's and Lovecraft's approaches to the urban uncanny represents a larger zeitgeist is beyond the scope of this essay, but it cannot be ruled out. Erik Mark Kramer and Soobum Lee describe rapid, increased urbanization, and the fact that on a larger scale, "for the first time in human history most of the people in one's social environment were strangers" (142). As such, groups "'outside' the normative structures of a dominating social order" (150) came to be seen as intrinsically threatening.

These discomfiting populations don't have to belong to different races; they merely have to be people who don't fit into any "socioeconomic structure" (148). Of course, in Lovecraft's time, new immigrants and people of color, coming into what had been a relatively homogeneous population that was, at least by him, perceived as having a shared cultural background, were immediately placed into the position of outsiders.

In this environment, the urban uncanny becomes a lens through which to view the individuals, isolated and possibly alienated among a vast city of strangers, who can view the environment through the lens of the urban uncanny, which once represented symbolic liminal states but is now the site of literalized, tangible fears. The presence of obvious outsiders, who can be easily marginalized, creates a target upon which angst-ridden urban explorers can project their fears.

The major psychological theories of the uncanny were published in between the writing of the Machen and Lovecraft tales: Ernst Jentsch's "On the Psychology of the Uncanny" (1906) and Sigmund Freud's "The Uncanny" (1919). Both writers' theories on the uncanny confront the ways in which others are both like us and unlike us, a conundrum that can be psychologically unsettling. Jentsch's views are more philosophical, with a broader description of the uncanny, relating it to the fact that "the traditional, the usual and the hereditary is dear and familiar to most people, and that they incorporate the new and the unusual with mistrust, unease and even hostility" (3). A person's sense of "the uncanniness of a thing," then, is bound up in "a lack of orientation," an inability to place the uncanny experience into one's sense of reality, the state in which one is at ease (2). Freud in contrast tries to pinpoint the uncanny in more tangible ways, for example, with his lengthy focus on automata in the stories of E. T. A. Hoffmann and examples from psychoanalytical case studies. The difference between these two major early definers of the uncanny reflects the similar shift from Machen's body of weird fiction to Lovecraft's.

Racial and cultural differences between groups of people have been described as falling into the "uncanny valley," the point on the spectrum at which something unhuman seems so close to human that it causes the most discomfort in a viewer. This has been linked to the idea of racial differences, for example by blogger Leigh Johnson in a series of essays on the concept of the uncanny valley: "We *believe* that the human/non-human distinction is a difference that makes a difference, just as we believe the same about racial differences, and we have a deep investment in maintaining the distinction between the real and the apparent . . . even in the case of racial identities, *which are almost entirely about the 'apparent'*."

While we now tend to view the "uncanny" in a broader scope, it's troubling to note that the original definitions hinged on an imperfect distinction between what is human and what is not, with automata being (for both writers) the clearest example of an uncanny object. When the uncanny is seen in racial terms, as it is in Lovecraft's work, an extension of those ideas would suggest that a view of certain populations as not quite fully human, while still being demonstrably similar to other people in almost every way, could place them in the uncanny valley. This in turn could cause a psychological unease that would not exist without the underlying perception that denies some people their humanity in the first place, and creates a feedback loop of uncanny perception.

As the larger existential fears once explored in literature become focused on ethnic minorities and the economically disadvantaged, the dehumanization of these groups of people renders them uncanny: like, but not like. Their inevitable presence in a space, the city, defined by its openness to difference, perpetuates a veneer of the uncanny over the cityscape. This idea has taken root and been further developed into contemporary times. Examples can be found that a fear of a perceived underclass has long been with us, including, for example, Dickens's urban criminals, in familiar novels such as *Oliver Twist*. Nonetheless, the presence of an urban uncanny in literature, with the language of the weird and mysterious used to reflect internal states of mind, was once much more prominent than in the modern day. The more general trend of urban symbolism has never really gone back to the pre-Machen depiction of the city primarily as a psychological landscape. Instead, when the urban underclasses appear in films and literary works, they frequently embody an individual's fears of the city's unknown elements. The mode of urban uncanny seen in Lovecraft's New York stories has flourished, particularly in horror films, not always fixed specifically on racial or ethnic difference, but focusing fears on socioeconomic outsiders, including people of color.

In films where the urban unease is not of a supernatural or science fictional nature, the threat is even more likely to be coded in overt racial terms, with depictions of violent street gangs or ghetto "thugs": described by Steve Macek as "the Savage Urban Other" (71). Cult horror films of the 1980s, a time of rapid social transition, could add an instant uncanny element with the presence of threatening homeless people, living in squalor outside the norms of the mainstream society, as seen in films such as *C.H.U.D.* and John Carpenter's *Prince of Darkness*.

In the times of Dickens, Thomson, and Machen, it was not generally thought that the poor should be excluded from the fabric of urban life. When the young De Quincey lived on the street, haunted by opium phantoms, the poverty-stricken population around him was not a threat; rather, he describes how prostitutes had "taken my part against watchmen who wished to drive me off the steps of houses where I was sitting," and was helped in illness by a young woman who had "scarcely wherewithal to purchase the bare necessaries of life." Contemporary representations of popular culture, however, tend to view a city's unluckiest occupants as threatening, in much the way Lovecraft did. The uncanny presumes a sense of stability, necessary for a context and contrast against which an element can be judged as belonging or not belonging. What does the uncanny mean in the modern world, where so much is changing at a faster pace than someone such as Machen or Lovecraft could have imagined? It is hard to know whether human beings will acclimate, experiencing less and less of a sense of the uncanny, in the absence of a *heimlich* to compare it to, or whether the uncanny will leak out, so what should seem familiar and homelike will all come to seem unsettling.

It is impossible to track accurately all the ways that images of the urban uncanny have changed through time, with so many complex factors affecting attitudes about urban life, and the hard-to-pinpoint nature of the uncanny. Still, as a pair of weird tales linked by their similar narratives and Lovecraft's reading of Machen, "The Red Hand" and "The Horror at Red Hook" provide glimpses of a "before and after" at a pivotal shift in the way the urban uncanny was used to symbolize human fears.

Works Cited

Collins, Jo, and John Jervis. *Uncanny Modernity: Cultural Theories, Modern Anxieties*. Basingstoke, UK: Palgrave Macmillan, 2008.

De Quincey, Thomas. *Confessions of an English Opium-Eater*. Project Gutenberg. 2005.

Dickens, Charles. *The Uncommercial Traveller and Reprinted Pieces etc*. New York: Oxford University Press, 1997.

Fisher, Mark. *The Weird and the Eerie*. London: Repeater Books, 2016.

Harman, Graham. *Weird Realism: Lovecraft and Philosophy*. Winchester, UK: Zero Books, 2012.

Jentsch, Ernst. "On the Psychology of the Uncanny" [Zur Psychologie des Unheimlichen] (1906), trans. Roy Sellars. *Angelaki* 2, no. 1 (1995). www.art3idea.psu.edu/locus/Jentsch_uncanny.pdf

Johnson, Leigh. "The Uncanny Valley 2: Racial Appearances." *ReadMore WriteMoreThinkMoreBeMore*. 10 October 2009. www.readmorewritemore thinkmorebemore.com/2009/10/uncanny-valley-2-racial-appearances.html

Kramer, Erik Mark, and Soobum Lee. "Homelessness: The Other as Object." In *Reading the Homeless: The Media's Image of Homeless Culture*, ed. Eungjun Min. Westport, CT: Praeger, 1999. 135–58.

Lovecraft, H. P. *Letters from New York*. Ed. S. T. Joshi and David E. Schultz. San Francisco: Night Shade Books, 2005.

Macek, Steve. *Urban Nightmares: The Media, the Right, and the Moral Panic over the City*. Minneapolis: University of Minnesota Press, 2006.

Machen, Arthur. "The Great God Pan." In *The Great God Pan and the Hill of Dreams*. Mineola, NY: Dover, 2006. 1–66.

———. "The Red Hand." In *The White People and Other Stories*. Ed. S. T. Joshi. Oakland, CA: Chaosium, 2003. 1–28.

Thomson, James. *The City of Dreadful Night*. Project Gutenberg. 2008.

Wolfreys, Julian. "The Urban Uncanny: The City, the Subject, and Ghostly Modernity." In Collins and Jervis 168–80.

Naming the Unnamable: Lovecraft's Return of the Text

Paul Neimann
University of Colorado, Boulder

Introduction

In all its brevity, "The Unnamable" (1923) is an exemplary H. P. Lovecraft tale. The narrator, (Randolph) Carter, is a recurring character and recognizable writerly stand-in for Lovecraft. The setting evokes New England's dark side, as Carter unearths a seventeenth-century legend about a local monster; descriptions feature typically florid vocabulary; encounters end in something like insanity. We find, in other words, a template for—and reflections on—a number of other works. In addition, Lovecraft offers commentary on literary realism's faults and on conflicts between art and commerce. For all these reasons, readers and editors have observed that we could do worse than approach this self-reflexive story by recalling the author's explicit comments on "weird" fiction—in essays or manifestoes such as "Supernatural Horror in Literature" (1927) or the *In Defence of Dagon* (1921) essays. The title, given the many familiar elements, has been taken to suggest a defining philosophical concern of Lovecraft's work: that which defies ordinary experience and representation, what we might call the meaning of horror.

But Lovecraft may disappoint as a theorist of the Unnamable—or perhaps should, if one expects novel reflections that predict recent ideas. Literary studies of neo-Gothic genres tend to treat the unspeakable in psychological terms, while others have recruited "weird" authors to projects of rethinking descriptions of the natural world. Lovecraft, however, treats his subject in more antiquated modes: as archivist, student of early modern aesthetics, and prose stylist. "Supernatural Horror in Literature," for example, can be described as, mostly, a learned catalogue of horror traditions that defines newer weird fiction using older aesthetics. The essay proceeds in circular Aristotelian fashion to define a genre in terms of an already intuited set of successful works that provoke the right emotions. Many of its best-known claims derive from Edmund Burke's *A Philosophical Enquiry into the Origin of Our Ideas of the Sublime and Beautiful* (1757). Discerning authors can descriptively exploit the biologically based fears that ground pious awe, primitive superstition, and true horror alike. Despite criticizing English Gothic's dated, too-tangible terrors ("secret murder, bloody bones, or a sheeted form clanking chains according to rule" [CE 2.84]), Lovecraft arguably recalls the way writers such as Ann Radcliffe and Mary Shelley formulaically deployed Burke's aesthetics to enhance fiction without necessary interest in real unknowns.

Similarly, whereas "Supernatural Horror in Literature" finds *The Castle of Otranto* (1764) lacking, Lovecraft bases later criticism on Horace Walpole's Gothic prescriptions for characters who react realistically to the unnatural. His claim that "we cannot expect all weird tales to conform absolutely to any theoretical model" (*CE* 2.84) implies that they might or ideally should; and he identifies that model mainly with mood-setting artifice. Edgar Allan Poe, accordingly, is complimented for his "scientific attitude" and "analytical knowledge of terror's true sources" (*CE* 2.101). These virtues, as in Poe's "The Philosophy of Composition" (1846), identify fear with calculated efforts at rhetorical effect more than metaphysical or psychic speculation. Poe's criticism even suggests cynicism or parody of commercialism and has supported, as Dennis Pahl notes, a "prevailing belief" among scholars that Poe's fiction carries greater "theoretical implications" than his essays (1). In Lovecraft's case, such a feeling easily dovetails with the position that while he succeeds as writer, "Lovecraft as a thinker just wasn't of any importance, whether as a materialist, an aestheticist, or a moral philosopher" (Rottensteiner 118).

Typically, that is, Lovecraft seems defiantly un-modern. His critical literary focus on composition and rhetoric predates a defining impulse of scholarship around horror genres since Freud: to discern "repressed fears and desires" and "residual conflict surrounding those feelings" (Clover 11). That drives cultural criticism that identifies, for example, *Invasion of the Body Snatchers* (1956) with Cold War anxiety, or John Carpenter's film *Halloween* (1978) as capturing "the end of the permissive, liberal 1970s" (Phillips 142). This thinking has often been applied to Lovecraft's work, convincingly tracing his terrors to, say, suppressed fears of human fragility or modernity, or his own xenophobia. Those who identify "The Unnamable" as a metafictional account of an abjection that recalls Freud's Uncanny or Lacan's Real also set the stage for those seeking distinct Lovecraftian philosophies. But Lovecraft's traditional aesthetics, or an account of borrowings from Burke, Walpole, Radcliffe, and Poe, should complicate efforts to find him a new theorist of the weird. Relatedly, his dated critical habits can seem irrelevant or less astute than his fictions, which may reveal the Unnamable in unconscious or oracular fashion.

This essay seeks a way between studies that treat Lovecraft's literary theory as ancillary to his fiction and those that, perhaps less convincingly, find him a postmodern theorist. I turn first to "The Unnamable" to explore the title concept many find at the center of Lovecraft's work. Briefly, the narrative establishes one character, Joel Manton, a proponent of philosophic and artistic realism, as the socially conventional foil for Randolph Carter, who champions the Unnamable as a worthy focus of his pulp fiction. While Carter, theorist of inexpressibility, most clearly figures Lovecraft, Manton can be read as voicing the author's thoroughgoing skepticism. The resulting quasi-Socratic dialogue advances Carter's aesthetic theories through several flawed iterations. Critics usually emphasize Carter's account of the unrepresentable, which seems confirmed by Manton's concluding encounter with the legendary Thing referenced in the story's title. Martyn Colebrook, for example, identifies the Lovecraftian Unnamable with "the paradox of representing entities, objects, and places that are beyond established modes of representation" (216).

Strangely, the pursuit of this theme leads many away from Lovecraft's explicit views on writing horror: He is seen unconsciously to produce monsters to decode, or appears as a pioneer of ideas not necessarily his own. Rather than risk bypassing or obscuring his aesthetics, I suggest returning to Lovecraft's notion that "a weird story whose intent is to teach or produce a social effect, or one in which the horrors are finally explained away by natural means, is not a genuine tale of cosmic fear" (CE 2.84). This has been taken to direct us to the ineffable or to writing strategies that summon it. Most directly, however, we find a belief that horror is not found outside, in any real, or in a story's social entanglements. Instead, Lovecraft consistently returns to the written text itself, and to the author's raw power to seduce and unsettle. That may frustrate desires for a more palpable weird, but there are reasons to consider this a horror as real as any.

Closing on the Unnamable

"The Unnamable" rewards close reading in surprising ways, given that Lovecraft often works through cumulative excess. A quick plot synopsis accommodates key phrasings directing us to the inexpressible. Randolph Carter and his friend Joel Manton are "speculating about the unnamable" (the focus of Carter's writing) in a cemetery with an "illegible" tombstone; Carter calls attention to a tree perhaps drawing on "unmentionable" underground nourishment, which he ties to an area legend; Manton accuses him of talking "nonsense," since there is "nothing" there (CF 1.397). Carter insists on the reality of a "thing" first described by Cotton Mather as the "impossible" result of unholy couplings between a local man and, apparently, livestock (CF 1.400-401). We are told townsfolk "did not dare to tell" of a sibling to the half-animal (CF 1.401). There are "innuendoes" about the "nameless" and "indescribable" (CF 1.401-2). Carter's own fictional version of the story, we are told, included a witness who "couldn't describe what it was that turned his hair grey" (CF 1.400). The companions are finally attacked by an "unseen" entity that is nevertheless partly described, and they go a bit mad (CF 1.404-5). Manton, as final witness, notes that the entity actually wasn't the beast or thing Carter tried to explain: *"it wasn't that way at all,"* he says. "It was everywhere—a gelatin—a slime—yet it had shapes, a thousand shapes of horror beyond all memory. There were eyes—and a blemish. It was the pit—the maelstrom—the ultimate abomination. Carter, *it was the unnamable!"* (CF 1.405).

Lovecraft's account of the unspeakable would appear to impeach Manton, a closed-minded bourgeois type, who serves mainly as a test subject for Carter's defense of the outré. A school principal who shares "New England's self-satisfied deafness to the delicate overtones of life," he holds that "only our normal, objective experiences possess any aesthetic significance" (CF 1.398). He favors, in art, "accurate, detailed transcripts of every-day affairs" (CF 1.398) and insists that

> We know things [. . .] only through our five senses or our religious intuitions; wherefore it is quite impossible to refer to any object or spectacle which cannot be clearly depicted by the solid definitions of fact or the correct doctrines of theology—preferably those of the Congregationalists, with whatever modifications tradition and Sir Arthur Conan Doyle may supply. (CF 1.397-98)

Against all this, Carter takes up, more or less, Lovecraft's critique of naturalist fiction that "clings to frequently felt emotions and external events" (CE 2.82). S. T. Joshi's *H. P. Lovecraft: The Decline of the West* helps identify Manton's vague pieties with the "muddled lower-middle-class mind" the author deplored (131–32).

Carter's "counter-attack" on Manton, an "orthodox sun-dweller," seems warranted, given the latter's feeling that "nothing can be really 'unnamable.' It didn't sound sensible to him" (CF 1.398–99). One senses an authorial hint opposing Manton. "Nothing" is truly unnamable precisely because it is not "sensible." Carter renews his defense of the supernatural captured in folklore and legend. Strangely, though, the tale suggests this is too domesticated, not quite the Unnamable. Carter describes, at best, what we might call the supra-sensory or paranormal. In a weak defense of his fiction he asserts the credibility of "old-wives' superstitions" like ghosts, including "psychic impressions," "spectral substances" and "living dead things" (CF 1.399). Manton, the yardstick here, remains "unimpressed." References to Manton's mild religious supernaturalism and faddish spiritualism—the fact that he "believ[ed] in the supernatural much more fully" than Carter—suggest the latter has not ventured far beyond his interlocutor (CF 1.398).

The discussion arguably questions Lovecraft's own Burkean formulations of primal feeling predicated on fear. Manton's real gripe with such fictions, it turns out, concerns a crude literalism that is actually the opposite of the sublime or unthinkable. "Nobody," he complains, "but a cheap sensationalist would think of having [the monster of legend] grow up, look into people's windows at night, and be hidden in the attic of a house, in flesh and in spirit" (CF 1.400). He suggests weird genre fiction fails not by exceeding experience, but because it relies on a reductive (fictive) materialism that mechanically excites readers' senses. We are asked to note a persistent tension in supernatural genres—between gestures at the ineffable and a diminution into plot device, monster, or special effect that inevitably occurs on the page. The debate recalls, for example, the giant helmet in Walpole's *Otranto*, which combines sublime supernaturalism with perhaps too-real description: "He beheld his child dashed to pieces, and almost buried under an enormous helmet, an hundred times more large than any casque ever made for human being, and shaded with a proportionable quantity of black feathers" (Walpole 19). The last phrase is comic; yet Lovecraft elsewhere commends the technique. Indeed, Manton derides

Carter's (Lovecraft's own) signature and opposing techniques of 1) presenting sublime horrors in exhaustively detailed prose and 2) simply insisting on the Unnamable by presenting a traumatized character unable to describe "what it was." These are "flagrant trashiness" (CF 1.400)—lapses into dubious conventions.

One danger for Carter appears to be that the Unnamable may derive chiefly from pulp fiction's vulgarity. Carter, recalling the real Lovecraft, reveals his work was censored in the conservative South and West while jaded New England readers ignored the "extravagance." His work is only unspeakable in the blunt sense of violating good literary taste with something "biologically impossible" (CF 1.400). Manton notes Carter's "lowly standing" as a writer and rejects the "puerile" cliché of having narrators "paralysed" by what is too awful to describe (CF 1.397). Here the Unnamable is—plausibly—what Manton more aptly derides as just impolite or "unmentionable" (CF 1.397). As a result, Carter draws unwarranted metaphysical conclusions from dubious narrative conventions.

A subsequent attempt to show the reality of the Unnamable leads to a more anthropological theory. In an ill-advised concession to Manton, Carter offers up "awful evidence" of Cotton Mather's outrageous account (CF 1.399). This turns on notions of the monstrous—the violation of conceptual categories, what is called unnatural according to categories or taboos. Here, bluntly, crossing boundaries is an unthinkable act of bestiality resulting in a Minotaur-like "hybrid" offspring. Again though, Lovecraft undercuts this familiar theory of horror, implying it is not truly inexpressible. Manton objects that "some unnatural monster" may have existed but that "even the most morbid perversion of Nature need not be *unnamable* or scientifically indescribable" (CF 1.402). Clearly we do not proceed beyond representation; by implication, a rationalist and materialist can reduce "abomination" to the merely deviant, nothing more than cultural or biological outlier.

Carter supplies an overlapping theory to the effect that Cotton Mather's shocking legend is remarkable for having excited the prurient interest of a supposedly pious Puritan. The (real) legend has origins in the stifled sexual imagination of the "Puritan age": "There was no beauty, no freedom," as confirmed by "poisonous sermons of the cramped divines. And inside that rusted iron strait-jacket lurked gibbering hideousness, perversion, and diabolism. Here truly was the apotheosis of the unnamable" (CF 1.400–401). Despite ambivalence about Freud, Lovecraft here treats horror in terms of desire or discontent, resulting from socialization, that remains within but is projected outward. This fits remarks in "Supernatural Horror in Literature" on early American superstition, including "unbelievable secret monstrosities." Colonial America's supernaturalism is built on

> the free rein given under the influence of Puritan theocracy to all manner of notions respecting man's relation to the stern and vengeful God of the Calvinists, and to the sulphureous Adversary of that God, about whom so much was thundered in the pulpits each Sunday; and the morbid introspection developed by an isolated backwoods life devoid of normal amusements and of the recreational mood, harassed by commands for theological self-examination, keyed to unnatural emotional repression. (CE 2.104)

This suggests a convergence of Lovecraft's and recent critical viewpoints. The narrative, however, moves past this plausible account of the inexpressible, and returns to what Carter confusingly describes as a point drawn from "aesthetic theory" that a "spectre" might constitute "in all loathsome truth the exquisitely, the shriekingly *unnamable*" (CF 1.403).

Some Names for the Unnamable

Overall, the story captures a lasting contradiction in Lovecraft's writing: we find ruthlessly modern efforts to demythologize fear as a product of human ignorance and prejudice. On the other hand, we find anti-Enlightenment convictions that horror lies beyond psychic or social explanation and remedy. Carter's lapse into unconsciousness and Manton's ranting have been taken to vindicate the conceptual coherence of un-representability. On the question of whether Carter's literary interests can be justified, many critics answer in the affirmative—taking Lovecraft to present or theorize "the paradox of representing entities, things, and places that are beyond representation" (Kneale 107).

Broadly speaking, engagements with Lovecraft's Unnamable have taken two paths. One, plausibly, finds the abject or unpresentable at the anxious center of Lovecraft's fictions, in his bigotry or possible misogyny, for example. Such criticism demythologizes Lovecraft much as he analyzes the feverish Puritan imaginary. In a recent collection, for example, Gina Wisker employs Lacanian traditions to read Lovecraft's women as "monstrous mothers of the more monstrous, as voracious excessively sexual seductresses, or predatory hags linked to devilish knowledge and power"

(36). David Simmons observes that Lovecraft's fiction "seeks to configure alien, and unknowable, others as internal threats to national, political, and psychological stability" (28).

In a twist, some writers find Lovecraft directly concerned with philosophical investigation. If we take "The Unnamable" as a metaphysical manifesto, Lovecraft may suggest that efforts to domesticate the unspeakable through cultural-historical analysis miss the point of that which obdurately resists interpretation. Maria Beville offers such a critique of scholarship's

> general preoccupation with the monster's subversive potential as a figuration of Otherness: a characterisation that counterpoints most aspects of 'mainstream' culture, history, and identity. Engaging with the cultural dynamics of the monster from this perspective, many studies invariably attempt to manage the monster in processes of classification. Such attempts to control the Otherness of the monster are seen in claims that the monster serves a social function as an embodiment of fear that enacts a purging and projection of our most basic anxieties. (1)

She turns instead to Lovecraft's Unnamable as a noumenal "absolute Other: a monstrous 'Thing' that is impossible to name and represent" (102). Related readings in "speculative realism" or "new materialism" take Lovecraft as a proto-philosopher or the figurehead for philosophies approximately concerned with reality beyond human language or consciousness, the non-human, or physical bodies. New materialisms include an array of writings with family resemblances to critical theory familiar to some as "thing theory" or eco-criticism; writers making substantial use of Lovecraft include Eugene Thacker, Graham Harman, and Donna Haraway.

These are likely contestable on their own terms. Beville and others, looking beyond cultural studies, may neglect the intrinsically linguistic and social aspects of Lacanian borrowings. Numerous critics have, similarly, questioned anti-semiotic accounts of an inaccessible real (Boysen 225–42). But, strictly speaking, I do not argue here that any of these are false or that Lovecraft does not hint at such notions. Neither do I intend to regard only authorial intent. Psychoanalytic interpretations, for example, convincingly explicate a Lovecraft who is not a fellow theorist. Some speculative ontologies may contain truth or utility. I do assert, however, that Lovecraft is not a writer of the Unnamables that inform these efforts. That means that some assertions about weird realities—those with strained, unfalsifiable readings of Lovecraft's fiction, or cherry-picked references to his essays—illuminate his texts much like those books that find the *Tao Te Ching* intuiting insights from quantum mechanics, in that it might and also obviously does not.

Instead, I wish to take up the more straightforwardly literary argument that locates weirdness in the effects of language. Many current readings use this as a starting point, even if their interests lie elsewhere. Stephen T. Asma, for example, finds Lovecraft, Freud, and Heidegger "trying to articulate [. . .] dark, unsettling experiences that could not be discursively communicated except in the poetic and visual expressions of artists" (186). That loosely connects the unspeakable to the literary text's rhetorical incommensurability—what now-neglected American "New Critics" treated as the poem's resistance to paraphrase or moral or philosophical synopsis. Indeed, Graham Harman's *Weird Realism: Lovecraft and Philosophy* (2012) makes unexpected use of Cleanth Brooks's New Critical notion of the "heresy of paraphrase" and its critique of attempts to capture literature in summary—that is, reduce it to a vehicle for ideas best expressed in other (more valued) discourses, as if merely an ornamented, emotive, or inexact description, or a dramatization of moral platitudes.

Brooks, in works like *The Well Wrought Urn* (1947), hoped to rehabilitate poetic language as truth-telling, but in distinct ways worthy of specialized study. In Harman's terms, Lovecraft is a writer of "noumenal" horror inasmuch as he employs descriptive strategies irreducible to regular propositional or referential statements about physical phenomena. That fits Brooks's claim that literary, non-referential speech takes the poem "out of competition with scientific, historical, and philosophical propositions" (226). In the same way, recent theorists of the Unnamable might be said to overturn the rhetorical values of Edmund Wilson's notorious attack on Lovecraft's "hack" writing and recover pulp trashiness much as New Critics recovered poetry from encroachments of scientific culture. One can, in fact, discern parallels between the New Critics and some recent critical theory. Both can be described as reactions against positivism, technological enframing, or utilitarian empiricism; both proffer poetic—or weird— truths in the social place of science or superstitions and faiths lost to skepticism and demythologization.

Appropriating Lovecraft to philosophy also breaks with the literariness treated by New Critics. For Brooks, to take a simple example, Robert Browning's figurative phrase "So wore the night" has a non-referential, unglossable meaning inseparable from senses of the word "wore" as operative in the context of his poem (184). This truth or image is not portable to

other speech, and really only exists by engaging the text. The literary function (its weird ontology) emerges, for Brooks, strictly in the irreducible po-
etic/fictional object, as distinct from supposedly equivalent claims or
creeds. He even suggests a poetic superiority to numinous religious truths,
since the latter are often, as he notes in his essay "Religion and Literature," paraphrased into a more literal "fairy tale with ethical implications"
(107). Here we find another parallel between new ontologies and New
Critics, in that vague invocation of quasi-religion has been regarded as a
weakness of both. These are distinct cases, though, in that weird realism
and its kin make, as Brooks says of religion, "some claim on our belief,"
while for him literature is its own experience—it "requires of us an out-
reach of the imagination; it does not require a commitment" (106). His
poetic religion was quite directly a religion of poetry and not of concealed
reality. But many critics succumb to heretical paraphrase in at least the
sense of treating Lovecraft's work as proof-text, inspiration, or unwitting
evidence for independent claims. Harman takes Lovecraft to be a great
writer of the modern era precisely because, "despite his apparently limited
interest in philosophy," he makes "tacit" gestures at metaphysics Harman
describes, in other discourses, in his own books (3). However much he is
celebrated as proto-theorist or performer of unspeakability, Lovecraft is ultimately a disposable element in these accounts. That suggests less a recu-
peration of horror writing than an inversion of Edmund Wilson's
snobbery—offering alternative truths by which to measure fiction, despite
Lovecraft's animus against writing whose "intent is to teach or produce a
social effect." Sure enough, having offered an account of reality or "philosophical themes" (232) to which writers could aspire, Harman finds numerous Lovecraft passages unsuited to neo-Heideggerian quibbles to be
stylistically deficient.

Lovecraft's closeness to formalist ideas most simply suggests the same
interest in texts as such, and powerful "suspension of disbelief" over realities, weird or otherwise. The *In Defence of Dagon* papers strikingly parallel
New Critical sensibility, but in terms truly comparable to their aesthetics:

> It is not the [imaginative writer's] business to fashion a pretty trifle to please
> the children, to point to a useful moral, to concoct superficial "uplift" stuff
> for the mid-Victorian holdover, or to rehash insolvable human problems
> didactically. (CE 5.47)

The writer's task is rather one of sheer composition aimed at affect. Lovecraft writes "purely and simply to reproduce a mood" (CE 5.49). The writer of imaginative horror is "a painter of moods and mind-pictures—a capturer and amplifier of elusive dreams and fancies"; he is a "myth maker" and "poet" of "moods"; "visions"; "memories"; because "Phantasy exists to fulfill the demands of the imagination" (CE 5.47).

In truth, there is little evidence for the philosopher of the weird con-structed by some—in a rough composite, one whose weird literature a) ex-presses novel metaphysical or cosmological views that b) inform his aesthetic theory and c) point to unrepresentable realms as d) a challenge Western traditions that e) provokes horror at human insignificance. Even an incomplete accounting suggests that, in fact, Lovecraft's brand of mate-rialism can adequately be equated with norms of experimental science (ex-isting "knowledge and experience" [CE 5.41; see also 5.76]) which led him, in his own accounts, to a freethinking but otherwise run-of-the-mill sense of mechanical determinism ("laws of Nature" [CE 5.39; see also 5.70; 5.76; 5.148]), natural selection, and astronomical discovery. He de-scribes his outlook, mostly formed by age thirteen, as the product of geog-raphy, geology, astronomy, and biology (CE 5.146). He takes from these a posture of scientific detachment (CE 5.41), acceptance of humankind's eventual demise, irreligion, and disbelief in transcendent truth (CE 5.143-48). He characterizes his sensibility, available to any hardheaded reader of science, as "calm, courageous facing of the infinite" (CE 5.43), stoic indif-ference, and philosophical cynicism (CE 5.75). When pessimistic he de-scribes human reality in aesthetic terms unconnected to horror, as tragedy and farce. Lovecraft saw the challenges materialist thought posed to the bourgeois and religious—but did not identify news of this upheaval with weird philosophy. He readily credits High Modernists, like T. S. Eliot, with the same ideas, though he deplores their alleged vulgar tweaking of common sensibilities. Far from wild philosophy, but against Modernism, he saw weird fiction as a gentlemanly return to imagination and aristocrat-ic excellence compatible with skepticism. He clearly describes Poe's weird "phantasy" as a (presumably fictive) relief from his own (true) rational sci-entism—not an insight into fantastic metaphysics. His aesthetics were not radical. He accepted traditional culture as a de facto civilizing force, re-mained committed to the superiority of classical authors, and saw weird literature carrying on their sensibility by other means.

Critical temptation to find Lovecraft naming a real Unnamable often seems an effect of loose reading. Lovecraft uses "weird" chiefly as an adjective and "the weird" to mark a genre, a feeling, and quality of writing (as in "weirdness"); there are dozens of uses in "Supernatural Horror in Literature," but none much suggests "the weird" as an extra-textual subject to which can be attached predicates in the sense that he describes any Thing. Taken at face value—and why not?—his central definitions suggest no claims about objects or metaphysics: "The one test of the really weird is simply this—whether or not there be excited in the reader a profound sense of dread, and of contact with unknown spheres and powers" (*CE* 2.84). The sole locus of weirdness is "simply" the reader's manipulated reaction to a construction (a sense as if). Readers confer success or failure, so implicitly the weird is nowhere except where it is felt (*CE* 5.48). Lovecraft therefore found the same effects in inferior and nonweird authors. That follows from his consistent regard for the total effect of plotted works. Unlike those who identify short passages with alternative realisms, a move that privileges any scrap of vague description, Lovecraft crucially links weirdness to the text's overall appeal. In short, while Lovecraft may be central to some "speculative realisms," it is unclear that speculative realism is any part of Lovecraft.

Horror on the Surface

On the contrary, where Lovecraft defends his fiction as built on truths about a cold "mechanistic cosmos" it is less to reveal ungrasped realities to all than to direct complacent readers to the scientific reality he thought available to all but the blinkered (*CE* 5.64). Recent readings find him pointing, via fiction, to the world's weirder background or to horrific existence; Lovecraft saw himself layering weird untruths over plain truths of empiricism that were horrific mainly to the unenlightened. The *In Defence of Dagon* papers show just this debate with (Manton-like) readers immune to fictional supernatural shock because their pieties barely allow for the scientific. That confirms Lovecraft's view of horror as an elite imaginative pastime, and shows an effort to re-conceive a high culture for an age of science. But the very drive to defend his fiction, rather than dismiss unworthy readers, shows his contradictory need to direct horror at those disinclined to appreciate it. His real foes are Victorianism and sentimentalism, and his fictional interventions are social, not metaphysical. Again one finds a conventional affiliation with formalism in advocating for literary or weird language that defamiliarizes what Carter in "The Unnamable" calls "hackneyed" reality (CF 1.398).

Along those lines, if we truly take "The Unnamable" seriously as a metafiction, Manton can be said to be attacked by just the kind of story he rejects—and forced to see an uglier reality than he admitted. In that, we see Lovecraft's wry imaginary revenge on obtuse readers. Freudian criticism would describe (Manton's) repressed truths as the source of fear subversively exploited by the artist. But Lovecraft more disturbingly identifies horror with the text itself—the way its ultimately illusory sensationalism works on both the skeptical and the too sophisticated. More notable than Manton's comeuppance is the way the tale utterly fails, in a number of ways, to vindicate Carter's theorizing about the "real" Unnamable still sought by some. The final horror defies his efforts to explain or predict the unspeakable. Even more importantly, Lovecraft's conclusion willfully fails to demonstrate any real or stylistic Unnamable that answers Manton's criticisms. Both Carter's debilitating shock and Manton's overly precise description ("gelatin" and "slime") are cheap genre clichés already faulted; instead of gesturing at the abject or weird, the ending contains all the crude failures attributed to low pulp writing. Lovecraft concludes satisfied that he can produce the proper emotional effect in exactly the writing his critics identify, in theory, as flawed.

For a related insight we might look to Victor LaValle's metafictional novel, *The Ballad of Black Tom* (2016), a thoughtful homage, criticism, and repurposing of Lovecraft's xenophobic "The Horror at Red Hook" (1927). In line with dominant critical and ethical modes, LaValle gives a voice to the unnamed monstrous Others of Lovecraft's story (immigrants and racially marginalized New Yorkers). His biographical note and dedication, though—"*For H. P. Lovecraft, with all my conflicted feelings*"([5])—invites us to consider the attraction of texts we may also deplore and disenchant; the Thing is not the monster we decode, but the text itself, as an object of pleasure built precisely out of its prejudices. Here one could recall, as well, that Carter/Lovecraft likely analyzes Cotton Mather's monster story correctly—as a product of sexual repression and hypocrisy. That implies that a benighted rural mob, fascinated and titillated by a bogus ur-legend, scapegoated and murdered an innocent man. In that sense, the largely misguided drive to find Lovecraft limning an actual horror or baroque reality just makes his point about the lure and triumph of his texts over common sense.

Works Cited

Asma, Stephen T. *On Monsters: An Unnatural History of Our Worst Fears.* New York: Oxford University Press, 2009.

Beville, Maria. *The Unnameable Monster in Literature and Film.* New York: Routledge, 2014.

Burke, Edmund. *A Philosophical Enquiry into the Origin of Our Ideas of the Sublime and Beautiful and Other Pre-Revolutionary Writing.* Ed. David Womersley. New York: Penguin, 1998.

Boysen, Benjamin. "The Embarrassment of Being Human: A Critique of New Materialism and Object-Oriented Ontology." *Orbis Litterarum* 73 (2018): 225-42.

Brooks, Cleanth, *The Well Wrought Urn: Studies in the Structure of Poetry.* London: Dobson, 1947.

————. "Religion and Literature." *Sewanee Review* 82, No.1 (Winter 1974): 93-107.

Clover, Carol J. *Men, Women and Chainsaws: Gender in the Modern Horror Film.* Princeton, NJ: Princeton University Press, 2015.

Colebrook, Martyn. "'Comrades in Tentacles': H. P. Lovecraft and China Miéville." In *New Critical Essays on H. P. Lovecraft,* ed. David Simmons. New York: Palgrave, 2013. 209-26.

Joshi, S. T. *H. P. Lovecraft: The Decline of the West.* Mercer Island, WA: Borgo Press, 1990.

Kneale, James. "From Beyond: H. P. Lovecraft and the Place of Horror." *Cultural Geographies* 13, No. 1 (January 2006): 106-26.

LaValle, Victor. *The Ballad of Black Tom.* New York: Tor, 2016.

Pahl, Dennis. "De-composing Poe's Philosophy." *Texas Studies in Literature and Language* 38, No. 1 (Spring 1996): 1-25.

Phillips, Kendall R. *Projected Fears: Horror Films and American Culture.* Westport, CT: Praeger, 2005.

Rottensteiner, Franz. Review of *H. P. Lovecraft: The Decline of the West* by S. T. Joshi. *Science Fiction Studies* 19, No. 1 (March 1992): 117-21.

Simmons, David. "'A Certain Resemblance': Abject Hybridity in H. P. Lovecraft's Short Fiction." In *New Critical Essays on H. P. Lovecraft,* ed. David Simmons. New York: Palgrave, 2013. 13-30.

Walpole, Horace. *The Castle of Otranto.* Ed. E. J. Clery. New York: Oxford University Press, 1996.

Wisker, Gina. "'Spawn of the Pit': Lavinia, Maceline, Medusa, and All Things Foul: H. P. Lovecraft's Liminal Women." In *New Critical Essays on H. P. Lovecraft,* ed. David Simmons. New York: Palgrave, 2013. 31–54.

Correlating the Contents of Lovecraft's Closet

Fiona Maeve Geist
and
Sadie Shurberg
Independent Scholars

> *I didn't know whether to kiss it or kill it!*
> —H. P. Lovecraft

Lovecraft: The Queer Fellow

Discussion of sexuality in the works of H. P. Lovecraft is difficult given the paucity of information. As Bobby Derie has noted, "Scholarship into Lovecraft's sexuality, sex life, relationships, and his attitudes and beliefs toward gender, sex in literature, and sexuality in life has been sporadic, but is an important and often overlooked element in understanding the Lovecraft Mythos" (13). Conversely there is a bewildering and extensive corpus concerning Lovecraft's racism ranging from apology to condemnation—especially contentious when discerning the role of Lovecraft's racism in his writing. The intersection of these two aspects of his persona remain little investigated, with notable exceptions.[1] This paper attempts to elucidate the contours of these interlocked aspects of Lovecraft and his corpus, articulating ways in which the confluence of his personal and ideological life shaped his literary output while evading the dead end of the reactionary position that argues Lovecraft was simply a product of his time and that his racism and sexuality are hermetically separate from his work.

---

1. These include Bruce Lord's "The Genetics of Horror" (2004), Bennett Lovett-Graff's "Shadows Over Lovecraft" (1997), Silvia Moreno-Garcia's "Lovecraft's Femme-Fatales" (2017), Joel Pace's "Queer Tales?" (2008), and Jeffery Andrew Weinstock & Carl H. Senderholm's *Age of Lovecraft* (2016).

Lovecraft's sexuality—and the related question of *whether* Lovecraft's sexuality had any bearing on his literary output—is an under-interrogated aspect of Lovecraft as a point of academic inquiry. Proffered suggestions, of varying degrees of plausibility, range from the claims that Lovecraft was asexual (Jones), (latently) homosexual (de Camp), had some trans-like identity integral to his homophobia (Pace), or was an indifferent heterosexual (Derie). The only substantiated information regarding Lovecraft and sexuality is his correspondence, claiming that his understanding of sexuality as a biological mechanism since childhood caused him to have little interest in sexual matters. Often remarked upon is that Lovecraft had almost exclusively male friendships, including several homosexual and bisexual friends. The most provocative suggestion is that there was a queer friendship between Lovecraft a young R. H. Barlow, as noted by Paul La Farge in the *New Yorker*. It is known that Lovecraft consummated his marriage to Sonia Greene (although the couple spent their honeymoon reconstructing "Under the Pyramids," a manuscript that Lovecraft lost the night before their wedding). Greene reported to interviewers that Lovecraft showed restrained affection for her and did not initiate sexual contact. The record of their marriage is incomplete, because Greene burned her correspondence with Lovecraft and several recorded interviews with her were not archived. Also remarked upon is how Lovecraft's mother wanted a daughter and grew his hair out until he demanded it cut at the age of six—alongside his declaration of being a girl as a child. This is the basis of the case that Lovecraft experienced some sort of gender variant identity, and it seems relatively weak. Finally, Lovecraft expressed homophobia in his letters and illustrated familiarity with psychoanalysis and sexology (although exactly what he read remains opaque). These facts lead Bobby Derie to conclude that:

> While there is no solid evidence that Lovecraft was a homosexual (which is to say, there is no written account or a proof of a homosexual affair or admission involving Lovecraft). . . . No proof is sufficient to remove the suspicions of those who choose to read a homosexual subtext into account of Lovecraft's life. That he married a woman and had sexual relations with her, or that he was derisive to homosexuals in his letters, is insufficient or even considered proof for those determined to believe [. . .] (47)

Some lingering questions remain because of the compelling question of the gay and bisexual men who were part of Lovecraft's circle of friends. As

Pace queries: "What was it about Lovecraft and his writing that drew these [gay and bisexual] men to it and to him?" (125). These relationships can lead to intriguing speculation, such as Paul La Farge's novel *The Night Ocean*, centered on the possibly romantic relationship between Lovecraft and Barlow. Barring the discovery of La Farge's fictitious *Erotonomicon*, which provides a Rosetta Stone to Lovecraft's sexuality, Lovecraft's actual sexuality must remain speculative.

Lovecraft: Aristocratic Racist

On the other hand, evidence of Lovecraft's racism is abundant, popping up in his voluminous correspondence and within his stories themselves. This includes Lovecraft giving enthusiastic, and, later, guarded praise for Hitler (*IAP* 939-40), arguing for the innate inferiority of non-"Aryans," composing screeds against immigrants (*SL* 2.68), articulating anti-Semitic conspiracies (*Letters to Rheinhart Kleiner* 119), defending lynching as a sad necessity, and invoking eugenic arguments for birth control on scientific and rationalist grounds (*SL* 5.197-201). Lovecraft's racism included an array of behaviors and beliefs; yet these reactionary opinions are frequently dismissed as Lovecraft being a product of his time. A claim advanced by Lovecraft's defenders is that his racism, while deplorable, is not germane when considering his literary merit. This argument is frequently espoused by S. T. Joshi, who frequently decries arguments that racism is a central—or exceptional—aspect to his writing. Joshi speculatively proposes that Lovecraft made no further positive statements about Nazism after 1936, arguing that this is evidence that Lovecraft repudiated his previous praise for the Nazi regime (*IAP* 941). Another important aspect of this defense is the claim that Lovecraft's admiration of Hitler was lukewarm and his support for the Nazi regime was tepid when contrasted with its ardent supporters, allegedly diminishing that the degree to which Lovecraft praised the Nazis. Relatedly, Joshi argues that Lovecraft's racial animus was typical of his contemporaries and, while they may lower our collective estimation of him as a person, has no bearing on his quality as a writer (*IAP* 1053-54). Implicitly this claim is married to the position that only a few of Lovecraft's works are tinged with a racist viewpoint.: "The Lurking Fear," "The Horror at Red Hook," and "The Shadow over Innsmouth" all are concerned with miscegenation. While this is a far from a comprehensive accounting for that particular racial thematic in the works of Lovecraft, it illuminates the particularity of their intersection in his literary output. Lovecraft's work is saturated with the intersections of sexuality and race despite his own lack of sexual ardor.

Interrogating Lovecraft's thought elucidates a common refrain concerning "the dangers of racial impurity, [which] are not uncommon themes in Lovecraft's work and letters" (Ellis 132). To a degree, Lovecraft espouses the explicitly white supremacist beliefs of many of his contemporaries. However, there is a disconnect between Lovecraft partaking in the racism of his contemporaries and the degree and frequency with which he expressed these views. Lovecraft's wistful longing for a bygone era, along with his uneven education—as he was primarily self-taught—provides anachronistic content to his racial animus. Lovecraft had a wide range of interests, but the actual content of his intellectual curiosity illustrates a number of persistent fixations that cause him to jettison contemporary thought. Franz Rottensteiner notes that there are large gaps in Lovecraft's knowledge of many subjects; of particular contention is Lovecraft's uncritical acceptance of archaic racist ideology largely derived from Ernst Haeckel (a German biologist, materialist, forerunner of eugenics and popularizer of the theory of polygenesis[2]) and William Benjamin Smith's publication *The Color Line: A Brief in Behalf of the Unborn* (1905). Although Lovecraft sought to educate himself, his sources were colored by his distinctive disdain for non-whites, which heavily skewed the sources upon which he drew.

Lovecraft's status as a "product of his time" is exculpatory only if studiously ignoring that while racism, anti-Semitism and xenophobia were unremarkable for his era, the rationale behind Lovecraft's views were decidedly out of sync with those of his contemporaries. For example, Lovecraft's poem "De Triumpho Naturae: The Triumph over Northern Ignorance" condemns the Civil War for defying God and Nature[3] by ending the institution of slavery in the United States. Lovecraft was certainly not alone in his views, but there are notable particularities to his racism reflecting the racial theories espoused by British imperialists—sensible given Lovecraft's Anglophilia, his totalizing view of race, and his extreme fear of 'acceptable' (Anglo-Saxon) whiteness besieged by alien Others. Lovecraft's views are sympathetic to the academic viewpoint developed in the

2. The theory of separate origin of racial groups rather than common ancestry.

3. Possibly conflated, although it is strange to see the staunchly atheistic HPL invoke the divine.

nineteenth century in which race plays a central role. In *Colonial Desire: Hybridity in Culture, Theory and Race* (1993), postcolonial theorist Robert J. Young writes:

> [. . .] racial theory, substantiated and "proved" by various forms of science such as comparative and historical philology, anatomy, anthropometry (including osteometry, craniology, craniometry and pelvimetry), physiology, physiognomy and phrenology, became [. . .] endemic not just to other forms of science, such as biology and natural history, to say nothing of paleontology, psychology, zoology and sexology, but was also used as a general category of understanding that extended to theories of anthropology, archaeology, classics, ethnology, geography, geology, folklore, history, language, law, literature and theology, and thus dispersed from almost every academic discipline to permeate definitions of culture and nation. Imperialistic doctrines of the diffusion of cultures describe equally well the way in which theories based on race spread from discipline and became one of the major organizing axioms of knowledge in general. Race became the fundamental determinant of human culture and history: indeed, it is arguable that race became *the* common principle of academic knowledge in the nineteenth century. (93)

In kinship with these theories, Lovecraft ideologically articulated that race was a totalizing construct indexed to a wide variety of knowledges. This accounts for his occasional references to polygenesis and obsession with the fossil record for differentiating the "types" of human being (Lovett-Graff, "Shadows over Lovecraft"). Lovett-Graff, for example, provides an answer to a quandary that vexed Joshi: what engendered Lovecraft's singular distaste for the Aboriginal population of Australia. The answer lies in Lovecraft's enthusiasm for Sir Arthur Keith and Thomas Henry Huxley's arguments that they are a separate race and less evolved than even "negroes" in Lovecraft's dim assessment. He maintained a theoretical separation of races understanding them as different species, exemplified his claims such as: "I have no active dislike for dogs, any more than I have for monkeys, human beings, negroes, cows, sheep, or pterodactyls" ("Cats and Dogs," *CE* 5.185). Within his iconic position of cosmic pessimism, Lovecraft at least incidentally maintains an indifference to "the races" as a whole while frequently engages in invective and bile *about* the explicit inferiority of non-Anglo-Saxons.

Further aligning Lovecraft's racism with the British imperial racist ideology is his pessimism regarding racial contamination and overthrow.

Several of his works are centrally concerned with a "lesser" race overpowering and usurping the superior race (e.g., "The Shadow out of Time"). His position diverges from the optimistic pronouncements of his contemporaries in mainstream eugenicists who believed genetic lines could be improved. Another tenant of the eugenic thought of Lovecraft's era was that eugenics could reverse "racial suicide." In direct opposition to that optimism seems to be his frequent utilization of "discovering" tainted ancestry ("Facts concerning the Late Arthur Jermyn and His Family," "The Shadow over Innsmouth"), inadvertent exposure to sexual contact with the Other ("Medusa's Coil," "The Thing on the Doorstep") or being (nearly) overwhelmed by the fecund hoards besieging noble humanity ("The Horror at Red Hook," "Polaris," "The Street"). There is a complement between these themes in the works of Lovecraft and the British imperialist fears of miscegenation, decay and cultural decline. As Young explains the position:

> [. . .] theories of racial difference as degeneration themselves fused with the increasing cultural pessimism of the late nineteenth century and the claim that not only the population of cities but the world itself, that is the West, was degenerating. Each new racial ramification of miscegenation traced an historical trajectory that betrayed a narrative of conquest, absorption and inevitable decline. For the Victorians, race and sex became history, and history spoke of race and sex. (175)

This view of history as being composed of race and sex and also decay and decline seems harmonious with Lovecraft's pessimistic racism concerned with tainted legacies, inhuman ancestry, and inescapable decline once a bloodline is compromised. Therefore it is instructive to turn to Lovecraft's works attending to the intersection of race and sexuality to excavate what this illuminates about Lovecraft. This should demonstrate the centrality of (sexualized) racism to his worldview expressed in his fiction.

As Ellis notes, "Lovecraft uses his fiction and poetry to develop both images of race and his racism, and it is instructive to see how he does so" (124). Given this intersection is a somewhat unique angle for approaching Lovecraft, some preliminary points should be addressed. We begin by examining physical (sexual) contact between a protagonist and a (racial) Other—a vein that has been tapped regarding the consanguinity of race and sexuality in the works of Lovecraft, specifically in "Medusa's Coil" and "The Thing on the Doorstep" (Moreno-Garcia; Pace; Waugh). Segueing into the concept of tainted ancestry in the works of Lovecraft, which reflects a prolonged engagement with the idea of racial (im)purity especially in "The Shadow over Innsmouth," from which the "Innsmouth look" as a sign of contamination gets its name, concluding with prolonged reflection on the racial logics structuring "The Call of Cthulhu" and "The Shadow out of Time," which are less about miscegenation breeding monsters than about reflecting how Lovecraft's cosmic pessimism emphasizes "noble" and "pure" cultures being torn down by lesser races. This engenders extended reflection on how the locus of sexuality and racism reassess Lovecraft's legacy.

Physical: The Abhorrence of Sexual Contact with the Other

"Medusa's Coil" and "The Thing on the Doorstep" are the "only [works] in which the overt concern of the plot is the erotic connection between a man and a woman; though Lovecraft may seem uncomfortable with such a subject, it is remarkable that given such a discomfort he does deal with the subject twice" (Waugh 137–38). Both stories are not simply the only ones about heterosexual coupling by Lovecraft, but both are similar in structure and outlook, often paired in critical literature. As Waugh summarizes:

> In both stories a rather weak young man consummates a marriage with a daemonic figure that leads him beyond the world we know; and in both stories the narration insists that an old, honorable family, represented [. . .] by a father, is destroyed [. . .] Finally, almost as an afterthought, the narrator assures the reader that the true horror lies in an act of miscegenation, in the first story with a fishlike creature, in the second story with a black. (138)

Both stories hinge on the macabre revelation of racial impurity: whether "contamination" is inhuman or non-white seems to be an immaterial consideration for Lovecraft. He at least assumes that monstrosity and non-whiteness are conflatable. As Moreno-Garcia confirms, "the revelation of Marceline's blackness is supposed to be more shocking than the discovery that Marceline's hair has a life of its own . . . and is able to attack people." In the case of "The Thing on the Doorstep" it is less shocking that sexual contact occurred between a protagonist and a woman possessed by her deceased father than the fact that she is of "tainted" Innsmouth ancestry.

Marceline and Asenath have further monstrous elements reflecting Lovecraft's intense disgust with miscegenation. Eugenic concerns over the potential for white-passing individuals to contaminate the bloodline of a "pure" family feature prominently. Considering that perspective, "the most monstrous element of Marceline and Asenath may be the ease with which they are able to infiltrate the world of the fit. They are both successfully passing as normal, healthy women" (Moreno-Garcia). Asenath is, notably, a match for Edward Pickman Derby, so that his father vehemently objects to what may seemingly challenge her *passing*, especially given that her connection to Innsmouth is suspected from the outset. Yet this courtship mirrors eugenic concerns of the inheritors of "pure bloodlines" falling into dissolution and forever tainting their legacy. The ultimate horror is how their successfully passing themselves as "normal" women (at least to their potential spouses if not their families) allowed them to ruin otherwise healthy (that is, white) families. Ultimately:

> [. . .] through Asenath and Marceline, Lovecraft makes manifest a number of eugenic concerns tied to women. Asenath and Marceline's racial ambiguity, deviant behavior and sexual allure brand them as unfit and serve as markers of their Otherness. This Otherness threatens not only the bodies of individual white men, but annihilates the family structure as a whole. This, of course, was what eugenicists feared: the decimation of the family and ultimately the nation. Although Asenath and Marceline never speak a line of dialogue, their silent bodies ultimately narrate a story of biological terror and triumphant destruction. (Moreno-Garcia)

Lovecraft's overtly sexual content is heavily influenced by racially animated fears. Pertinently the stories are framed by a the repulsion/desire reaction regarding Asenath and Marceline; as Others who "pass" as nominally acceptable pairings for the men they doom. Their monstrous intrusion destroys not only their spouses but their family legacy. Both pairings are ultimately fatal and fail to produce a compromised and tainted family line. The horror is one of the *end* of families rather than their *monstrous continuation*. Moving from discussions of sexual pairings as such in Lovecraft's work flows into his utilization of hereditary degeneration as the basis of horror.

Genealogical: The Catastrophe of Heredity

Lovecraft's "Facts concerning the Late Arthur Jermyn and His Family" conjoins the fatal seduction by a monstrous woman—whether white passing or passing for human—with Lovecraft's fixation on aberrations in racial purity dooming a family line. Lovett-Graff summarizes "Arthur

Jermyn" as concerning "a body that has been sacrificed to the uncontrollable forces of evolution, history, and sexual desire" ("'Life Is a Hideous Thing'" 381). The story is classic Lovecraft, opening with reflection on how knowledge leads to shattering conclusions as Arthur Jermyn immolates himself triggering an investigation. In a recurring Lovecraftian trope, the reader witnesses the consequences of the protagonist seeking forbidden knowledge: madness, disturbing personal revelations, and damnation. At the foreground of this "forbidden knowledge" are direct and symbolic evocations of racist discourses about miscegenation. Jermyn burns himself after querying about his family's decline over five generations, climaxing in his stunning revelation that his great-great-great-grandmother was a humanoid ape explicating their degraded condition. Paired with this decline is a drop in class status and a physical degeneracy generations after the initial "corruption" takes place. This illuminates features relevant to Lovecraft's idiosyncratic racist worldview. For Lovecraft, humanity is only differentiated by proximity to primates and, relatedly, differentiation between "species" is by degree rather than by type. Within Lovecraft's biological determinism, there is not a particularly compelling difference between species other than degree of evolution—which accounts for why Lovecraft's racist remarks frequently center on the presence of simian features he believes are essential to nonwhites. For Lovecraft, evolution is not a linear progression but an ongoing process where it is possible to devolve like the Jermyn clan. Biological imperatives win out, regardless of Jermyn's erudition, he opts for suicide when confronted with his simian ancestry. His decision, though horrifying, is *rational* within Lovecraft's framework because the "truth" of Arthur's ancestry is inescapable. The horror hinges on the possibility that even "noble" stock can find itself defiled by the infusion of impure blood. Lovett-Graff elaborates:

> Lovecraft is artful enough in his profound racism to rework [the] obvious association [between nonwhites and primates] into something just as racist, but presumably far more frightening to his supposed white audience. By emphasizing the capacity of whites and apes to interbreed, a phenomenon typically reserved for nonwhites, Lovecraft transforms his white ape goddess into a far more frightening figure. Instead of mediating white evolutionary ancestry through blacks, Lovecraft goes for his reader's racist juglar by suggesting the inherent power of physical reproduction to drag even the most

"advanced" human species down to the level of their primate ancestors. ("'Life Is a Hideous Thing'" 378)

The horror implicit in this account is one rooted in Darwinian evolution—humans are descended from apes—but with the further contention that it is possible for evolutionary progress to ebb allowing "fears of a degenerate ancestry take center stage as the fundamental horror of contemporary existence" (373). Interestingly, Jermyn's great-great-great-grandmother—the ape goddess—bookends the story, being revealed only in the conclusion. "The Shadow over Innsmouth" follows a different structure concerned with a similar revelation. Importantly, the hybrid offspring of the Deep Ones and Innsmouth residents are discussed and seen throughout the text, rather than revealed as a shocking conclusion.[4] The choice of Lovecraft to depict the monsters themselves is bound up in his fascination with monstrous embodiment—conceptually bound to many of Lovecraft's racist tendencies.

Monstrous embodiment, so termed by literary theorist Jay McRoy, can be viewed as a means of tracing "a locus of dread," intimately bound up in discourses of "regression and degeneracy common to early modernist sociological tracts on criminality, evolution, and eugenics" (335). This is thoroughly entwined with the racial anxieties concerning contamination expressed through the hybrid offspring of Innsmouth. In this sense, "The Shadow over Innsmouth" is not simply a cautionary tale about miscegenation. It conveys the consequences of the narrator's decision to cross an ethical and racial line he is warned not to approach. Through depictions of the Deep Ones, Innsmouth inhabitants, and their hybrid offspring, Lovecraft creates figures of racialized revulsion and horror that deliver to the reader fears of miscegenation alongside assumedly non-racialized horrors of the unknown, decay, deception, and occultism. Like Marceline and Asenath, the inhabitants of Innsmouth remain mute and are often obscured from view, shadowed, murmuring behind closed doors and hiding in boarded houses. From the outset, Innsmouth and its inhabitants are things to be observed, described, investigated, and explored by the protagonist and, by proxy, the reader. The text itself is arranged around the visibility of the consequences of cross-breeding between humans and Deep Ones, a logic Rieder explains in terms of the "colonial gaze [which] dis-

---

4. The story opens with the destruction of Innsmouth by the federal government and the relocation of its inhabitants to camps. However, the revelation of the nature of the inhabitants is not withheld until the story's conclusion.

tributes knowledge and power to the subject who looks, while denying or minimizing access to power for its object, the one looked at" (7). This gaze further "helps to maintain and reproduce the political and economic arrangements that establish the subjects' respective positions" reinforcing the structured positions of subject and object while operating in a framework of exaggeration and spectacularization characteristic of speculative fiction (15–16).

Exemplary of this discourse of visibility is the dialogue between the ticket clerk and narrator regarding the spectacular "strangeness" of Innsmouth's inhabitants. The ticket clerk begins his description of Innsmouth highlighting its relative isolation from its neighbors and poor reputation before concluding:

> [t]he real thing behind the way folks feel is simply race prejudice—and I don't say I'm blaming those that hold it. I hate those Innsmouth folks myself [. . .] I s'pose you know [. . .] a lot of our New England ships used to have to do with queer ports in Africa, Asia, the South Seas, and everywhere else, and what queer kinds of people they sometimes brought back with 'em [. . .]
>
> Well, there must be something like that back of the Innsmouth people [. . .] it's pretty clear that old Captain Marsh must have brought home some odd specimens [. . .] There certainly is a strange kind of streak in the Innsmouth folk today—I don't know how to explain it, but it sort of makes you crawl [. . .] Some of 'em have queer narrow heads with flat noses and bulgy, stary eyes that never seem to shut, and their skin ain't quite right. Rough and scabby, and the sides of their necks are all shrivelled or creased up. (CF 3.163)

Innsmouth inhabits a spectacular 'Otherness' as both a location and a population. Regarding the first, Innsmouth is described as cut off from the rest of the world existing in geographical isolation. Thus, the narrator's excitement over entering uncharted territory ripe for exploration, discovery, and observance; all qualities bound up in colonial discourses concerning land, settlement, and contact with non-Western peoples (McClintock). There is also a particular emphasis on the embodiment of the inhabitants themselves, the "Innsmouth look" described in terms of their physiognomy and phenotype—along with miscegenation (in its typically understood sense) with the amalgamated spawn of the Deep Ones and Innsmouth inhabitants, marking them as truly Other. The extolling of the embodied otherness of the inhabitants of Innsmouth is strikingly similar to language used in eugenic tracts on the features of "dominant" and "lesser races." Despite the revulsion inspired by the residents of Innsmouth, the narrator is determined to go there. He learns that their physical abnormality comes from interbreeding with the Deep Ones before being confronted with their hideous forms—the sort of revelation that often dooms Lovecraftian protagonists.

The epilogue details the aftermath of this revelation as the narrator discovers he is a great-great-grandson of Obed Marsh, tainted with Deep One ancestry. This parallels "one-drop" blood quantum rules that dictated any non-white ancestry was grounds for racialized Otherness in the United States. Confronted with this knowledge and his metamorphosing body, the narrator gives into "the Innsmouth shadow which had so darkly coloured my imagination" (CF 3.228). Pivoting on the "shadow" hanging over Innsmouth, the language describing Innsmouth and its imaginative impact are cloaked in racialized symbolism: the sinister shadow corrupting and contaminating the narrator's mind or the "darkly coloured" imagination. That it is "darkly coloured" reinforces the racialized nature of the corruption on a symbolic level, tapping into what Toni Morrison, in *Playing in the Dark: Whiteness and the Literary Imagination* sees as literary symbols and images that often equate whiteness with light and purity while casting blackness as shadow, sinister intent, and evil (22). The narrator, aware that his uncle committed suicide after learning of his own taint—echoing Arthur Jermyn—begins transforming physically. However, instead of ending this heritage shocked by the revelation, the narrator embraces it, concluding that he—along with his cousin—will "go to marvel-shadowed Innsmouth. We shall swim out to that brooding reef in the sea and dive down through black abysses to Cyclopean and many-columned Y'ha-nthlei, and in that lair of the Deep Ones we shall dwell amidst wonder and glory forever" (CF 3.230). The narrator's rapturous embrace of his monstrosity is intended to horrify the reader; while there are reclamatory readings of the finale, they seem to be working against Lovecraft's position that this is a chilling possibility. Becoming inhuman arguably makes the narrator a race-traitor in a profound manner. However, this transgression is not intended by Lovecraft to be radical or progressive; instead it complicates and problematizes the notion of identification. The passage, given Lovecraft's sympathies, was intended to express of the fear of race-suicide—a corollary to the fear of miscegenation expressed in Lovecraft's fiction—that is "never [. . .] far from the surface of Lovecraft's conceptions" (Buhle 203-4). This raises the question of what it means to be identifying with a protagonist that expresses desire to be Other, to be monstrous, to be repulsive?

Lovecraft doesn't answer these questions in "The Shadow over Innsmouth," but it is clear that the narrator is corrupted by his exploration into the forbidden knowledge of Innsmouth. Embracing his Innsmouth heritage, the narrator comes to embody the monstrous Other— a threat to those who delve too deeply into forbidden knowledge. Lovecraft's description of the narrator embracing his hybrid Innsmouth heritage is decidedly negative in its tone. The narrator is cursed by his own actions, embodying a monstrous choice that positions him against the perceived "natural order" of anti-miscegenation, white supremacy, and eugenic sentiments. The horror of actively *joining* the ranks of inhumanity— rather than opting for suicide like Arthur Jermyn or the narrator's uncle— accentuates the ways in which hereditary corruption expresses the entwined nature of sexuality and race in Lovecraft works. Further, the narrator's decision to reject humanity and give in to his transformation, aligning himself with the Deep Ones and other horrors from the Lovecraft mythos, provides an entry point to the final aspect of how profoundly these issues influenced his literary output.

Cosmic: Racism among the Stars

A potential objection to the insistence on the importance of Lovecraft's racism—and its conjoined relationship to sexuality—is his endorsement of a total pessimism rooted in the contingency of biological life. If Lovecraft's cosmicism contends that godlike alien horrors will awaken when the stars are right and annihilate all life, does his racist outlook matter? To illustrate the centrality of Lovecraft's sexualized racism, we turn to Lovecraft's popular and enduring story "The Call of Cthulhu." We argue that at the heart of his vision there is a call for European ethnocentrism with universalizing pretensions in the face of monstrous forbidden knowledge constantly threatening to contaminate his protagonists. Far from universalizing pessimism, the existential dread undergirding Lovecraftian cosmic horror is predicated upon the dehumanization and subjugation of non-white populations, aghast that white supremacist racial hierarchies could be overturned.

"The Call of Cthulhu" is not only among Lovecraft's best-known and widely read works, it also provides "the first comprehensive view of Lovecraft's cosmicism" (Klinger 123). Lovecraft's enduring anti-mythology is defined less by humanity's attempt to understand and place themselves in the order of the cosmos and more by the "impossibility of an understanding of the universe" (124). This theme, of the impossibility of comprehending the universe and its horrifying and monstrous contents, is central to many of Lovecraft's stories; however, the universal scale in "The Call of Cthulhu" is unique. Central to the story is the theme of forbidden knowledge that is among the hallmarks of Lovecraft's writing, including "monstrosity, biological horror, occult mysteries, noir-like investigations, and cosmic pessimism" (McRoy 337). Lovecraft opens the story by evoking the caustic implications of the knowledge that humanity is irrelevant to the inner workings of the universe:

> The most merciful thing in the world, I think, is the inability of the human mind to correlate all its contents. We live on a placid island of ignorance in the midst of black seas of infinity, and it was not meant that we should voyage far. The sciences, each straining in its own direction, have hitherto harmed us little; but some day the piecing together of dissociated knowledge will open up such terrifying vistas of reality, and of our frightful position therein, that we shall either go mad from the revelation or flee from the deadly light into the peace and safety of a new dark age. (CF 2.21–22)

The seemingly universal dread described in this simultaneously undergirded by racializing language and imagery indicative of larger anxieties concerning race and the threat of cross-cultural contact explicit in the tale. The cosmic horror contained within "The Call of Cthulhu" is arguably the clearest distillation of Lovecraft's cosmic pessimism. In the face of malevolent extraterrestrial beings, apocalyptic conspiracies and worlds beyond human comprehension, race still matters. Lovecraft's erudite, white protagonists become corrupted by uncovering cults and endangering themselves through proximity to otherworldly aims, non-white characters are consistently rendered as subhuman, monstrous and active collaborators with inhuman annihilating forces that engender the "deadly light" of revelation.

The globe-spanning cults—always racialized—actively worship dread Cthulhu, the alien who will eventually rise signaling the end of civilization—despite being temporarily stalled in the course of the story. Despite this defensive action, "his ministers on earth still bellow and prance and slay around idol-capped monoliths in lonely places" assured of his return (CF 2.55). This linkage between the inhuman Cthulhu and his (sub)human worshippers bridges the two types of monstrous embodiment in Lovecraft's fiction McRoy outlines. There are unspeakable non-human entities that threaten moral order and existential comfort by their very existence. Juxtaposed with the truly alien first category is the second, consisting of the multi-racial underclass that is characterized by degeneracy, decay, and unruliness (335). While all life may be equally contingent given the grand scale of cosmic pessimism there is a disjunction between the role of Lovecraft's white protagonists actively staving off the return of the Great Old Ones and the attempts by non-whites to usher in their return.

This theme is not exclusive to "The Call of Cthulhu," Lovecraft's writing prominently features Anglo-Saxons beset by hordes of "lesser" races—including embarrassingly and overtly racist stories such as "He" and "The Horror at Red Hook"—repeated in stories which make little, if any, direct mentions of race such as "The Shadow out of Time." Briefly, the story concerns the Great Race of Yith and its ability (and need) to project their minds into other individuals. The Great Race maintain a great library city that contains the history and future of many races including humans constructed on Earth 250 million years in the past beset by a savage race of half-polypous creatures (although, notably, the bodies inhabited by members of the Great Race on Earth are not their original bodies but ones they occupied to escape the destruction of their race and planet). In short, the human narrator who switched bodies with one of the Great Race and dwelled in its library city discovers in his own time that the Great Race was overwhelmed by the creatures and destroyed—although they mass-projected their minds again. Thematically, this connects Lovecraft's obsession with the "noble" beset by the "savage" while additionally reflecting his outlook of cosmic pessimism. Surmising this position, and Lovecraft's views on race and sexuality as a whole, Bruce Lord contends that:

> [. . .] for Lovecraft, the "natural" act of reproduction is not equated with life, but with degeneration, decay, and eventually death. Lovecraft's primary conception of humanity as an insignificant species dwarfed by the sheer scope of the universe and the indifferent horrors that occupy it thus is coupled with another, equally horrific fate. Humanity, as portrayed in Lovecraft's fiction, is not only incapable of resisting the impact of racial and hereditary degeneration, but also incapable of maintaining itself 'properly' via sexual reproduction, an act that for Lovecraft gives birth to nothing but nightmare.

Overwhelmingly, Lovecraft's literary output expresses a philosophical outlook implicitly rooted in issues of sexuality and race—views that, with notable exceptions, are odious to many readers.

Conclusion

Unsurprisingly, a vexed reviewer may concede that confronted "with the racism, misogyny, and the semicomical monsters, including hissing six-foot penguins, [they] may well, out of exasperation and distaste, lay the book aside" (Baxter). Lovecraft's creative output awkwardly and vitriolically stumps for a variety of loathsome positions; his racist views simply spark the most controversy. Confronting this is unavoidable insofar as Lovecraft reconfigured generic traditions of forbidden knowledge and monstrous figures and imbued them with racial and colonial logics that were regressive even for his era while exerting considerable influence on contemporary horror and weird fiction. Yet grappling with these issues and confronting them directly allows one to understand Lovecraft's work at a level that ignoring the racist and colonial logics he espoused cannot; this is essential to taking Lovecraft seriously as literature. It does not behoove anyone to accept that Lovecraft is a pioneer of genre fiction while acknowledging his less savory aspects of his literary output. Certainly, it is equally true that Ezra Pound was an anti-Semite and unrepentant fascist but also an integral figure in the world of poetry. Both aspects of his life are necessary to evaluating *him*. Apologetics simply cheapen the complicated relationship that many readers have with Lovecraft himself. Rather than denial, this calls for serious inquiry into Lovecraft to accurately assess his literary contributions. This is not a call to censor the works of Lovecraft, as some claim, but an appeal to take him seriously that includes sustained reflection on repugnant works such as "The Street" and "The Horror at Red Hook." The re-envisioning of Lovecraft's work through the eyes of those he explicitly derided is ongoing. Such work as Victor LaValle's *The Ballad of Black Tom* and Ruthanna Emrys's *Winter Tide* indicate promising inroads rather than stale pastiche. Yet they also beg the question whether moving through Lovecraft's racist legacy will open up scholarly and creative avenues for works that operate in universes, worlds and monstrous planes far beyond the influence of H. P. Lovecraft.

Works Cited

Baxter, Charles. "The Hideous Unknown of H. P. Lovecraft." New York: *New York Review of Books*. 18 December 2014. www.nybooks.com/articles/2014/12/18/hideous-unknown-hp-lovecraft/

Buhle, Paul. "Dystopia as Utopia: Howard Phillips Lovecraft and the Unknown Content of American Horror Literature." *Minnesota Review* 6, No. 1 (2011): 118-31.

Derie, Bobby. *Sex and the Cthulhu Mythos*. New York: Hippocampus Press, 2014.

Ellis, Phillip A. "The Construction of Race in the Early Poetry of H. P. Lovecraft." *Lovecraft Annual* No. 4 (2014): 124-35.

Emrys, Ruthanna. *Winter Tide*. New York: Tor, 2017.

Jones, Nick. "Strange Flesh: The Use of Lovecraftian Archetypes in Queer Fiction." burnttongueblog.wordpress.com/serialized-posts/ 2016.

Klinger, Leslie S., ed. *The New Annotated H .P. Lovecraft*. New York: Liveright, 2014.

La Farge, Paul. "The Complicated Friendship of H. P. Lovecraft and Robert Barlow, One of His Biggest Fans." *New Yorker*. 9 March 2017. www.newyorker.com/books/page-turner/the-complicated-friendship-of-h-p-lovecraft-and-robert-barlow-one-of-his-biggest-fans

———. *The Night Ocean: A Novel*. New York: Penguin Press, 2017.

LaValle, Victor. *The Ballad of Black Tom*. New York: Tor, 2016.

Lord, Bruce. "The Genetics of Horror: Sex and Racism in H. P. Lovecraft's Fiction." Personal blog. www.thephora.net/forum/archive/index.php/t-41907.html. 17 November 2014.

Lovecraft, H. P. *Letters to Rheinhart Kleiner*. Ed. S. T. Joshi and David E. Schultz. New York: Hippocampus Press, 2005.

Lovett-Graff, Bennett. "'Life is a Hideous Thing': Primate-Geniture in H. P. Lovecraft's 'Arthur Jermyn.'" *Journal of the Fantastic in the Arts* 8, No. 3 (1997): 370-88.

———. "Shadows over Lovecraft: Reactionary Fantasy and Immigrant Eugenics." *Extrapolation* 38, No. 3 (1997): 175-92.

McClintock, Anne. *Imperial Leather: Race, Gender and Sexuality in the Colonial Contest*. New York: Routledge, 1995.

McRoy, Jay. "There Goes the Neighborhood: Chaotic Apocalypse and Monstrous Genesis in H. P. Lovecraft's 'The Street,' 'The Horror at Red Hook,' and 'He.'" *Journal of the Fantastic in the Arts* 13 (2003): 335–51.

Moreno-Garcia, Silvia. "H. P. Lovecraft's Femme Fatales: Monstrosity, Race & Sexuality." www.vexmosaic.com/h-p-lovecrafts-femme-fatales-monstrosity-race-and-sexuality/ , 2017.

Morrison, Toni. *Playing in the Dark: Whiteness and the Literary Imagination.* New York: Vintage, 1993.

Pace, Joel. "Queer Tales? Sexuality, Race and Architecture in 'The Thing on the Doorstep.'" *Lovecraft Annual* No. 2 (2008): 104–38.

Rieder, John. *Colonialism and the Emergence of Science Fiction.* Middletown, CT: Wesleyan University Press, 2008.

Rottensteiner, Franz. "Lovecraft as Philosopher." *Science Fiction Studies* 19, No. 1 (1992): 117–21.

Senderholm, Carl H., and Jeffrey Andrew Weinstock. *The Age of Lovecraft.* Minneapolis: University of Minnesota Press, 2016.

Smith, William Benjamin. *The Color Line: A Brief in Behalf of the Unborn.* New York : McClure, Phillips, 1905.

Waugh, Robert H. "The Ecstasies of 'The Thing on the Doorstep', 'Medusa's Coil' and Other Erotic Studies." *Lovecraft Annual* No. 4 (2010): 136–62.

Young, Robert J. C. *Colonial Desire: Hybridity in Theory, Culture and Race.* New York: Routledge, 1995.

Lovecraft Meets the Mummy: Orientalism, Race, and Monstrous Egypt in "Imprisoned with the Pharaohs" and "Out of the Aeons"

Troy Rondinone
Southern Connecticut State University

> "The East . . . Egypt . . . truly, this dark cradle of civilisation was ever the well-spring of horrors and marvels unspeakable!"
> —H. P. Lovecraft, "Under the Pyramids" (1924; CF 1.442)

The mummy in the Western imagination has long held the status of dangerous mystery. Wrapped and preserved, beholden to an ancient faith created by a primordial civilization and erupting into the present world thanks to a mysterious technology of human preservation, the mummy evokes dreams and nightmares of race, colonialism, appropriation, and even romance. The allure of the mummy dates from the Middle Ages, but our modern vision of the mummy took shape during the nineteenth century, when the rapid production of professional, institutionalized knowledge combined with print technologies, advancing literacy, and a fascination with colonial subjects that mummies drew crowds. A helpful way of understanding this process is the concept of *Orientalism*. As Edward W. Said observed, the East is, in part, a construction of the Western imagination, an exotic Other that serves as exemplar of mystery, danger, heretical knowledge, and racial backwardness. This difference begets definitional distinctions against which the West can measure its own superior culture.

The American public has drunk deeply at the well of Orientalism. Bold Anglo-Americans have sought self-aggrandizing adventure in the Eastern Other in pulp thrillers, novels, films, the art of the nineteenth century and recent cinema and short films. Writing of classic Hollywood horrors starring Boris Karloff and Lon Chaney, Laurence Michalek writes, "The Middle East of the Mummy movie represents despotism, old age, de-

191

cay, death, and superstition; the Western archaeologists who dominate the Mummy represent democracy, youth, vigor, life, and science" (4). Recent notable instances of the orientalist trend include the fantastical subhuman Persians in the hit film *300* (2006) and the ghastly beasts in the big-budget Tom Cruise vehicle *The Mummy* (2017). In the former film, Scottish actor Gerard Butler turns back hordes of menacing Persian warriors until finally overwhelmed by a cascade of cheap-shot arrows. His (clearly white) Spartans resist the Eastern hordes in manly fashion; in their tragic demise we rediscover the redemptive power of supporting "freedom" at all costs. As a surviving Spartan lieutenant tells 10,000 "free Greek" warriors about to engage the Persian "barbarians" at the film's end, "This day we rescue a world from mysticism and tyranny!" Western light versus Eastern darkness can hardly be more apparent. In *The Mummy,* a white American tomb raider (Cruise) gets infected by an ancient Egyptian curse while looting treasures in Iraq. The mummy's curse results in a blight of undead descending on London.

Both *300* and *The Mummy* play their part in maintaining orientalist themes apparent since Napoleon's forces began sending back reports from their 1798 foray into Egypt (Fritze 157–61). Ever since, Orientalism has served to generate stories of exotic mystery and to stoke fears of alien incursion, including the mummy tales of H. P. Lovecraft. This essay examines how Lovecraft employed orientalist themes to articulate prominent Western fears and longings (but mostly fears) in his work. His stories "Under the Pyramids" and "Out of the Aeons" are firmly within the mainstream of popular thought.

When Napoleon traveled to Egypt, he brought with him 167 scholars. He was genuinely intrigued by the ruins of the once-powerful world civilization, telling his troops before his battle with the Mamelukes, while indicating to the pyramids in the distance, "Soldiers, from these heights forty centuries of history look down upon you" (Brier 46). The general (he was not yet Emperor) viewed many ruins there, and he himself raced up the side of the Great Pyramid. It was this trip that engendered the field of Egyptology, marked by the establishment of the Institute d'Egypte in Cairo in August 1798. As Edward W. Said writes, Napoleon's mission "gave birth to the entire modern experience of the Orient" (87). In short order, a torrent of artifacts, from pottery and jewels to obelisks and mummies, flowed west.

Public interest in mummies grew apace of its Egyptomania. Some scholars have called the protracted Egypt fad "Mummymania." Travelers regularly brought back mummy-mementos legally in the early nineteenth century and, after an 1835 antiquity protection law, illegally. Imagined mummies abounded. The first mummy fiction, Jane Webb London's *The Mummy! A Tale of the Twenty-Second Century* (1827), tells how the mummy of Pharaoh Cheops gets awakened with electricity in 2126. She goes on to critique the problems of a future England. Théophile Gautier's fantastical "The Mummy's Foot" (1840) has the mummified foot of an Egyptian princess, bought in a Parisian shop as a paperweight, sparking a dream in which the narrator finds the princess, with whom he falls in love but chooses not to marry. In 1845, Edgar Allan Poe published "Some Words with a Mummy" in the *American Review*. In this satirical story, a group of men use electricity to resuscitate a mummy named Allamistakeo, who proceeds to discourse on the lack of progress evident in the nineteenth century as compared with his own antique day. The mummy explains that people lived much longer in ancient Egypt, and that embalming is a means of preserving life in a kind of hibernation state.

Museums were soon filling with mummies, and mummy-unwrapping parties became all the rage (as alluded to in Poe's story). But all was not fun and games. The mummy could bring bad luck, too. The idea of the mummy's "curse" probably dates back to the Middle Ages (Day 188–89n11), but in the nineteenth century it represented an awareness of participatory guilt in Western imperial meddling. In Louisa May Alcott's "Lost in a Pyramid, or, the Mummy's Curse" (1869), for instance, a pyramid raid yields seeds stolen from a female mummy. In the words of Jasmine Day, the seeds "sap [. . .] the vitality [of the raider's] bride, who becomes like a living mummy" (46). Similar curses come in stories by Sir Arthur Conan Doyle ("The Ring of Thoth," for instance) and Bram Stoker (*The Jewel of Seven Stars*).

In 1922, British Egyptologist Howard Carter unearthed King Tutankhamun's tomb in the Valley of the Kings. The spectacular find, which yielded, among other things, the mummified remains of King Tut himself, inflamed the public's imagination. Pop culture swarmed at the discovery, inspiring a Mummymania that has never quite ended. The Tut-boom begat a wave of films, art, stories, and songs (the first, "Old King Tut," came out in 1923; see Brier 169). Lovecraft was riding this wave when he teamed up with Harry Houdini in 1924.

The world's greatest escape artist, Houdini had a harrowing story to tell, published as "Imprisoned with the Pharaohs" in the May–June–July issue of *Weird Tales*, although Lovecraft's preferred title was "Under the Pyramids." Houdini had been fascinated with the exotic East since he was a young man, even dressing as a yogi to bilk gullible tourists of cash during the Columbian Exposition in Chicago in 1893. As his fame grew, Houdini purchased a number of mummies and remained enraptured and financially interested in the Orient. His final planned escape, while straitjacketed, locked in a coffin, and buried in a sand chamber, explicitly evoked Egypt. The poster shows his body inside the coffin leaning against a stone tomb in the desert, the Sphinx looking on in the background. Unfortunately, Houdini died before he could execute this daring escape. His body was transported from Detroit to New York in the same coffin. (Kalush and Sloman; Goto-Jones 176).

In "Under the Pyramids," Houdini recounts a visit to Cairo he made with his wife in 1910. In the account, Houdini arrives and is taken around the city by his guide, Abdul Reis el Drogman. When Drogman gets into a fight with a Bedouin, Houdini breaks it up, but the seething combatants are compelled to agree to an ancient rite of combat atop the pyramid of Giza. Houdini cannot resist attending the fight, which turns out to be a ruse to test the great escape artist. He is captured, bound, and thrown into a deep pit. After wriggling free, Houdini drops into an abyss. Following a draft, he descends ever deeper, stumbling about in the dark and arriving in an enormous underground chamber. It is there he finds an army of mummies, many of which are half-animal atrocities.

Under the pyramid, Houdini is faced with a ceremony wherein monstrous priests (including King Khephren and his ghoul-queen Nitokris), commanding legions of mummies, offer sacrifices to an abominable five-headed creature. Using all his resources, Houdini manages to escape, at the last moment finding himself before the Great Sphinx in the desert. Here he grasps the abominable truth. The great stone Sphinx actually represents a real monster. The five-headed thing is in fact the paw of a monstrous beast! In the last sentence, he blandly reports: "But I survived, and I know it was only a dream" (*CF* 1.450). In other words, though Houdini has once again proven his amazing escape skills, he assures us that his real-life skepticism of the supernatural remains intact. He has his cake and eats it too.

But Houdini did not write the story. The great escape artist's name was affixed to a typically Lovecraftian creation written by Lovecraft himself. According to S. T. Joshi, Houdini had originally tried to pass off the tale as "an actual occurrence," but Lovecraft, hired on by *Weird Tales* owner J. C. Henneberger to ghostwrite it, "quickly discovered" it to be "entirely fictitious." Lovecraft composed a story that Joshi (and I) finds to be "entirely Lovecraft's in its prose and largely in its conception" (*A Dreamer and a Visionary* 191). As Lovecraft explained in a letter to James F. Morton of February 1924, "It seems this boob [Houdini] was (as he relates) thrown into an ancient subterraneous temple at Gizeh [. . .] I gotta idea he tries to put over his Munchausens as straight dope, in which he figures most heroically. But if Henny [Henneberger] and Hoodie [Houdini] give me a free hand—then b'gawd I'll pull a knockout!" (*JFM* 67). Indeed, sentences such as "It was very gradually that I regained my senses after that eldritch flight through Stygian space" (CF 1.434) leave little in question.

"Under the Pyramids" follows Said's argument that the Orient is less a real place than a dreamscape of Otherness upon which to juxtapose Western rationality and cultural superiority. Take for example this description of Cairo:

> Old Cairo is itself a story-book and a dream—labyrinths of narrow alleys redolent of aromatic secrets; Arabesque balconies and oriels nearly meeting above the cobbled streets; maelstroms of Oriental traffic with strange cries, cracking whips, rattling carts, jingling money, and braying donkeys; kaleidoscopes of polychrome robes, veils, turbans, and tarbushes; water-carriers and dervishes, dogs and cats, soothsayers and barbers; and over all the whining of blind beggars crouched in alcoves, and the sonorous chanting of muezzins from minarets limned delicately against a sky of deep, unchanging blue. (CF 1.421)

This long, Arabesque sentence draws us into a strange land in which a map would be of no use. Lovecraft tells us the place is "alluring," but the allure is due to its menacing quality. As he notes, the sights there disclose the "darker charm of Pharaonic Egypt" (CF 1.422) with its "abnormal, animal-headed gods in the ancient Nilotic pantheon" (CF 1.425). And though the ancients might be long gone, "the elder magic of Egypt did not depart without leaving traces," with "fragments of a strange secret lore and priestly cult-practices" still in evidence (CF 1.431). And of course we will learn that the ancients are not really gone.

The inhabitants of Lovecraft's Cairo are both ignorant and dangerous. We find "chattering youths [who] pulverise mustard in the hollowed-out capital of an ancient classic column—a Roman Corinthian, perhaps from neighbouring Heliopolis, where Augustus stationed one of his three Egyptian legions" (CF 1.421–22). Carrying on in ignorance of the architectural wonders all around them, these folk are unworthy of controlling the place and its riches. Yet the dangerousness of Houdini's experience also alludes to something else, a warning perhaps. Many Americans felt that cultural superiority did not necessarily require conquest. As American politician William Jennings Bryan phrased it, in reference to naval battles in the Spanish American War, "shall we contemplate a scheme for the conquest of the Orient merely because our ships won a remarkable victory in the harbor of Manila?" (quoted in Kinzer 15). In other words, we must watch that our vast superiority not lure us into British-style empire, with its rejection of popular sovereignty and endless entanglements. Beneath this is the notion that imperial reach might open the door to new waves of non-white immigrants. Lovecraft, an Anglophile, probably did not embed a critique of England within his tale, though he certainly tapped the Anglo-American worry about being entranced and wrecked by "alien" civilizations.

The true danger of the ancient Orient is evident in Egypt's architecture, especially at night. This is when the pyramids haunt us with their "dim atavistical menace" (CF 1.429). In Cairo, Houdini sees a populace infected by its past, demonically possessed of "strange secret lore and priestly cult-practices." The "horror and unwholesome antiquity of Egypt" (CF 1.434) is evident in everything. Its "grisly alliance" with "the tombs and temples of the dead" (CF 1.434) inspire dread in the rational Western mind. Even his Western education conspires to undermine his confidence: "If only I had not read so much Egyptology before coming to this land which is the fount of all darkness and terror!" (CF 1.438).

Of importance here is Lovecraft's lovingly detailed horror-portrait of mummies and mummification. It is part and parcel of the horror-culture of Egypt. He writes,

> All these people thought of was death and the dead. They conceived of a literal resurrection of the body which made them mummify it with desperate care, and preserve all the vital organs in canopic jars near the corpse; whilst besides the body they believed in two other elements, the soul, which after its weighing and approval by Osiris dwelt in the land of the blest, and the obscure and portentous *ka* or life-principle which wandered about the upper and lower worlds in a horrible way, demanding occasional access to the preserved body, consuming the food offerings brought by priests and pious rela-

tives to the mortuary chapel, and sometimes—as men whispered—taking its body or the wooden double always buried beside it and stalking noxiously abroad on errands peculiarly repellent. (CF 1.438-39)

The ultimate horror of mummification rests in its transgression of boundaries, making it a perfect representation of the unwanted infiltration of the Eastern Other. It is decadent and deviant, employing the conceit of playing God by performing blasphemous rituals. This Egypt represents the upturning of the upright and rational West. The most famous technology of ancient Egyptian religion, mummification, yields "perverse products of decadent priestcraft." This perversity is made horribly manifest in the animal-human combinations, the "*composite mummies* made by the artificial union of human trunks and limbs with the heads of animals in imitation of the elder gods" (CF 1.439). Such transgressions summons the racial science of Lovecraft's day, in which many educated Anglo-American minds viewed racial categories as something of a sliding scale towards animality. Progressive America, writes historian Jackson Lears, was imbued with a "pervasively racist atmosphere" from the top-down (95). Degrees of humanity became scientifically quantifiable by means of racial classification. In the composite mummy, one sees an ancient religion in a racially suspect region reducing humanity in ghastly ways. Lovecraft worried a great deal about racial infection of America's "blood." In a letter to J. Vernon Shea of 25 September 1933 he wrote, "Wherever superior races have absorbed large doses of inferior blood, the results have been tragic. Egypt is one case—& India presents a still more loathsome extreme" (JVS 158).

Trapped under the pyramids, Houdini encounters the monstrous mummies first hand. He hears

the morbid and millennial tramping of the marching things. [. . .] The training of unhallowed thousands of years must lie behind that march of earth's inmost monstrosities . . . padding, clicking, walking, stalking, rumbling, lumbering, crawling . . . and all to the abhorrent discords of those mocking instruments. And then . . . God keep the memory of those Arab legends out of my head! The mummies without souls . . . the meeting-place of the wandering *kas* . . . the hordes of the devil-cursed pharaonic dead of forty centuries . . . the *composite mummies* led through the uttermost onyx voids by King Khephren and his ghoul-queen Nitokris. (CF 1.445)

These composite mummy hordes echo contemporary worries about the subhuman Asiatic and Eastern European "hordes" then "flooding" American shores. This fear would culminate in the infamous Immigration Act of 1924, which specifically targeted immigrants not from Northern and Western Europe. The Act would not be undone until 1965.

Nearly a dozen years later, Lovecraft ghostwrote another mummy-inspired tale, "Out of the Aeons," for Hazel Heald. Joshi has observed that "there is abundant evidence that Lovecraft wrote nearly the entirety of all five stories" of hers ("A Note on the Texts" xvi). Lovecraft himself informed Clark Ashton Smith, "I should say I *did* have a hand in it . . . . . I wrote the damn thing!" (*DS* 594). As a point of evidence, I found the word "Cyclopean" used twelve times. "Out of the Aeons" concerns an incident involving a museum mummy. The mummy in question is a fearsome object delivered by one Capt. Charles Weatherbee of the freighter *Eridanus*, bound from Wellington, New Zealand, to Valparaiso, Chile. On his voyage Weatherbee had found an uncharted island with structures of "prehistoric Cyclopean masonry" adorning it. Here he found a strange mummy "of a medium-sized man of unknown race," frozen in "a peculiar crouching posture." It is a terrifying sight:

> The face, half shielded by claw-like hands, had its under jaw thrust far forward, while the shrivelled features bore an expression of fright so hideous that few spectators could view them unmoved. The eyes were closed, with lids clamped down tightly over eyeballs apparently bulging and prominent. Bits of hair and beard remained, and the colour of the whole was a sort of dull neutral grey. In texture the thing was half leathery and half stony, forming an insoluble enigma to those experts who sought to ascertain how it was embalmed. In places bits of its substance were eaten away by time and decay. Rags of some peculiar fabric, with suggestions of unknown designs, still clung to the object. (CF 4.406)

Also found is a mysterious cylinder containing a "baffling scroll of unknown hieroglyphs" (CF 4.407).

The mummy is placed in a "hall of mummies . . . esteemed by historians and anthropologists as harbouring the greatest collection of its kind in America," including "typical examples of Egyptian embalming" as well as "mummies of other cultures" (CF 4.405). Weatherbee's mummy is T'yog, "High-Priest of Shub-Niggurath and guardian of the copper temple of the Goat with a Thousand Young" (CF 4.414). Over the course of the tale, we learn that T'yog once tried to battle the "hellish god or patron daemon Ghatanothoa" (CF 4.412) who lived beneath a fortress on the island. Each year, a cult that worshipped Ghatanothoa sacrificed a dozen male "warriors" and a dozen "maidens" to satisfy the deity. Finally T'yog went in to face the creature. He cleverly armed himself with a special scroll that would protect him from Ghatanothoa and perhaps even "restore the Dark God's petrified victims" (CF 4.415). But the jealous High Priest of Ghatanothoa's cult snuck into T'yog's room and replaced the scroll with a similar one that would be useless against the beast. As result, T'yog entered the fortress never to return. That was 175,000 years ago. Now found, the mummy of T'yog sits in the museum.

The narrator (the museum's curator, the stolidly Anglo-Saxon sounding Richard H. Johnson) tells how two men break into the museum after hours to steal the mummy but instead are found dead, apparently as result of the mummy's eyes opening and staring at them. One of the intruders in in fact instantly mummified himself. The story concludes when an autopsy is conducted on the mummy and its brain is found to be very much alive and "*pulsing*" (CF 4.432).

Just as with "Under the Pyramids," this story banks on the horrors of the racialized, non-white Other to frame its tale. Though this tale is not about Egypt, the "mummy" is a beastly creation from an ancient civilization and its very real, transgressive gods. In this case, the mummy is not a recruit but a punishment for violating the will of the evil god, with a hellish immortality inflicted on the victim, who is aware and yet trapped for hundreds of centuries. Brought into New England by Charles Weatherbee, the mummy in turn infects the land by drawing to it a steady stream of racially retrograde visitors. For example, we read how, thanks to the mummy, a "stream of freakish foreigners" arrive to "infest the place" (CF 4.424). These include "persons of strange and exotic aspect—swarthy Asiatics, long-haired nondescripts, and bearded brown men who seemed unused to European clothes" (CF 4.421) as well as "a dark, turbaned, and bushily bearded man with a laboured, unnatural voice, curiously expressionless face, clumsy hands covered with absurd white mittens, who gave a squalid West End address and called himself 'Swami Chandraputra'" (CF 4.410). In a time in America when the fear of "subhuman" immigrants from far-off lands pouring in challenged the primacy of the Protestant Anglo hierarchy, such physical signifiers summoned a whole network of terrors. In this case, "dark" types from Asia and the Pacific Islands are infiltrating a bastion of displayed scientific knowledge. Tellingly, this particular bastion trucks in items gleaned from imperial conquest. The idea of the mummy's "curse," since at least the nineteenth century, has been connected not only to fear of the Other but also to imperial guilt over despoiling indigenous cultures. Guilt and fear mix well in museums, where visitors peer at bizarre items that, in other circumstances, might appear to be "stolen." "Out of the Aeons" seems to suggest that one such item might bring with it horrors very much alive and interested in evil deeds.

The mummies Lovecraft presents in "Under the Pyramids" and "Out of the Aeons" attend different functions in service of each narrative. In the first tale, mummies are monstrous echoes of Egypt's blasphemous past returning to the present, manifestations of the undeath of an ancient religion, and of the lurking terror hovering in the pale of Western rationalism. They lumber about beneath the earth to represent the underlying and dangerous difference of Eastern culture. In "Out of the Aeons," the mummy attracts racially degraded Others into the stolid Anglo-Saxon fortress of Massachusetts. It is a source of infection, a magnet for evil cultists. It is also a symbol of the maliciousness of an ancient demon-god who delights in creating curses that last, well, for aeons. This is no Egyptian god, of course, but like the "blasphemies" of Egypt, this creation extends its dark ways into American life.

The mummies in both stories share much in common. For one, they are emblems of Oriental horror. As Said notes, representations of Arabs and Muslims communicate a "fear" that they will "take over the world" (287). The takeover by the Oriental Other could occur in a variety of ways—in immigration, cultural creep, anti-rational intellectual infection, etc. In "Under the Pyramids," mummies are pawns of a dark pantheon of gods and immortal priests. They are hybrid in that they are trapped between life and death and between humanity and animality. Lovecraft's *"composite mummies"* communicate this. This interstitiality can be seen still today in cultural productions, as in the hybrid monstrosities living among the Persian hordes in the film *300*. In this case, we find a goat-headed man luxuriating in Xerxes' harem. The belief that subhuman races literally contain animal genetics is an old racist canard, one inscribed into academic science in the Progressive America in which Lovecraft lived.

In "Out of the Aeons" the interstitial quality of being simultaneously alive and dead, as with the pulsing brain and the opening of the mummy's eye, resonates with philosopher Noël Carroll's argument that monsters embody "categorical transgression" and "impurity": "Many monsters of the horror genre are interstitial and/or contradictory in terms of being both living and dead: ghosts, zombies, vampires, mummies, the Frankenstein monster, Melmoth the Wanderer, and so on [. . .] Also many monsters confound different species: werewolves, humanoid insects, humanoid reptiles, and the inhabitants of Dr. Moreau's island" (32, 34). The composite mummy does this and more. Not only are species conflated; impurity is manifested culturally. The dark land of Egypt gets physically embodied in the wrapped ghouls lurking under the pyramids. Further, the pyramids, those massive, long-disused structures climbing towards the heavens, evoke both wonder and terror. What happens *beneath* them can only be bad.

When Lovecraft wrote "Under the Pyramids," the discovery of King Tut's tomb was on everyone's mind. He even references a time "when Tut-Ankh-Amen mounted his throne in distant Thebes" (CF 1.422). The supposed "curse" that afflicted the discoverers of Tut tells us more about popular culture than Egyptian history. The hideous, decadent mummy stoked the imaginations of Lovecraft's contemporaries and undoubtedly informed the Mummymania of which Lovecraft's mummy stories are a part. His mummies—part of the "padding, clicking, walking, stalking, lumbering, crawling" monstrosities beneath the pyramids—recall dangerous immigrants in such stories as "The Horror at Red Hook."

The danger of the East—its peoples, religions, culture, and history—resonated with Lovecraft and his audience. This was a high-water mark of xenophobia, when laws and academic science came together to condemn entire global regions into the abyss of backwardness and degenerate raciality. At the same time, there was an allure. As Said explains, ever since antiquity the Orient has been conceptualized as "a place of romance, exotic beings, haunting memories and landscapes, remarkable experiences" (1). In Lovecraft's hands, the allure becomes nightmare. The romance of Cairo devolves into a warren of hidden passageways and subterranean labyrinths. The exotic characters draw him (as Houdini) to witness a pyramid-top battle only to trap him in a devious deception. Even outside Egypt, in "Out of the Aeons," mummies can entrap "haunting memories" that remain locked in the skull for 175,000 tortured years. The landscapes of the mummies are terrible, be they in Egypt or a strange island in the Pacific. In these stories the "remarkable" becomes the uncanny—Lovecraft's ultimate weapon of terror. In his hands reality dissolves before the very eyes of the rational Western man.

Works Cited

Brier, Bob. *Egyptomania: Our Three Thousand Year Obsession with the Land of the Pharaohs.* New York: St. Martin's Press, 2013.

Carroll, Noël. *The Philosophy of Horror; or, Paradoxes of the Heart.* London: Routledge, 1990.

Day, Jasmine. *The Mummy's Curse: Mummymania in the English-Speaking World.* London: Routledge, 2006.

Doyle, Sir Arthur Conan. "The Ring of Thoth." 1890. In *The Best Supernatural Tales of Arthur Conan Doyle.* Ed. E. F. Bleiler. New York: Dover, 1979. 202–22.

Fritze, Ronald H. *Egyptomania: A History of Fascination, Obsession and Fantasy.* London: Reaktion Books, 2016.

Goto-Jones, Chris. *Conjuring Asia: Magic, Orientalism, and the Making of the Modern World.* Cambridge: Cambridge University Press, 2016.

Joshi, S. T. *A Dreamer and a Visionary: H. P. Lovecraft in His Time.* Liverpool: Liverpool University Press, 2001.

———. "A Note on the Texts." In H. P. Lovecraft, *The Horror in the Museum and Other Revisions.* Ed. S. T. Joshi. Sauk City, WI: Arkham House, 1989. xv–xviii.

Kalush, William, and Larry Sloman. *The Secret Life of Houdini: The Making of America's First Superhero.* New York: Atria, 2006.

Kinzer, Stephen. *The True Flag: Theodore Roosevelt, Mark Twain, and the Birth of American Empire.* New York: Henry Holt, 2017.

Lears, Jackson. *Rebirth of a Nation: The Making of Modern America, 1977–1920.* New York: Harper, 2009.

Michalek, Laurence. "The Arab in American Cinema: A Century of Otherness." *Cinéaste* 17, No. 1 (1989): 3–9.

Said, Edward W. *Orientalism.* New York: Vintage Books, 1978.

Stoker, Bram. *The Jewel of Seven Stars.* London: Heinemann, 1903.

The Cosmic Drone of Azathoth: Adapting Literature into Sound

Nathaniel R. Wallace
Independent Scholar

"Om//the first sound, the cause of the universe, itself a drone."
—Owen Coggins and James Harris (7)

Elements of H. P. Lovecraft's fiction were adapted during his lifetime by artists who illustrated his stories in pulp magazines, such as *Weird Tales*. What is less well known is that he was approached to approve two sound-based adaptations of his work. In July 1932, Harold S. Farnese sought permission from Lovecraft to set two sonnets of his *Fungi from Yuggoth* cycle to music. With Lovecraft's approval, Farnese composed musical settings for "Mirage" and "The Elder Pharos"—meant to be sung as songs. Lovecraft never received the sheet music, and indeed was not aware that Farnese completed the work. (He declined to collaborate with Farnese by writing a libretto for *Fen River*, an operetta that Farnese wanted to compose.) Around seven months later, *Weird Tales* editor Farnsworth Wright attempted to purchase rights for a radio dramatization adapted of "The Dreams in the Witch House." Lovecraft rejected that request, citing the necessity of "integrity of form" that creates "atmospheric effects" (*SL* 4.155). Long after Lovecraft's death, actors narrated his work for sound recordings, and musicians began to adapt his works to sound.

Of Lovecraft's fictional gods, Azathoth is the one most identified with sound. Considered together, his descriptions of the deity represent an inconsistent but universe-altering voice amidst an alien ensemble of drums and flutes. Commenting on the unique configuration of the deity, Graham Harman, a noted proponent of object-oriented ontology, categorized Azathoth as an instance in Lovecraft's work "in which both the object and its features resist all description" (234). Despite the linguistic and ontological challenges posed by the deity, nearly thirty-five Azathoth-related pieces have been produced by composers and musicians, the earliest being the British psychedelic band Arzachel in 1969 (see table 1).

One essential point of Harman's treatise on Lovecraft's philosophy is his contention that the author's fiction does not translate well to literalization, since its effectiveness in conveying mood rests on metaphor and associations among textual elements (9). This paper examines how Azathoth, a collection of metaphorical references and descriptions of sound, freed from the restrictions imposed by copyright, has undergone since Lovecraft's death in

"Azathoth" (2018) by Ramiro Roman. Used by permission of the artist.

1937 a similar process of *musicalization*, or the adaptation of literature into sound. Musicians have approached the task of adaptation along a spectrum, by quoting sections from the original text through lyrics, by incorporating drums and flutes described or alluded to in Lovecraft's original texts, or by emphasizing in contrast the gaps between these elements and the cosmic drone or noise.

The focus of the current analysis is the last approach, one whereby musicians build upon the outlines of the deity's descriptions, almost like a nascent score, focusing on atmosphere and mood often mediated to a certain extent with drone sounds. A *drone* is a note or chord sustained or repeated over time within a composition. Azathoth-related pieces in this mode require an element of sound design and repositioning of the audience to listen directly and experience the fictional concept itself, the original text being performed as though the musicians were proxies for the deity's sound qualities, rather than a mere description through lyrics. Separated from the original context, recorded musical performances become iterations of the concept of Azathoth, without the baggage of narrative, while offering the possibility of achieving the unity of effect that caused Love-craft to balk at potential sound adaptations. These aesthetic differences are evaluated for their significance within a specific selection of Azathoth-related pieces that represent the "merciful cloak" Harman emphasizes re-garding the deity of recognizable sounds, versus a more complicated and less knowable musical portrayal, tracing a map of compositions located be-tween recognizable human-associated sounds and the cosmic and incom-prehensible sounds of Azathoth (240).

The Musicalization of Azathoth: A Scale of Comprehension

Lovecraft objected strongly to the notion of audio adaptations of his work, arguing that since "the force of any carefully written story depends on atmospheric effects peculiar to the original wording" that his "demands for integrity of form are justified" (SL 4.155). But musicians can employ distinct methods in adapting Lovecraft's Azathoth-related texts using approaches that avoid the "dialoguer's unconscious caricaturing" (SL 4.155) by building "vague impressions & atmosphere" (Letters to Robert Bloch and Others 229) potentially by what Lovecraft describes in his suggestion to Henry Kuttner regarding "non-mundane" stories, that involve a "certain amount of human filtration or interpretation" (CLM 240). This "parallelism" he refers to, at least in music, can be "comprehensible" through some minimal reference made to human-centric elements, such as the flute, drums and vocals, that are intentionally diverged from in order to create a mood of "awed listening" (SL 5.258, CE 2.84). The primary qualities of the pieces chosen for the analysis of musicalization of Lovecraft's literature lean toward music that is performative of Azathoth-related text rather than appropriative, a simulated audio verité experience rather than one experienced by a "surrogate" listener, or the vague and atmospheric in music rather than structures found in conventional popular music. As the following analysis demonstrates, these categories are not all binary and are rather discursive from piece to piece, though the differences highlight how these approaches can play off of one another. As Graham says of real objects, they "cannot be exhausted by any sum total of specific experiences or linguistic propositions, but to some extent resist all perception" (237), much as adaptations of any given text are distinct interpretations.

The origin of Azathoth can be traced to an entry in Lovecraft's com-monplace book that tersely stated "AZATHOTH–hideous name" (CE

5.222). Only pieces bearing this "hideous name" in their titles have been chosen for analysis, since alternative wordings or mere allusions in the lyrics to Azathoth place too much emphasis on the interpretation of lyrics rather than on an examination of sound. A title may well affect the way a musical piece is received, but this analysis proceeds with the assumption, made by Margery B. Franklin, Robert C. Becklen and Charlotte L. Doyle, regarding a painting's connections to its title, that "qualities and forces of organization inherent in the artwork determine how it is perceived" (108). A musical piece may bear the name *Azathoth,* but its actual features prompt the listener to respond and focus on particular components based upon its structure. Indeed, according to Joseph Norman, a good number of Lovecraft music adaptations are in the "metal" genre, and when it comes to Azathoth, nearly a third of the thirty-four pieces bearing variations in their titles can be classified as such (193). Reber Clark remarked that most musical adaptations of Lovecraft are "programmatic, making [them] dependent on non-musical information such as a title, an image, a verbal introduction, or something else other than the music." Pieces that lean heavily on such an approach, especially those quoting the source material, largely connect with Lovecraft's work through caricature of the original literature, in that the original text is laid over the skeleton of existing popular music structures, such as metal, which can be contrary to the cultivation of a certain mood.

Lyrics and singing are related to communicating to the listener, or "telling" the listeners in a performative manner, as Linda Hutcheon observes in *A Theory of Adaptation,* whereas the Azathoth pieces examined here focus on the immersion of the audience "through the perception of the aural" (22). The difference can be derived from Lovecraft's own letters, in which he states that "human characters must not assume too great importance" (*CLM* 229) and that conversation and dialogue "detract [. . .] from the atmospheric tension" (*CLM* 204) of his style of writing. An audience listening to a telling focuses on the method and style of the telling rather than on the mood the narrative's various parts work together to express. The teller does the heavy lifting; the listener must interpret the language of the tale and the way it is performed, calling attention to the human speaker. At the opposite end of the spectrum, immersion and atmosphere stem from sources that do not call attention to their performative nature, especially the human interventions. The more an aural work can convey mood without the thumbprint of human agency, the more difficult it is for listeners to orient themselves and to create a relationship based upon comprehension.

The difference this analysis seeks to highlight is the manner in which each would-be adapter draws recognizable elements of the original into a composition. Since Azathoth is portrayed as a deity, unconcerned with human affairs, it is significant that Azathoth and its related ensemble of musicians contains anthropomorphic elements, in the presence of a mouth and in the fact that the Other Gods perform what is essentially an interpretation of the rituals associated with Dionysian Mysteries, Bacchanals, and witch-cults. It is the performing of music and the recording of sound, however, that determine the degree of comprehensible anthropomorphic qualities versus more complicated and less recognizable ones. The difference is based entirely upon the degree to which composers and producers seek to mask the human element in representing Azathoth through sound. Indeed, Lovecraft very much valued ambiguity, infinity, and purposelessness in the arts and attempted to describe the essence of what he idealized in music in the following passage:

> I can get the idea of music in the abstract. I always think of strange, delicate fragments of half-heard melody associated with the ethereal and visionary worlds of cosmic memory or sunset glamour—even though I can form no concrete impression of what those fragments are, or what they are remotely like. What I hate worst in music, I guess, is *definiteness*. I like it to remain vague and cosmic. (*Essential Solitude* 299)

Examining the terms "vague" and "cosmic," one finds that the former stands for the opposite of definiteness and comprehensibility in that the music Lovecraft describes is difficult to discern and connect with familiar musical qualities.

Musicalization of texts that constitute the known qualities of the fictional deity Azathoth would be based on the removal of the "surrogate observer," as Harman labels the fiction-embedded witness, and would provide a simulated audio verité experience of what the deity might sound like if it actually existed and the listener possessed the ability to hear it (Harman 259). These interpretations of Azathoth would have certain similarities with the original text, incorporating elements of instrumentation and sound. The "orchestrated prose" that Fritz Leiber has seen in Lovecraft's use of repetition of major descriptions and themes within a single work, as Azathoth as used in *The Dream-Quest of Unknown Kadath* and "The Dreams in the Witch House," does not function in the same manner within the resulting adaptations of the original texts (Leiber 13). These adaptations are stand-alone pieces that for the most part are contiguous within the object rather than disruptive or contrasting, with the exception of Arzachel's composition.

Of thirty-four recordings bearing a variation of the title of "Azathoth," only eleven readily fit the category of performative adaptations of literature (Table 1). Most deviate from the standard pop duration of three to five minutes, coming in either as shorter or much longer recording times. All but the piece by Arzachel were produced within the last fifteen years, probably indicating a decline in the cost of recording, and also a resurgence of Lovecraft-related media, especially as practitioners within the genre of drone and ambient music have taken up horror-related themes.

Table 1. Compositions with *Azathoth* in the title

Band / Composition	Track No. (Length)	Album Title (Year of Release)	Genre
Arzachel / "Azathoth"	2 (4:25)	*Arzachel* (1969)	Psychedelic rock
Flint Glass / "Azathoth"	4 (0:31)	*Nyarlathotep* (2003)	Dark ambient
Ungl'unl'rrlh'chchch / "Azathoth"	3 (9:37)	*Ungl'Unl'Rrlh'Chchch* (2003)	Drone
Bird from the Abyss / "Intro-Beginning at the Center of Chaos-Azathoth and Flutes"	1 (1:54)	*I* (2009)	Experimental
Nettless / "Azathoth"	3 (8:01)	*From Beyond* (2010)	Dark ambient
Aklo / "Azathoth"	10 (5:38)	*Titan Blur* (2013)	Dark ambient
Abysmal Growls of Despair / "Azathoth"	4 (21:20)	*Lovecraftian Drone* (2014)	Funeral doom metal
Cryo Chamber / "Azathoth 1"	1 (54:24)	*Azathoth* (2015)	Dark ambient
Cryo Chamber / "Azathoth 2"	2 (64:57)	*Azathoth* (2015)	Dark ambient

Of particular significance to a discussion of the literary origins of musical adaptations is the nature of how music is dominated by the initial medium in which it is embedded. In *The Musicalization of Fiction*, Werner Wolf focuses upon literature that contains elements connected to music. Applicable to the current analysis is his description of intermedia and the dominance of one medium over another where they intersect (38). Wolf describes the process thus:

"covert" or indirect intermediality can be defined as the participation of (at least) two conventionally distinct media in the signification of an artefact in which, however, only one of the media appears directly with its typical or conventional signifiers and hence may be call the dominant medium, while another one (the non-dominant medium) is indirectly present 'within' the first medium (41).

The passages in Lovecraft's work regarding Azathoth illustrate a case of literature dominating sound within its own medium, so it is logical that when adapters derive music from these sources, the literary qualities tend to prevail and are much more likely to be signified within a new interpretation, which is especially the case in the genre of metal.[1] Lovecraft's descriptions of Azathoth offer not an exact musical model but rather a set of texts from which musicians may selectively draw, almost like an aleatoric technique, which produces indeterminate music.[2] Comparison of Lovecraft's Azathoth-related texts to a Fluxus score is appropriate, since they are intermedia, or as Michael Nyman states, "something that falls between different media [. . .] between poetry and performance" and yet the resulting caricature is captured as a sound object (79).

It is significant to note that the very concept of adapting objects into other media is not external to Lovecraft's texts, as he included numerous instances of humans doing just that. He explained such a process in "The Dreams in the Witch House," writing "Half the chants of the Sabbat were patterned on this faintly overheard pulsing which no earthly ear could endure in its unveiled spatial fullness" (CF 3.269). Those mysterious musicians carrying out the "Walpurgis-rhythm" (CF 3.269) were taking their cues from Azathoth, this beyond space, and adapting it through cultural practices. Similarly, in The Dream-Quest of Unknown Kadath, Lovecraft describes the inhabitants of Inganok as maintaining "the rhythms of the Great Ones," most likely the same Other Gods who use their music to

---

1. Joseph Norman has stated that HPL's mythos is one of the more notable fictional-based cultures featured in the metal genre (194).

2. When asked how he would adapt Azathoth, Reber Clark responded, "If I was scoring a movie (or something with a visual reference) of Azathoth I'd opt for large orchestra and aleatoric techniques. Something random, jarring and chaotic. I would attempt to surprise the audience by my approaches—maybe quiet and subtle with interspersed loud chaos."

counter Azathoth (CF 2.161).[3] In terms of adaptation, Lovecraft implies in his fiction that the cosmic sounds of Azathoth and its court are something constantly adapted by humans and ushered into an approximation of reality. This coincides with Graham Harman's connecting Azathoth to the "neo-Platonic theory of emanation" whereby everything in existence is derived from an initial and more profound reality; however he notes that Azathoth exists as metaphor with its status as an object and qualities (209). How, then, can a musician create music based upon a metaphor? The rituals Lovecraft alludes to in his descriptions, such as the Dionysian Mysteries and the Bacchanals, had a certain level of historical evidence; but is it really a metaphor, as Harman suggests, or an indeterminate prescription?

The Voice of Azathoth: Beyond Comprehension

Despite Azathoth's place the top of Lovecraft's hierarchy of deities, its literary origins are confined to a very small percentage of his overall work. All told, Azathoth is mentioned in seven of Lovecraft's writings, The most significant descriptions are in *Fungi from Yuggoth*, *The Dream-Quest of Unknown Kadath*, and "The Dreams in the Witch House."[4] As noted, Lovecraft first mentioned Azathoth in his commonplace book; he then made another entry regarding "A terrible pilgrimage to seek the nighted throne of the far daemon-sultan *Azathoth*" (CE 5.222). These brief references have no connection to sound per se, but the second speaks to the potential Orientalist source for the fictional god and its ability to possess matter.[5]

---

3. Indeed, in *The Dream-Quest of Unknown Kadath*, music signifies the god Azathoth indirectly, as the god is never seen first-hand but only heard, and in other cases Carter experiences the sound of Azathoth second-hand through the musical performances and interpretations of its followers.

4. Azathoth is mentioned briefly in "The Whisperer in Darkness," "The Horror in the Museum," "The Thing on the Doorstep," and "The Haunter of the Dark."

5. The term *sultan* can be traced to the thirteenth-century English term "used [to describe] indiscriminately of Muslim rulers and sovereigns" (*Online Etymology* 2015). HPL's use of *sultan* highlights Azathoth's place at the top of his fictional hierarchy. His use of *daemon* can be interpreted in several ways, a notion that Eugene Thacker elaborates upon in *In the Dust of This Planet: Horror of Philosophy, Volume 1*. He introduces two characterizations relevant to this current analysis: "a placeholder for some sort of non-human, malefic agency that acts against the human," and an allegory for

In *The Dream-Quest of Unknown Kadath*, Lovecraft begins a transition of Azathoth from a vaguely anthropomorphic figure into an abstract cosmic ritual possessing and accompanied by sounds.[6] As the protagonist Randolph Carter is described descending into the Dreamlands in the narrative, Lovecraft offers several clues as to what Azathoth sounds like:

> [. . .] that shocking final peril which gibbers unmentionably outside the ordered universe, where no dreams reach; that last amorphous blight of nethermost confusion which blasphemes and bubbles at the centre of all infinity—the boundless daemon-sultan Azathoth, whose name no lips dare speak aloud, and who gnaws hungrily in inconceivable, unlighted chambers beyond time [. . .] (*CF* 2.100)

This passage defines Azathoth in entirely new ways, giving it distinct elements associated with sound, specifically a voice. The deity "gibbers" and "blasphemes," which are both elements of speaking. Connecting those descriptions with the verb "gnaw" and "muttered" from the sonnet "Azathoth," it appears that the entity possesses a disembodied mouth in which an inconsistent but degrading voice is produced that undermines the order of the universe. Indeed, the deity seems to emit a never-ending stream of consciousness, emanations of words, like ancient oracles, or "speaking in tongues," all beyond the comprehension of the human protagonist. The point of the description is to render the deity's speech indecipherable to the reader, a manner of producing sound that is similar to what Jean François Augoyard and Henry Torgue have termed "linguistic drone" (43). Expressing intelligible words, even if they are tied in with the deity, breaks the illusion of actually hearing a sound representation of a concept and is much in line with the "overfacile language-learning" Lovecraft found that most science fiction literature employed (*CE* 2.181).

In "The Dreams in the Witch House," Lovecraft's allusions to the na-

---

humanity's inability to understand, represented with the repetitive acts of invasion and possession" (27). HPL's use of the word in his commonplace book in entry 196—"Daemons, when desiring an human form for evil purposes, take to themselves the bodies of hanged men"—would seem to conform to this idea of Azathoth engaged in a type of possession (*CE* 5.232). One can see in later texts that Azathoth possesses the universe, and in some cases, humans as well, such as Walter Gilman in "The Dreams in the Witch House."

6. Before HPL added these details to Azathoth in *The Dream-Quest of Unknown Kadath*, he described the Other Gods in his prose poem "Nyarlathotep" (1920).

ture of this enlarged mouth are less explicit, and the voice seems to become much more frantic and intense. Lovecraft describes the space associated with Azathoth as "shrieking" and "roaring," using variations of that last word at least four times. Significant to the current analysis, the fourteenth century definition of "to roar" became associated with drone, creating one of the most definitive links between the deity and the genre (Meyer, 2012). Depending on Lovecraft's description of the deity's voice, it contains no melody but is dissonant and without a discernible pattern.[7]

The Azathoth pieces performed by singers who refrain from communicating lyrics largely decenter the significance of voice, rendering vocals as just another instrument among a multitude of sounds. The descriptions Lovecraft used to portray Azathoth find their way into several compositions, beginning with the very first musical adaptation created in 1969 by the band Arzachel. The psychedelic rock song on *Arzachel* initially contains hymn-like singing by bassist Mont Campbell, the lyrics paraphrasing Lovecraft's description of the god, as in the passage, "Azathoth the mighty centre of confusion." Though the lyrics are about a subject matter that might be obscure to the general public, they are sung in a flat and intelligible manner with heavy reverb that conforms to the English audience's expectations, and they would not have been out of place on a typical Sunday at most churches in England at the time, with the exception of the drums and bass, which are not unduly emphasized. During the drone-infused break that begins at the 2:11 mark, there is an indecipherable muttering where the singer seems to be speaking gibberish until a low wailing coincides with feedback-infused keyboards and guitar. The remarkable aspect to this disruption is that the very production of the vocals changes, as they become buried in the mix and exist only as another discordant sound. The

---

7. There is likely a relationship between the voice of Azathoth and Nyarlathotep since in *Fungi of Yuggoth* Nyarlathotep identifies itself as the "messenger" of Azathoth (AT 89). If Nyarlathotep communicates to others on Azathoth's behalf, it must share some aspect of the god. There is some contention over who possesses the character of Akeley in "The Whisperer in Darkness." If Nyarlathotep is to whom HPL refers, it is clear that it possesses a drone-like voice. HPL describes the drone qualities of the deity's speech: "It was like the drone of some loathsome, gigantic insect ponderously shaped into the articulate speech of an alien species" (CF 2.488). The use of "drone" here emphasizes the eleventh-century English origins of the word, which was strongly associated with the bee (Myer 2012). This insect-like sound, which accentuates the character's speech, locates its origins outside time and space.

reverb that characterized the previous vocal passages is removed, and they lose their ethereal presence and become something more guttural, incomprehensible, and immediate. The "known & accustomed objects" (*DS* 263) of sound here represented by the hymnal-form becomes a cultural reference point for a greater vocal departure, representing a similar rupture that characterizes Azathoth in *The Dream-Quest of Unknown Kadath* and "The Dreams in the Witch House." In a similar but drawn-out approach, The Abysmal Growls of Despair's "Azathoth" (2014), includes a male vocalist initially singing the name Azathoth between withering and murmuring, largely within the same vocal line. Within these lines there is established by a band, a dynamic between a kind of comprehensible chant, challenged by utterances of an indiscernible type, that creates an ongoing rupture that eventually transitions into loud droning distorted bass explorations.

"Azathoth" by the United Kingdom band, Ungl'Unl'Rrlh'Chchch, on its self-titled album (2003) comes closest to holding qualities to what Lovecraft described in his work and is often associated with drone music as a genre, though without the presence of a flute. The band includes Dave Terry of the drone group, Bong (Thundarr and Belegure). "Azathoth," at 9:37, is not particularly long; however, through its repetitive and unchanging structure and use of a single, slow-tempo drumbeat, Ungl'Unl'Rrlh'Chchch's piece maintains the feeling of a stable and ceaseless playing of drums and rhythm.

Ungl'Unl'Rrlh'Chchch's vocals do not include lyrics or represent an act of verbal communication, but only exist as a meditative hum or chant amidst the drone of the vibration of the bass string. Significantly, an indiscernible deep voice hums a guttural sound throughout the piece, conforming to Lovecraft's description of the deity "muttering" and "gibbering." The vocal accompaniment appears to represent the deity directly rather than using language or lyrics to describe it indirectly. Since the rhythm of the piece never changes, it creates an order that is contrasted by the variations of the vocalist's humming. This sonic dynamic is analogous to the chaotic and changing voice of Azathoth which is ever-challenged by the patterned flutists and drummers who attempt to create a semblance of order against the deity. Similarly, "Azathoth" (2009) by Bird from the Abyss contains layers of chanting, and mumbling against a heavy drone, as well as flutes, all creates a similar but more chaotic dynamic between instruments and vocals. Bands that have used vocals as an extension of the fictional god have done so largely within the spirit of the original text in their reluctance to communicate, but rather interact with the order or chaos of the instrumentation of a given piece.

Other Gods: A Cosmic Ensemble of Flutists and Drummers

Often overshadowing Azathoth in Lovecraft's texts is its ensemble of Other Gods who inhabit the same central space. Beginning with *The Dream-Quest of Unknown Kadath* (1926–27), Azathoth loses its status as a singular entity and becomes irrevocably connected with the Other Gods who endlessly dance and play the flutes and drums to counter and contain the deity. In terms of sound elements related to these creatures, Lovecraft remarked that Azathoth resides "amidst the muffled, maddening beating of vile drums and the thin, monotonous whine of accursed flutes" (*CF* 2.100). The nature of these individual instruments and their affective qualities will be examined in detail, but first it is important to note that Lovecraft appears to have appropriated in conceiving Azathoth a similar sound-based relationship as the Anglo-Irish author Lord Dunsany and his creator god MĀNA-YOOD-SUSHĀĪ, and Skarl the Drummer featured in *The Gods of Pegāna*, published in 1905.[8] Unlike Dunsany's relationship, in which MĀNA-YOOD-SUSHĀĪ is kept from destroying his creations by the ceaseless drumming of Skarl, Lovecraft's iteration of this idea produces active and ongoing conflict between the central god Azathoth and its antithesis of sound in the Other Gods.

The other significant influence concerning Lovecraft's Azathoth and its relationship to musical performance is the manner in which Lovecraft broadly appropriated music-related rituals, including Dionysian Mysteries, Bacchanals, and those mentioned in Margaret Murray's *The Witch-Cult in Western Europe* (1921), to create the general outlines of the Other Gods.[9] Indeed, it is this strand of ritual, though much more alien and not related to human beings, that Lovecraft positions at the center and top of the hierarchy of being in his fictional world. In a letter to Robert E. Howard, Lovecraft, further tying the deity to ritual, elaborated upon his knowledge concerning witch-cults:

> The semi-annual orgies (April 30 and Nov. 30) were what came later to be known as *sabbats*. In the main, they consisted of dances and chants or worshippers—mostly female, but presided over by a male hierophant in shaggy animal disguise, called simply 'The Black Man' (*MF* 70).

---

8. HPL first mentions the fictional god in a letter he wrote in 4 September 1923, to Maurice W. Moe (*MWM* 132).

9. HPL probably learned about witch-cults through Murray's book, shortly after it was published in 1921 (Waugh 117).

These concepts were explored in "The Dreams in the Witch House," but Lovecraft switched the source of "Nature" to Azathoth, and "The Black Man" was positioned as just another identity of the shape-shifting Nyarlathotep. It is significant that Murray originally stated, "The music was always as an accompaniment of the dance; the instrument in general use was a pipe" (136). Clearly Lovecraft felt that the rituals and the instruments that accompanied them held some kind of power, and in drawing on these elements to create Azathoth, he brought this concept into his literature. On a more literal level, Lovecraft alludes to real historical cultural practices that involved human musical performance, a process explained eloquently in Robert H. Waugh's essay "The Witch-Cult in New England." Metaphorically, one could interpret his appropriation of such practices in the creation of his central, most important god, as analogous to Friedrich Nietzsche's central conceit in *The Birth of Tragedy*. This sentiment, that the Dionysian Mysteries spawned a significant development in the arts and human culture that existed in some form for nearly two millennia, is replicated on a cosmic scale in the form of this fictional deity.

Lovecraft describes flutes in direct association with Azathoth in six stories, largely using the same wording: "thin, monotonous whine of accursed flutes" (CF 2.100). "Monotonous" here can be specifically linked to stasis in music, a quality in drone which Joanna Demers says "avoids conventional harmonic or melodic goals but also music that takes specific steps to obscure any sense of the passage of time" (93). This description parallels Azathoth and the Other Gods residence in "unlighted chambers beyond time" in that Lovecraft describes these sounds as endless. In terms of pitch, the "whine" indicates a high pitch, while the modifier "cracked" used in *Fungi from Yuggoth* alludes to a discordant or even atonal sound (AT 89). Interestingly, this same sonnet speaks to the effect of the flutes, "Whence flow the aimless waves whose chance combining / Gives each frail cosmos its eternal law" (AT 89). This leads the reader to infer that the sounds of the flutes textured over one another, randomly colliding in space to create a deep organizational pattern from which the universe is based within Lovecraft's fictional cosmology.

Of the nine pieces examined in this analysis, only a few contain actual flute sounds, demonstrating that musicians performing the texts related to Azathoth appear to be reluctant to musicalize this aspect of the deity, perhaps because many of them do not possess such a skill or have no suitable flutist available. In his interpretation on the material, the French funeral doom artist Abysmal Growls of Despair begins his composition with what sounds like rain falling against a surface. Then a single tom-tom drumbeat sets a slow tempo for the piece until 1:07, when a single flute plays in a high register, alternating a half step. Thus the repetitive elements essentially shift from the beat of the drums to the notes of the flute during this portion of the song, as the percussion ceases. The flute in this instance, with its lack of dynamics and flat sound, is less a driving element and more of an instrument bridge maintaining the former tempo of the drums until its discontinuation at 4:40. when a heavily distorted bass drones until it takes up a similar progression of notes, only at a lower register with frequent departures from the original time signature.

The Cryo Chamber Collective on its 2015 album recorded two "Azathoth" pieces, the second of which contains a flutelike instrument beginning at the 16:04 mark out of a total length of 64:57. The flute is layered in the piece at regular, medium-in-duration intervals, largely at the crest of a drone crescendo, sometimes punctuated with the irregularly struck high hat and assorted percussion such as wood blocks. Here the flute serves to emphasize the beginnings of a segment of tension-filled, drawn out drone. In "Intro—Beginning at the Center of the Chaos—Azathoth and Flute" by Bird from the Abyss, a dynamic flute can be heard initiating a chaotic, ever-moving set of bass-heavy drone sounds that twist and pivot off what seems to be the prime mover of the piece, the style seems vaguely, stereotypically Middle Eastern, hearkening back to Lovecraft's original Orientalism that characterized Azathoth in his commonplace book.

Though the "muffled" drums (CF 2.211) are emphasized in the descriptions of the Other Gods in *The Dream-Quest of Unknown Kadath*, they become a "cosmic pulsing" in "The Dreams in the Witch House" (CF 3.269). The percussion becomes less sharp, more flat in aspect, the main quality of its nature collecting adjectives such as "monstrous" and "cosmic," "which no earthly ear could endure in its unveiled spatial fulness" (CF 3.269), a foreshadowing of the damage that the protagonist, Gilman, suffers at the end of the story once his ear drums are ruptured. The main quality of the instrumentation is "maddening," which can be interpreted as high-tempo, loud, or indefinite, though it is largely a term that seems tied to affect rather than definitive qualities of their playing. Joanna Demers describes such music as related to drone: "Their long durations and loud volumes test our limits of concentration and, in some cases, our tolerance for pain" (92). The central quality of these drums, as described by Lovecraft, seems to be their ability to cause anxiety and discordance in the human listeners, which is a difficult scenario to translate directly into music. It is not clear what type of drums Lovecraft is referring to; however, the *tympanon*, "a frame drum beaten with the hand," was often used in Dionysian rituals in Ancient Greece (Apel 247, 881).

One might expect compositions attempting a more strict interpretation of Lovecraft's descriptions of Azathoth to employ tympanon-like drums, such as is featured in the wine festival scene in the film *Seconds* (1966), or Haitian Djouba drumming as captured by Alan Lomax, an American ethnomusicologist in the mid- to late 1930s. However the use of drums in Azathoth-related pieces is far more tied to traditional rock music, giving the pieces a much more conventional spin on the instrument. Arzachel's piece "Azathoth" is a low-tempo composition characterized by Clive Brooks's steady drumbeat, which barely changes even during the psychedelic dirge toward the end of the composition. The incorporation of percussion is not particularly emphasized and probably derives from the configuration of the band and qualities that establish this piece as a hybrid between a traditional hymn and a psychedelic rock song.

Ungl'Unl'Rrlh'Chchch departs from traditional Western rock music but in a methodical and stripped-down manner. Percussion is provided by a kick drum/bass drum with a slightly loose head played with a mallet. To the extent that it is "maddening," one might characterize the lack of dynamics in the band's performance over the course of the 9:37 track as conforming to this description. Abysmal Growls of Despair uses a tom-tom in a similar manner, only the musician begins the piece with drums as a means of establishing a tempo, only to depart later from it with a distorted bass once the drums cease.

Perhaps the most interesting use of percussion in these pieces is in two long tracks recorded by the Cryo Chamber Collaboration. Vast stretches of are filled with ever-changing drone and ambient sounds, with the sporadically singular drum-beat at a very low tempo, only to depart from the pieces after a brief duration. The first instance of this is at the 17:10 mark on the first track, where a slow drum can be heard, punctuated with what sounds like reverb and filter-heavy screaming. At 36:58, there is a stark pounding on a cymbal or sheet metal that repeats at a very slow and drawn-out tempo. On the album's second track, at 17:20, a drum again is struck. At 30:17, a regular-emitting electronic pulse drum sounds and helps to form a contrast with the ambient and ambiguous reverb-drenched sounds, perhaps made with a synthesizer. This lends the piece a moment of organization that has no comparison with the rest of the album.

The musicalized descriptions of Azathoth conducted by these musicians, in focusing on indecipherable vocals and on flute and drums, adds a human quality of the music that demonstrates affinities with known music, allowing for "a point of departure" for "excursions into the outside cosmic gulfs" in a way similar to Lovecraft's cherished architecture in his literature (*DS* 200).

Cosmic Drone: The Music of the Spheres

At the other end of the spectrum of the comprehensible in music, and related instruments, lies that which is difficult for a casual listener to process, since the nature of the sound might not be categorizable or attributable to any particular instrument. It lacks a discernible origin that might help the listener determine intent or context. This analysis proposes that drone in the pieces examined here provides a significant source for the musicalization of gaps inherent within the original texts, and also serves as a supplementary and dominant mediation of the instruments that are adapted into music. The tensions that Graham Harman finds within the object of Azathoth and the qualities that represent it are not entirely transposed to the new medium, since it exists as a potential ensemble of sounds and a metaphor, paralleled with sound qualities that incorporate known instruments juxtaposed with vague drone sounds that mask their identity.

In a key scene in *The Dream-Quest of Unknown Kadath*, the narrator describes a sound that seems either connected with or underneath Azathoth, which Randolph Carter encounters on his flight toward the deity and the deeper universe. The narrator describes this music as a "droning in faint chords that our own universe of stars knows not" and goes on to say: "It was a song, but not the song of any voice. Night and the spheres sang it, and it was old when space and Nyarlathotep and the Other Gods were born" (*CF* 2.210). Here Lovecraft alternates and seems to conflate the droning sounds of the outer spheres and with sounds made by the Other Gods, who possess flutes and drums. The description of this sound has distinct similarities to the Myth of Er as described by Plato and Aristotle, especially when combined with a passage from "The Whisperer in Darkness" that mentions Azathoth and "black aether at the rim" (*CF* 2.487). Indeed, the ancient Greek Myth of Er, as told by Aristotle, detailed a process by which the celestial bodies in heaven created friction that caused a type of drone sound (Hollander 29).[10] Aristotle describes the process as celestial spheres grinding against one another to create a drone sound that humans all hear at birth and later become so used to that they no longer hear it later in life. To deepen the connection between Azathoth and the Myth of Er, in "The Dreams in the Witch House," Lovecraft depicts Azathoth as such a force of sound that it ruptures the eardrums of Walter Gilman following the climax of the narrative.

As Reber Clark has indicated regarding Lovecraft's work, "Many have come to know HPL (or think they know HPL) through gaming, music, or the movies. None of these come close to what Lovecraft's work actually is and what it is saying and can do." This notion is certainly correct in terms of music, with so much of it based on a subculture of metal, as Joseph Norman has demonstrated; however, he would argue that there is a distinct strand of music that Lovecraft repeatedly references in his work, especially in connection with Azathoth, specifically drone music. A thorough review of his fiction reveals that Lovecraft saw drone as similar to what Owen Coggins conceptualizes, a translocal and transdimensional music that stands in for the cosmic (84). Significantly, Lovecraft references "droning" or "drone" in several stories beyond the Azathoth-related pieces mentioned herein, including "Poetry and the Gods" (CF 4.20), "From Beyond" (CF 1.195), "Hypnos" (CF 1.331), "The Festival" (CF 1.414), "Under the Pyramids" (CF 1.445), The Case of Charles Dexter Ward (CF 2.243, 290, 336, 346), "The Last Test" (CF 4.84), Fungi from Yuggoth (AT 84, 93),"The Curse of Yig" (CF 4.120), and "The Thing on the Doorstep" (CF 3.351). These works contain direct references to drone-related characteristics, providing an important body of Lovecraft's work from which to derive certain aural qualities that represent the incomprehensible.

What seems like a subtle sound quality described in the background of The Dream-Quest of Unknown Kadath emerges in the foreground in many of the pieces examined in this analysis, using drone as an auditory locus. Elements of vocals, flutes, and drums seem to exist merely as secondary in their inclusion in these compositions. Lovecraft would argue, however, that

---

10. HPL's reference to these processes in "Supernatural Horror in Literature" alludes to both Azathoth and the Myth of Er in a key passage, referring to "the scratching of outside shapes and entities on the known universe's utmost rim" (CE 2.84).

there needs to be something identifiable, or the presence of "accustomed objects" as he labels such phenomena, in order to assist an audience in giving the more incomprehensible phenomena "significance" (DS 263). For instance, the dark-ambient artist Flint Glass released "Azathoth" on *Nyarlathotep* (Trémorin), which is rather brief at 31 seconds. The piece opens with a medium blast of electronic noise and contains an electronic pulse that registers throughout the composition with occasional variations. The piece includes a deep oscillating sound in the background, almost as though it were recorded underwater. This sounds remarkably like the passage in "The Dreams in the Witch House" where the narrator describes "veiled cosmic pulsing," almost as if a sound from the outside were pressing against the sounds of reality (CF 3.269). Toward the end of the piece there is an oscillating sound accompanied with what sounds like either a fire or a consistent scrapping noise. This might be difficult for some audiences to grasp since there is little in the piece to which they can relate, or at least to which they can assign some sort of orientation. Similarly, the Finnish artist Nettless, has an ambient piece "Azathoth" on his album *From Beyond* (2010). Nettless's "Azathoth" is much longer, at 8:01, and contains keyboards with a sustained drone throughout the piece while lacking individual breaks between notes. Certain minor-sounding sound effects and backward-masked oscillating elements function as adornments to the aural reference of the drone. This form too does little to ingratiate the listener, beyond using certain buildups and progressions to draw the listener in through its rich textures of sounds. Its relationship to the original descriptions of Azathoth is largely only in reference to the title, and a subtext that may be difficult to summon for the listener without vocals or drums and flutes.

Ungl'Unl'Rrlh'Chchch's piece based on Azathoth is not accompanied by a flute; it balances the slow drumbeat with a high-pitched drone sound from an electric organ or synthesizer. The electric organ does not use individual notes distinctively; rather, it has two notes played continuously throughout by one of the band members, giving the composition a strong underlying consistency when juxtaposed with the low drone's slightly shifting and modulating aural vibrations. The low drone is probably produced with a bass guitar, either with an E-Bow or a violin bow used on one of the lower wound strings. This musical repetition produces what Michael Ballam of Utah State University deems a mental state in which "The human mind shuts down after three or four repetitions of a rhythm, or a melody, or a harmonic progression" (5). Although the listener is engulfed by the hypnotic drone sounds in conjunction with the slow-beating drum, the vocalist's humming produces the equivalent of a yogic "OM" or mantra that can be intoxicating for the listener.

Though it perhaps leans a little too closely to the comprehensible in its use of lyrics, Arzachel uses drone in exactly the way that Lovecraft uses Azathoth in "The Dreams in the Witch House," as a musical disruption of two approaches continuous within itself. Steve Hillage's Stratocaster, eerie-sounding keyboards courtesy of Dave Stewart's Hammond L122 organ, and minimal but subtlety punctuating Fenton Weill bass guitar by Mont Campbell, produces a collision among opposing poles of comprehensibility (Vinall). Indeed, Gary Hill calls the piece "rather fitting to its Lovecraftian roots, feeling like a psychotic, psychedelic funeral dirge throughout much of the piece" (28). The piece is only 4:25 long, but its slow pace and repetitive nature creates the impression in the listener that the piece goes on for a long period of time. The structure breaks down at 2:12, when the droning discordant sounds are taken up by guitar and keyboard, and it almost sounds like an entirely different piece intrudes, until 3:28 when the band return to the previous theme.

Cryo Chamber Collaboration, an ensemble of twenty-five ambient artists, took the opposite approeach when it released a double album devoted to Azathoth in 2015. Bands such as Kammarheit and Aseptic Void contributed sound elements, all synthesized into an organic whole. Edward Rinderle of Heathen Harvest has described the work as having "a random, almost improvisational feel to it," and its sound "seems to reflect the formlessness and untold awe of Azathoth rather than a sense of panic and annihilation." The clear difference between this production and other pieces discussed herein is that it is much longer and stretches more toward the infinite than to the digestible. With so many artists involved in the project, it is nearly impossible for a listener to detect individual contributions, which certainly has the effect of depersonalizing the music and hiding the human agency in the sound object. Though both tracks largely contain droning synths, the inclusion of flute sounds and percussion sporadically in the compositions creates an immersive aural simulation of Randolph Carter's journey in between and back and forth from "the spheres" (CF 2.248) that constitutes Azathoth's origins, to the deity itself.

Conclusion: The Word and Sound

Returning to the initial foundation of musicalizing Lovecraft's literary descriptions of Azathoth, it is significant that all but one of the nine piecess discussed in this analysis have largely been created over the last couple of decades and that this development is likely to continue apace. As more such pieces are produced, a kind of micro-genre is established, causing other musicians to undoubtedly take up the pursuit. The reasons for this are voiced eloquently by Graham Harman with reference to Azathoth in his contention that "an empty proper name is all that can be used to designate something for which no tangible qualities are available" (36). The absence of such qualities and Azathoth's relationship with music in Lovecraft's writings compels would-be adapters to attempt their own interpretations. The edict that "these words could not nor should never be put into sound" is an ideal that runs contrary to the fundamental human desire to mimic phenomena with which artists have a relationship, and it is just as much a provocation as it is a limiting statement (Van Elferen 89).

The musical interpretations of Azathoth analyzed here demonstrate that there are musical scenarios in the text that can indeed be simulated. Instead of quoting the original text, musicians take it as prescription and play off elements of the comprehensible versus the incomprehensible in order to achieve that "awed listening . . . [of] the scratching of outside shapes and entities on the known universe's utmost rim" (CE 2.84) through music that Lovecraft sought to cultivate in his stories. In directly attempting to replicate the sonic textures indicated in his fiction, the musicians taking such an approach place the sound directly into the reality of the listener, hence, what Edmund Burke wrote regarding the sublime, "The nearer it approaches the reality, and the further it removes us from all idea of fiction, the more perfect is its power" (3). Such music is present and immersive, not just described. The drone-related compositions pertaining to Azathoth of the type discussed here do not encroach on a second-hand narrator but rather enter our own space and our own ears. That the public is largely exposed to lyric-centric adaptations, largely in the genre of metal, veils Azathoth under conventional cultural practices, and creates a larger rift between the incomprehensible and mysterious original text and the musical compositions based upon it.

Works Cited

Apel, Willi. *Harvard Dictionary of Music*. Cambridge, MA: Harvard University Press, 1969.

Augoyard, Jean François, and Henry Torgue. *Sonic Experience: A Guide to Everyday Sounds*. Trans. Andrea McCartney and David Paquette. Montreal: McGill-Queen's University Press, 2006.

Ballam, Michael. Quotation. Sayan Nag, Shankha Sanyal, Archi Banerjee, Ranjan Sengupta, Dipak Ghosh "Music of Brain and Music on Brain: A Novel EEG Sonification Approach." Presented at the International Symposium on Frontiers of Research in Speech and Music, at NIT, Rourkela, 15–16 December 2017. Cornell University Library. 2017. arxiv.org/abs/1712.08336.

Burke, Edmund. *A Philosophical Inquiry into the Origin of Our Ideas of the Sublime and Beautiful*. 1757. Charlottesville, VA: Ibis, 1989.

Clark, Reber. E-mail Interview. 10 July 2017.

Coggins, Owen, and James Harris. *Sustain//Decay: A Philosophical Investigation of Drone Music and Mysticism*. Middletown, DE: Void Front Press, 2017.

Demers, Joanna. *Listening through the Noise: The Aesthetics of Experimental Electronic Music*. New York: Oxford University Press, 2010.

Disciglio, Dann. "The Dynamisms of Drone." In *Sonic Tendencies: An Analysis of Noise, Phonography, and Drone in Sound Art and Experimental Music Practices*. Amherst, MA: Hampshire College, 2015.

Franklin, Margery B.; Beklen, Robert C.; and Doyle, Charlotte L. "The Influence of Titles on How Paintings Are Seen." *Leonardo* 26, No. 2 (1993): 103–8.

Harman, Graham. *Weird Realism: Lovecraft and Philosophy*. Alresford, UK: Zero Books, 2012.

Hill, Gary. *The Strange Sound of Cthulhu: Music Inspired by the Writings of H. P. Lovecraft*. Lexington, KY: Music Street Journal, 2006.

Hollander, John. *The Untuning of the Sky: Ideas of Music in English Poetry, 1500–1700*. Princeton, NJ: Princeton University Press, 1961.

Hutcheon, Linda. *A Theory of Adaptation*. New York: Routledge. 2006.

Leiber, Fritz. "A Literary Copernicus." 1949. In *Discovering H. P. Lovecraft*, ed. Darrell Schweitzer. Holicong, PA: Wildside Press, 2001. 7–16.

Lovecraft, H. P. *Letters to Robert Bloch and Others*, ed. David E. Schultz and S. T. Joshi. New York: Hippocampus Press, 2015.

————, and August Derleth. *Essential Solitude: The Letters of H. P. Lovecraft and August Derleth*. Ed. David E. Schultz and S. T. Joshi. New York: Hippocampus Press, 2008.

Meyer, Robinson. "The History of Drone Music Culminates in 'Now That's What I Call Drone'." *The Atlantic*. July 26, 2012. www. theatlantic.com/technology/archive/2012/07/the-history-of-drone-music-culminates-in-now-thats-what-i-call-drone/260330/

Murray, Margaret Alice. *The Witch-Cult in Western Europe: A Study in Anthropology*. Oxford: Clarendon Press, 1921. arxiv.org/abs/1712. 08336.

Norman, Joseph. "'Sounds Which Filled Me with an Indefinable Dread': The Cthulhu Mythopoeia of H. P. Lovecraft in 'Extreme' Metal." In *New Critical Essays on H. P. Lovecraft*, ed. David Simmons. New York: Palgrave Macmillan, 2013. 193–208.

Nyman, Michael. *Experimental Music: Cage and Beyond*. New York: Cambridge University Press, 1999.

Online Etymology Dictionary. Search term "Sultan." www.etymonline.com/. Accessed 2015.

Thacker, Eugene. *In the Dust of This Planet: Horror of Philosophy, Volume 1*. Arlesford, UK: Zero Books, 2011.

Van Elferen, Isabella. "Hyper-Cacophony: Lovecraft, Speculative Realism, and Sonic Materialism." In *The Age of Lovecraft*, ed. Carl H. Sederholm and Jeffrey Andrew Weinstock. Minneapolis: University of Minnesota Press, 2016. 79–96.

Waugh, Robert H. "Dr. Margaret Murray and H. P. Lovecraft: The Witch-Cult in New England." 1994. In *A Century Less a Dream: Selected Criticism on H. P. Lovecraft*. Holikong, PA: Wildside Press, 2002. 112–23.

Wolf, Werner. *The Musicalization of Fiction: A Study in the Theory and History of Intermediality*. Amsterdam: Rodopi, 1999.

Discography

Abysmal Growls of Despair. "Azathoth." In *Lovecraftian Drone*. France: Band-camp, 2014. abysmalgrowlsofdespair.bandcamp.com/album/lovecraftian-drone

AKLO. "Azathoth." In *Titan Blur*. Utah: Bandcamp, 2013. aklo-lovecraftian. bandcamp.com/album/titan-blur.

Bird from the Abyss. "Azathoth." In *Bird from the Abyss*. Finland: Bandcamp, 2011. birdfromtheabyss.bandcamp.com/.

A Cryo Chamber Collaboration. *Azathoth*. Bandcamp. Cryo Chamber. Portland, OR: Bandcamp, 2015. cryochamber.bandcamp.com/album/azathoth.

Hillage, Steve; Campbell, Mont; Brooks, Clive; and Stewart, Dave. "Azathoth." By Arzachel. In *Arzachel*. London: Evolution label, 1969.

Netless. "Azathoth." In *Earth Mantra*. Boston: Netlabel, 2010.

Rinderle, Edward. "A Cryo Chamber Collaboration—Azathoth." In *Heathen Hearst*, 2015. heathenharvest.org/2015/12/02/a-cryo-chamber-collaboration- azathoth/.

Terry, David, and James Baker. "Azathoth." By Ungl'Unl'Rrlh'Chchch. *Ungl'unl'rrlh'chchch*. Sea Ranch, CA: Bandcamp, 2014.

Trémorin, Gwenn. "Azathoth." By Flint Glass. In *Nyarlathotep*. San Francisco: Brume Records, 2006.

Vinall, Antony. "Memories of Uriel." In *Arzachel*. London: Evolution, 1969. Egg Archive, 2007.

Contributors

Ian Fetters is a researcher of the weird and the 2017 fellow for the S. T. Joshi endowed research fellowship at Brown University. He is also the first recipient of the Donald Sidney-Fryer fellowship for Clark Ashton Smith-related archival research in 2018. His fellowship project "Icy Portents of Doom: Clark Ashton Smith's Hyperborean Cycle and the Polar Mythos" will be presented at the University of California Berkeley in the fall of 2019. The research conducted during both fellowships is part of a larger work in progress tentatively titled *Polar Rhetorics*. Other areas of interest include Antarctic fiction, rhetoric and composition, English language teaching, and the fiction of Jeff VanderMeer and Brian Evenson. Ian has a master's degree in English Literature and has taught part-time in the English department at Cal Poly in San Luis Obispo. He is a library specialist at the Robert E. Kennedy Library in San Luis Obispo.

Fiona Maeve Geist is a former academic whose work has appeared in *Trans Studies Quarterly*, *Lamplight Literary*, *Dead Reckonings*, and *CLASH Media*. She works on pen and paper RPGs and occasionally writes fiction.

Edward Guimont is a Ph.D. candidate at the University of Connecticut Department of History. His research focuses on nationalism in the late British Empire, with a particular focus on settler colonialism in Africa and the creation of mythical alternate histories to justify imperialism. His scholarship has also been published in *The Tufts Historical Review*.

Ray Huling is a Ph.D. candidate in the Department of Communication at the University of Massachusetts Amherst. He is a folklorist whose research explores the role of creative expression in the formation and experience of community, with a special focus on the folklore of those who work in sustainable food. His scholarly publications concern film and literature as well as folklore, and he has written a memoir, *Harvesting the Bay*, that presents Rhode Island's shellfishing industry as a model of sustainable food production. He is writing a book on ecology and the sustainability of excessive practices, such as sacrifice and festivals.

Karen Joan Kohoutek, an independent scholar and poet, has published in various journals and literary websites on the weird fiction of Robert E. Howard and Arthur Machen. She has written on a wide range of other popular culture, especially cult horror and Bollywood films. Her upcoming publications include an essay on *Mystery Science Theater 3000* and the Gamera films for *Giant Creatures in Our World: Essays on Kaiju and American Popular Culture*, which will be published by McFarland, and a reference guide to St. Louis Cemetery #2 in New Orleans, through Skull and Book Press. She lives in Fargo, North Dakota.

Sean Moreland is a writer, editor, and educator whose essays on Gothic, horror and weird fiction in literary, cinematic, and sequential art media, have appeared in many collections and journals, most recently *The Oxford Handbook of Edgar Allan Poe*. They edited *The Lovecraftian Poe: Essays on Influence, Reception, Interpretation and Transformation* (Rowman & Littlefield, 2017) and *New Directions in Supernatural Horror Literature: The Critical Influence of H. P. Lovecraft* (Palgrave, 2018). Their short fiction and award-winning poetry has recently appeared in *Over the Rainbow: Folk and Fairytales from the Margins, Lackington's*, and *Black Treacle*. They teach courses on horror fiction, American literature, comics, sequential art, and digital cultural studies at the University of Ottawa and occasionally blog, review, and conduct interviews at www.pstdarkness.com and is @OmNaes on Twitter.

Paul G. Neimann, Ph.D., teaches the University of Colorado Boulder. His background in eighteenth-century literature informs his interest in the Gothic and weird in book and film. He has taught courses on horror genres, popular culture, and related theory. He is at work on a study of early modern thinking about church and state, and recently published an essay on Jonathan Swift.

Heather Poirier is a writer/editor living in Washington, D.C. After teaching at the university level for ten years and working at a biomedical research center with a world-class researcher for five years, she moved to Washington, where she works as a senior editor at a precision oncology journal. Ms. Poirier has published articles on Lovecraft and detective fiction and is working on the intersection of those topics with the work of Edgar Allan Poe, Jorge Luis Borges, and the HBO series *True Detective*.

Lúcio Reis-Filho, Ph.D. University Anhembi Morumbi, is a film critic and historian specializing in the relationships between cinema, history, and literature, with a focus on the horror genre. Addressing the echoes of H. P. Lovecraft in Clive Barker's works, he wrote "Demons to Some, Angels to Others: Eldritch Horrors and Hellbound Religion in the Hellraiser Films," in *Divine Horror: Essays on the Cinematic Battle Between the Sacred and the Diabolical* (McFarland, 2017). He also wrote essays on zombies in contemporary Latin American films, published in journals such as the *SFRA Review* and horror-themed anthologies, and contributed a biographical study of George Romero to a Brazilian anthology on world independent cinema. Currently, he investigates the works of Lovecraft and its cinematic adaptations in the late twentieth century, theme of a piece published in *Abusões* in 2017.

Troy Rondinone is a professor of history at Southern Connecticut State University. He received his Ph.D. in history at UCLA, and his areas of scholarly interest include working-class history, economic history, and radical studies. He has published articles in *American Quarterly, Journal of American Studies,* the *Journal of the Gilded Age and Progressive Era, Connecticut History, Lovecraftian Proceedings,* and *Labor Studies.* He has written entries in the *Oxford Bibliographies in Latino Studies* and the *Cambridge Companion to Boxing.* His first book was *The Great Industrial War: Framing Class Conflict in America, 1865–1950* (Rutgers University Press, 2010). University of Illinois Press published his second book, *Friday Night Fighter: Gaspar "Indio" Ortega and the Golden Age of Television Boxing,* in 2013. *Nightmare Factories: The Asylum in the American Imagination* is due out from Johns Hopkins University Press in 2019. He is the recipient of the Norton Nezvinsky Trustees Research Award for 2010.

Sadie Shurberg is an undergraduate student at Hampshire College, where she studies English and Cultural Studies. She is interested in the liberatory potential of speculative fiction, Gothic horror, the history of Euro-American colonial and racial logics, and fan community creations. She is in the process of completing a senior thesis on racial and cultural politics of H. P. Lovecraft's recent popular revival. Shurburg loves reading horror and pulpy science fiction, playing story-heavy video games, and listening to fast and loud music when not writing.

Elena Tchougounova-Paulson received her Ph.D. at the Department of Theory and Methodology of Philology and Art (A. M. Gorky Institute of World Literature, Russian Academy of Science, Moscow) in twentieth-century Russian literature, dedicated to the theoretical analysis of Russian Symbolist poet Alexander Blok's poetry and prose. She has worked as head of the Communications Department and research fellow and publisher at the Research Information Centre at the Russian State Archive of Literature and Art, Moscow. As a textual scholar and translator, she participated in *Ukrainian Nationalist Organizations in the Second World War: Documents, Alexander Dovzhenko: Diaries, Alexander Blok–L. D. Mendeleeva-Blok: Correspondence (1901–1917)*, and other projects. She is now an independent researcher, residing in Cambridge and specializing in Russian and American literature, Ukrainian studies, textual studies, theory and history of literature, and horror studies. As a Lovecraft scholar, she has presented such papers as "Fantastic London: Dream, Speculation and Nightmare" at the Institute of English Studies, University of London, "On the Problem of Eschatological Perception in the Works of H. P. Lovecraft and Alexander Blok: Cities and Their Phantasms," at the Dr. Henry Armitage Memorial Scholarship Symposium, 2017, "Document and Ego-Document in Silver Age Culture," and "'God, When Creating, Wrapped His Heart in Dark Fabrics': Neo-Gothic Concept in Blok's Diaries and Notebooks," at the A. M. Gorky Institute of World Literature.

Nathaniel R. Wallace is an independent scholar living with his wife in Athens, Ohio. He received his Ph.D. from Ohio University's Inter-disciplinary Arts program in 2014 and wrote his dissertation "H. P. Lovecraft's Literary 'Supernatural Horror' in Visual Culture" (available on OhioLINK) on visual adaptations of the author's work. The chapter "The 'Inside' of H. P. Lovecraft's Supernatural Horror in the Visual Arts" was revised and published in *Lovecraftian Proceedings No. 2*. With his latest scholarship on musical adaptations of Azathoth included in this publication, he seeks to expand the scope of his studies to examine weird fiction's connection to sound.

Appendix: Abstracts of Papers Presented at the Dr. Henry Armitage Memorial Scholarship Symposium, NecronomiCon Providence, 17–20 August 2017

Dennis P. Quinn, Chair

The Dr. Henry Armitage Memorial Symposium aims to foster exploration of Lovecraft's cosmic mythology and how that mythology was influenced by, and has come to influence, numerous other authors and artists before and since. The Lovecraft Arts & Sciences Council (the organizer of NecronomiCon Providence) organizes this symposium of new academic work to explore all aspects of the writings and life of famed weird fiction writer H. P. Lovecraft, including the influence of history, architecture, science, and popular culture on his works, as well as the impact he has had on culture. The Armitage Symposium consists of the latest cutting-edge research on Lovecraft, topics related to Lovecraft, and his circle.

Matthew Beach
Independent Scholar
"Lovecraft's Consolation"

H. P. Lovecraft's vision of humanity's place within cosmic space and time has often been noted for its bleakness if not its horror. My talk makes the case for a more complex view of how Lovecraft understood his cosmic philosophy by exploring one of its overlooked dimensions: consolation. Drawing on archival research, I focus on how Lovecraft adapted his theories of cosmic time in his correspondence to console those who were suffering. In his letters, Lovecraft speaks of offering consolation by providing a "telescopic" view of time and space. To help relieve pain, make it more endurable, or simply put it in perspective, Lovecraft contextualizes the reader's local suffering within a larger framework of time. To explore the consoling dimension of Lovecraft's philosophy, I focus on what I argue are letters of consolation from Lovecraft to Helen V. Sully, beginning in 1933 and continuing until Lovecraft's death. In his letters, Lovecraft seeks to alleviate Sully's (emotional) pain and suffering by reminding her of the insignificance of humanity within the cosmos. For Lovecraft, the impersonality of the cosmos represents a relief from the intense individuality of human pain and suffering. I argue that Lovecraft's letters of consolation offer insight into the complexity and range of his cosmic philosophy. I suggest that his letters represent the human side of Lovecraft's philosophy, which in his stories appears more impersonal or nonhuman. His cosmic philosophy, developed in his stories and his correspondence, contains the potential for both horror and a unusual form of consolation.

Eric Berardis
Independent Scholar
"The Death of the Artist: H. P. Lovecraft and the Nihilism of the Text"

The artist's influential role in society has been the topic of debate since ancient Greek times. A polarized debate between critics and philosophers alike developed a schism in thought, with one side believing that an artist has the power to change society and others holding that only the artist's works can be judged and not his or her influence on them. Invoking the nihilistic writings of Friedrich Nietzsche, the nonfiction treatises of H. P. Lovecraft, and the criticism of S. T. Joshi, Donald R. Burleson, and Vivian Ralickas, this study investigates the function of the artist in American Gothic literature, specifically in Lovecraft's fiction, a topic that, until now, has not been adequately addressed in critical discourse. This study addresses the gap in the critical debate by exploring Lovecraft's constant of cosmic indifferentism in relation to Nietzsche's definition of nihilism and the state of the American artist in a burgeoning literary community reliant of realistic details in art. The question is discussed in relation to Lovecraft's essay "Nietzscheism and Realism" (1921), accused of being nihilistic and pessimistic, and in several of Lovecraft's best-known texts. This study pits his philosophy and texts against established American Gothic texts such as "The Legend of Sleepy Hollow" (1820) and *The Narrative of Arthur Gordon Pym of Nantucket* (1838). Lovecraft's texts suggest that the relationship between artists and their creations exposes its own death as a concept;

that the artist as creator is dead because of society's need for realism and the only value it can have is relevant only to the individual, not to the whole of civilization. I argue that, because Lovecraft's fiction signals that the artist is dead, the time is ripe for a radical reevaluation of how we alienate an artist from its creation, acknowledge its influence, and examine how readers perceive the artist's version of reality.

Ash Darrow
Independent Scholar
"Your Eldritch Horror Is in Another Castle:
The Quest for Cosmicism in Gaming"

Lovecraftian fiction is more abundant than ever. Lovecraftian themes and Mythos characters are becoming ubiquitous in our media. At the center of this growth is Lovecraft's impact on gaming. Lovecraft's presence in gaming has grown from the tabletop RPG to awkward gimmick titles like *Cthulhu Monopoly* (2016) and *Cthulhu Yahtzee* (2015). With Lovecraftian gaming so pervasive, how do Lovecraftian games interact with his cosmicist philosophy? Lovecraft expressed a central notion that humanity, as both a body of individuals and a concept, has no meaningful significance when viewed from geological or cosmic time scales. This runs contrary to the core experience expressed by most games. Gaming, at its core, is built upon ludic mastery. That is to say, games are designed to be conquered by their players through stories and gameplay that empower the player over adversity. This is a direct contradiction to Lovecraft's cosmicism. Survival horror challenges player empowerment, but it still offers validity to the player's experience and eventual empowerment. Cosmicist gaming, on the other hand, rejects the validity of empowerment by subverting narratological and ludic tropes. Games such as *BloodBorne* (2015) and *Devil Daggers* (2016) use cosmicism as a guiding principle, while other, more expressly "Lovecraftian" games, such as *Call of Cthulhu: Dark Corners of the Earth* (2005), fail to grapple with Lovecraft's philosophy and become bogged down in the Mythos. This paper explores the successes and failures at attempting to systematize Lovecraft's philosophy.

Ian Fetters
Cal Poly San Luis Obispo
"Lovecraft's Dark Continent:
At the *Mountains of Madness* and Antarctic Literature"

This paper focuses on H. P. Lovecraft's novel *At the Mountains of Madness* and its place in both the Lovecraft and Antarctic literary traditions. I propose two research questions: first, what can an in-depth analysis of Lovecraft's writing process, specifically focused the meticulous realism of the polar setting and its relationship to other influences, reveal about the novel's place in Lovecraft's oeuvre? Second, how might that repositioning contribute to granting the novel a greater place in the canon of Antarctic fiction? I use primary sources from the John Hay Library's H. P. Lovecraft Papers to answer these questions. Textual analysis of original handwritten and typewritten manuscripts help to decipher the novel's writing process and to make connections between the novel and its nonfiction and fiction influences, such as Admiral Byrd's 1928–30 Antarctic expedition and Poe's *Narrative of Arthur Gordon Pym*. Primary sources from the Bradford Swan Antarctic special collection are also used in identifying the nonfiction elements upon which Lovecraft draws in drafting the novel. I argue that in the novel Lovecraft's polar realism is not only spot-on, but it also is the crucial element that contributes to a greater representation of the continent than previous fictional attempts had up to that point in time. I also reference primary source correspondence from the Lovecraft collection in connection to the developments in writing process noted in the manuscript textual analysis. Lovecraft's letters to colleagues help to contextualize his writing of the Antarctic and its effect on his storytelling. From these sources I conclude not only that *At the Mountains of Madness* is a stellar achievement in Lovecraft's pursuit of horrific verisimilitude that warrants further investigation into other works from or around the period of the novel's conception, but also that the novel stands to be recognized as the head of the Antarctic fiction tradition for its polar realism and its appreciation of the Antarctic continent as a locus of adventurous expectancy.

Fiona Maeve Geist and Eli Shurberg
Independent Scholars
"A Correlation of Contents: Mapping the Intersections of Queerness and
Negativity in the Works of Lovecraft"

Excavating queerness from Lovecraft seems, on surface, like a fruitless
endeavor. What little information there is about his sexuality is
overwhelmingly heterosexual (his brief unsuccessful marriage to Sonia
Greene) and themes of sexuality seem divorced from his cosmic mythos.
In spite of the seeming futility of this project, Lovecraft himself and his
work are suffused with a sexuality—one which is itself very much queer.
This is not an endeavor to *reclaim* Lovecraft as a queer exemplar. The
purpose of this proposal is to interrogate the *incomprehensibly* queer aspects
of his life and writing. This entails engagement with Lovecraft through a
lens that takes his asexuality (and that of his characters) juxtaposed with
the fear of fecund masses and interspecies breeding to be significant
aspects of his work that have been frequently neglected *as* sexual.
Following scholars such as Heather Love, this is not a redemptive project
that seeks to apologize for the disturbing and sexualized aspects of
Lovecraft's work, but instead to contextualize them and trace their
unsettling influences. Of specific import is Lovecraft's unapologetic racism—often a focus of critical work regarding Lovecraft—and the
genealogies of corruption that saturate his work. Lovecraft's entwined
racism and repulsion regarding sex is occasionally quite overt—"The
Horror at Red Hook" frequently gets dishonorable mentions and critical
drubbing for such content, but the argument that it is a ubiquitous
phenomenon has been neglected in terms of critical attention. Mining this
vein, including tracing stylistic choices in his critically acclaimed and
pseudonymous work, attempts to launch a new space for scholarly
attention to Lovecraft's work.

David Goudsward
Independent Scholar
"Innsmouth, Florida"

Lovecraft makes no secret in his correspondence that Innsmouth is based
on Newburyport, Massachusetts, a town he first visited in 1923 and visited
repeatedly, including a trip in October 1931. Within a month of that visit,

he began to draft of "The Shadow over Innsmouth." Newburyport is un-questionably the primary inspiration for geography, both as both an ideal-ized version of itself and as its own antithesis in Innsmouth, with the narrator paralleling Lovecraft's tourist destinations in Newburyport. During his first visit to Florida earlier that year, Lovecraft wrote to August Derleth that, although St. Augustine was his favorite Floridian location, a glass-bottomed boat ride from Miami to the coral reefs in Biscayne Bay had sparked an idea for a story set around a reef in the tropics. A tropical story never materialized, but his next story features the partially hidden Devil's Reef off the coast of Innsmouth. The letter to Derleth is the first clue that his visit to St. Augustine contributes as much influence as, if not more than, Newburyport on "The Shadow over Innsmouth." Placing Lovecraft's St. Augustine travel destinations in context to the story, they serve as vital plot points.

Edward Guimont

Independent Scholar

"At the Mountains of Mars: Lovecraft's Relationship with the Red Planet"

This paper explores the influence of the planet Mars in H. P. Lovecraft's fiction. From a young age, he was interested in astronomical observations of the red planet. But Mars and its hypothetical inhabitants are almost entirely absent from Lovecraft's fictional universe. I maintain that both scientific and fictional representations of Mars and the possibility of Martian life can be seen to be influences on Lovecraft's conceptions of cosmicism and of powerful alien entities indifferent to humanity. Lowell's nonfiction treatises and the novels of H. G. Wells and various imitators depict advanced, non-anthropomorphic Martians who are morally indif-ferent to humanity and engage in the construction of massive engineering works, but for all their technology are unable to avert their civilization's decline from the inexorable forces of nature—all themes later found in Lovecraft. I explore some of the reasons that Lovecraft may not have wanted to depict Mars and Martians explicitly, including the planet's heavy use in works of allegory and satire; its associations with the Soviet regime; and its being a favorite locale of innumerable mediocre pulp space operas. I show that *At the Mountains of Madness* can be read as effectively being a "Mars story," as its themes (scientific explorers in advanced vehicles journeying to a distant frozen wasteland, where they uncover the remains of an advanced ancient alien civilization felled by climate change) parallel the tropes of contemporary Mars-set fiction, including a trilogy of stories written by Lovecraft's friend, Clark Ashton Smith. I conclude by exploring Lovecraft's influence on subsequent works of Martian fiction, and note how Wells's much less popular second Martian novel *Star-Begotten* (1937) can be interpreted as a recognizably "Lovecraftian" work.

Perry Neil Harrison

Independent Scholar

"Anthropodermic Bibliopegy and the Literature of H. P. Lovecraft"

In his short story "The Hound" (1922), H. P Lovecraft describes among the belongings of the unnamed narrator and St. John, "a locked portfolio, bound in tanned human skin, [holding] certain unknown unnamable drawings which it was rumored Goya had perpetrated but dared not acknowledge." While at first this document seems simply to be another artifact in the pair's macabre collection, a closer examination shows that this detail is rooted in the real-life practice of anthropodermic bibliopegy—the binding of books in human skin. This study demonstrates that Lovecraft drew upon the anthropodermic bookbinding practices of the nineteenth and early twentieth centuries while creating his fictional folio and characters. Specifically, I argue that the narrator and St. John share indisputable traits with real-life owners and producers of skin-bound books. Carolyn Marvin links those who created and owned such books with "a desire for personal recognition within . . . [an] upper-class avocation of rare-book collecting." The pair is not formally of the upper class, but the narrator takes pains to present their tastes in a way that echoes those of the cultural and aesthetic elite of the time. By demonstrating that the characters in "The Hound" possess the same upper-class artistic tastes as the real-life owners of anthropodermic books, I demonstrate that Lovecraft situated his narrative within a larger, real-world tradition.

Ray Huling

Independent Scholar

"Lovecraft, Bataille, and Sacred Terror"

Had they met in the summer of 1936 and had each known a thing or two about the other, Georges Bataille would have refused to shake H. P. Lovecraft's hand—and Lovecraft would likely have refused Bataille's. By this time, Bataille had founded Acéphale, a secret society that, among other things, practiced a taboo against shaking hands with anti-Semites.

Lovecraft would have found Bataille's pornography and sexual habits too revolting for politesse. This mutual disgust is important to keep in mind when exploring connections between Lovecraft and Bataille, an exploration that has excited numerous scholars in recent years. Not only do their worldviews, their philosophies, and their dramatizations of their ideas exhibit many parallels, so do their experiences: they both described feelings of horror in confronting the limits and implications of science and the animality of sex, for example. Yet Bataille and Lovecraft ended up writing from the poles of the extreme left and the extreme right, respectively. What is the meaning of this? My paper not only considers Lovecraft from a leftist position, it also establishes Lovecraft's fiction as a confrontation with sacredness, in Bataille's sense of the sacred as communication. The keys to this analysis are fascism, a phenomenon that fascinated them both, and eroticism, a phenomenon Bataille dived to the bottom of and into which Lovecraft hardly dipped a toe. Bataille sought to counter fascism with his own violent myths, with cultic rituals and sacrificial expenditures that would leave the world too exhausted for war-making. He failed. Lovecraft's sensibilities conformed to and even occasionally exceeded those of the fascists and those of the most continent prudes of his day. But it is Lovecraft's mythologies that endure and inspire to this day, even among those of the anti-fascist, anti-racist left. Lovecraft failed, too, precisely because he has a cult following and because of the sort of followers in his cult. I argue that a meditation on these failures can help to illuminate a path toward a future success, in contemporary leftist terms.

Joshua D. King

University of Virginia

"Reviewing Lovecraft's Cause of Death:

A Clinicopathological Conference"

H. P. Lovecraft died on 15 March 1937 at the age of forty-six. His death has been ascribed to intestinal cancer, with chronic nephritis (kidney disease) as a secondary cause; however, the basis for this is by no means firmly established. Lovecraft had no confirmatory testing to establish this diagnosis, nor was an autopsy performed. Cause of death was largely established by physical exam and symptoms alone. Kidney failure is somewhat unexplained; its duration, cause, and significance to his health are uncertain. Medical professionals regularly determine patient cause of death without fully supportive information; this was even more true in Lovecraft's day. Studies in the modern era evaluating the accuracy of the cause of death listed on death certificates find that 25 to 50 percent of these causes are disproved at autopsy. At the time of Lovecraft's passing, many diagnostic tests considered routine today were unavailable. It is improbable that causes of death were more accurate in his day. Throughout his life, particularly in his final years, H. P. Lovecraft mentioned bothersome symptoms in his voluminous correspondence. Using Lovecraft's own words about his health and daily practices as written in numerous letters, and the few existing records concerning Lovecraft's medical condition, an appreciation of Lovecraft's health in decline can be achieved. These data are used toward informed speculation on possible health conditions that Lovecraft suffered from, assessment to the extent possible whether his recorded cause of death is consistent with available data, and discussion of possible alternate causes of death.

Karen Joan Kohoutek
Independent Scholar
"Red Hand, Red Hook: Machen, Lovecraft, and the Urban Uncanny"

From Thomas De Quincey and James Thomson to twentieth-century horror films such as *C.H.U.D.*, urban environments have been depicted as sites for the fantastic and the uncanny. Many artists and thinkers have contributed to the genre's tropes, but weird writers Arthur Machen and H. P. Lovecraft can be seen to exemplify a pivotal period in the development of the urban uncanny, as it shifts from an inward, psychological experience to one that focuses outward, projected onto threatening populations within the city's boundaries. Machen was a habitual wanderer of the city streets, experiencing its strangeness and the resultant personal unease. He translated his sense of London's mystery into more concrete tales of crime and menace, well illustrated by "The Red Hand," in which a community of under-evolved "troglodytes" functions mostly as a red herring, although it does turn out to exist in the background of the tale. Lovecraft extended that example in his xenophobic New York stories, "He" and "The Horror at Red Hook," the latter of which opens with a quotation from "The Red Hand." In these tales, the city's uncanny elements are displaced onto marginalized groups, a sinister demographic depicted as uncanny and threatening to the larger (assumed Anglo-Saxon) society and its values. In Lovecraft's case, such fears were reflective of his personal discomfort with different ethnic groups and socioeconomic classes. Similar symbolic fears continue to be seen in contemporary popular culture, where the urban underclasses frequently embody the individual's fears of the city's unknown elements, especially when they occur in groups (such as gatherings of homeless persons or youth street gangs). The major psychological theories of the uncanny were published between the writing of the Machen and Lovecraft tales, and can be used to explore how this trend further developed into contemporary times, when individuals, isolated and alienated among a vast city of strangers, focus their fear of its unknown elements on ethnic minorities and the economically disadvantaged.

Fred S. Lubnow
Independent Scholar
"The Lovecraftian Solar System: A Tour of Our Cosmic Neighborhood
through the Eyes of H. P. Lovecraft"

H. P. Lovecraft had a lifelong love of science, and of all the disciplines astronomy was his favorite. From 1906 to 1918 he gazed into the heavens each night, occasionally visited the Ladd Observatory, and recorded the movement and appearance of celestial objects articles written for local newspapers. Lovecraft documented his observations regularly, and although he never became a professional astronomer, he incorporated his observations and knowledge into his tales of cosmic dread and horror. Lovecraft admitted that when he initiated his exploration of the cosmos he largely "ignored the abysses of space" and focused primarily on the moon and the potential habitability of it and the other planets. This presentation focuses on how Lovecraft incorporated into his tales what was known about the solar system in the early twentieth century and how our view of the solar system has changed over the last nearly 100 years. It uses many of Lovecraft's tales to present a view of the solar system in the "Lovecraftian Universe" and, where possible, compares Lovecraft's ideas to past and current scientific investigations. Tales discussed include "The Whisperer in Darkness," "The Colour out of Space," *The Dream-Quest of Unknown Kadath,* and "The Shadow out of Time." The presentation uses Neil deGrasse Tyson's categorization of the solar system, which includes five families of bodies: terrestrial/rocky planets, the Asteroid Belt, the gas giant planets, the Kuiper Belt (which includes Pluto), and the Oort Cloud of comets. Finally, the presentation explores components of the solar system of which Lovecraft was unaware but which may yield some Lovecraftian discoveries or horrors.

Anders Lundgren
Independent Scholar
"Mike Mignola and The Lovecraft Circle: Inspiration and World Sharing"

With this presentation, I offer insights into some of the stuff that makes the cartoonist and writer Mike Mignola and his work tick. I'm not aiming for the annotated version of his long-running series *Hellboy*; that would take several volumes. I simply wish to trace some of the influences back to their sources and analyze what function they serve for the stories. A brief introduction to Mignola's work is provided for those unfamiliar with it. Among the topics I discuss are connections between H. P. Lovecraft's writing and Mignola's comics. In what way does Mignola's approach differ from all the others that have been inspired by the Yog-Sothothery over the years? A case in point is Alan Moore, who recently wrapped up *Providence*, his twelve-issue dissection of all things Lovecraftian. I demonstrate how two very different temperaments taking inspiration from the same source can yield very different results. But the net is cast wider than that. In Mignola's work we find traces of H. P. Blavatsky (1831–1891) and the Theosophists, the Zermatism of Stanisław Szukalski (1893–1987), various hollow earth theories, and Hyperborea as encountered in the writings of Clark Ashton Smith (1893–1961) and Robert E. Howard (1906–1936). A fictitious country is not all Mignola got from Howard. He also took the notion of telling the story of his main protagonist in a disjointed fashion, jumping back and forth in the chronology of his life. Time travel of a different sort is something else Howard explored in stories such as "Kings of the Night," featuring his Pictish hero Bran Mak Morn. This is mirrored in the miniseries *B.P.R.D. Hell on Earth: The Abyss of Time* Nos. 1–2, written by Mignola and Scott Allie, and drawn by James Harren with color work by Dave Stewart. Which brings us to the last topic: what are the similarities and differences between how the Lovecraft Circle, Mignola, and his many collaborators go about writing stories in a shared world?

Rolf Maurer
Independent Scholar
"Through a Lens Dark and Lightly:
The Cosmicism of E. E. Smith and H. P. Lovecraft"

Despite his general dismissal of the space adventure form competing for pages in *Astounding Stories*, *Weird Tales*, or the other pulps of his day, H. P. Lovecraft, the self-styled antiquarian throwback trapped in the twentieth century, surprisingly enough had a fan in none other than E. E. "Doc" Smith, generally regarded as the father of science fiction's space opera sub-category. Their worldviews as to humanity's future and place in the universe as either hopelessly vulnerable or expansively anthropocentric merit scrutiny as literary examples of the anticipation and uncertainty defining the years in which their careers overlapped and, in the case of Doc Smith, how his narrative perspective has an ongoing resonance as part of our contemporary hi-tech societal self-definition, compared with Lovecraft's more cyclical appeal. Among the areas to be examined in this paper are the writers' respective attitudes toward the exotic and the Other in their writing (be it revulsive or inclusive, human-like or radically different), the contrasting role of Lovecraft's characters as learned-but-fragile pawns of higher powers, versus Smith's irrepressibly optimistic, learn-as-you-go heroes facing similar extra-dimensional challenges, as well as what the authors' attitudes and use of technology in their fiction reveals about particular sociopolitical and economic inclinations.

Ann McCarthy
Independent Scholar
"The Pathos in the Mythos: Real Feeling in Lovecraft and LaValle"

In *H. P. Lovecraft: Against the World, Against Life*, Michel Houellebecq posits meaninglessness as a central Lovecraft theme, claiming that Lovecraft "destroys his characters, invoking only the dismemberment of marion-ettes." This reading is borne out somewhat in the popular conception of Lovecraft. That is to say, everybody knows Cthulhu, but no one mentions Albert N. Wilmarth. I intend to speak about Albert N. Wilmarth and some others. Their lives contain fascination and suffering. Discussing *Melmoth the Wanderer* in "Supernatural Horror in Literature," Lovecraft praises "the white heat of sympathetic passion on the writer's part which makes the book a true document of aesthetic self-expression." My goal in this paper is, through close reading, to locate this passion as it is manifested in *The Case of Charles Dexter Ward*, "The Whisperer in Darkness," "The Rats in the Walls," and also in Victor LaValle's *The Ballad of Black Tom*, a recent retelling of "The Horror at Red Hook." The characters' relationships with history and one another, their rich feeling, need not be diminished by any perceived futility in relation to the larger universe. The seeking, the passion for data, the consultation of primary sources, the attachment to past and present Providence that obsess young Charles Dexter Ward constitute an academic romance, an ecstasy of research and humanism. "The Whisperer in Darkness" continues the theme of academic engagement, adding the element of friendship. The bonding of Wilmarth and Akeley over their shared interest in the mythos, and their collaborative antiquarian sleuthing through correspondence, comprise the warm human core of the story. "The war ate my boy," Delapore says at the climax of "The Rats in the Walls." His grief over his son's maiming and eventual death from injuries sustained in World War I precipitates his relocation to Exham Priory, and his ultimate break with civilization. No marionette, he! Finally, it is useful for comparison here to look at the centrality of the father-son relationship in *Ballad of Black Tom*.

Shawn McKinney
Hillsborough Community College, Florida
"The Madness of Minds: Consciousness and Materialism in
H. P. Lovecraft's Fiction"

An interesting facet of Lovecraft's fiction is that he explored the unknown real. Space is real, it is not a unicorn or a squared circle, but the nature and extent of space is still unknown. Time is real, but we still are not sure what time is. Dimensions beyond our perception are real, the math says, but it is difficult to explain exactly what they are. Among these other, more obvious Lovecraftian cosmic horror elements is another unknown real: consciousness. In Lovecraft's fiction consciousness is real, and its possession is not restricted to human beings. Various beings can swap their consciousness between bodies and throughout time. Entire Dreamlands exist that humans can access only with their mind. What makes Lovecraft's attention to consciousness more interesting is his belief in materialism. The type of materialism he advocated was that everything that was real was, ultimately, made of something like matter and causally connected to every other real thing: like the cosmos is a great machine. The great philosophical issue of the mind for millennia has been whether consciousness is composed of matter or if it is made of something other than matter (and if so, how does that work?). I am not the first person to find Lovecraft's treatment of consciousness philosophically interesting. Lovecraft's work has been characterized as advocating a pseudo-Platonic, nonmaterialist ideal of mind. The topic was touched upon at this very conference in 2013, where his work was claimed to promote a pseudo-materialist theory called epiphenomenalism. I investigate whether Lovecraft's work presents a more or less consistent theory of what consciousness is, and whether that theory is reconcilable with his materialism. I find that the answer to both questions is probably yes.

Sean Moreland
University of Ottawa
"Shadows out of Space, Colours out of Time:
The Cosmic Horror of Junji Ito and Charles Burns"

This paper considers how Lovecraft's ideas of weird fiction and cosmic horror are uniquely suited to the formal characteristics and conceptual possibilities of comics as a medium, and more specifically how the work of mangaka Junji Ito embodies something of the "cosmic outsideness" that Lovecraft identified as the sine qua non of weird fiction. Ito acknowledges Lovecraft's influence in interviews and commentaries, but he is not known primarily for visual adaptations of Lovecraft, instead developing a unique approach to the weird. Yet his exploration of the formal and structural possibilities of sequential art embodies the principles of weird fiction, as adumbrated by Lovecraft in "Supernatural Horror in Literature" and articulated at greater length in his letters and other critical writings. I focus on Ito's *Uzumaki* and his more recent *Fragments of Horror*, graphic texts that share an unsettling interrogation of our human perspectives on spatial and temporal relationships. Making subversive use of fascinatingly detailed linework and the relationship between panels and interpanel gutters, these texts suggest a momentary disruption of "the galling limitations of space and time," a trait Lovecraft viewed as the central goal of cosmic weird fiction.

Byron Nakamura
Southern Connecticut State University
"Will the Real Lovecraft Please Stand Up: An Example of Intertextuality
in the Work of Frank Belknap Long and H. P. Lovecraft"

H. P. Lovecraft's great Roman dream of 1927 was published in two variants, one borrowed (with Lovecraft's permission) and incorporated into
Frank Belknap Long's short novel *The Horror from the Hills* in 1931 and the
other published posthumously as a stand-alone tale entitled "The Very
Old Folk" in 1940. Lovecraft himself wrote that Long had used his dream
text originally described in a series of letters without any "linguistic
change" (*SL* 4.334). This is to say, Lovecraft understood that Long had not
made any alterations to the original text of Lovecraft's description of his
dream in a letter to Long (which no longer exists). Yet is this case? Despite
Lovecraft's assertions that the dream text had been preserved in *The Horror
from the Hills* unchanged from his original letter, there is strong stylistic
and structural evidence to the contrary. If we analyze and compare
Lovecraft's stylistic peculiarities, use of grammar and syntax, and
vocabulary with the extant versions of the great Roman dream of 1927 in
correspondence to Donald Wandrei and Bernard Austin Dwyer to Long's
version, it appears that Long either edited or rewrote Lovecraft's dream
text to fit his own style. Lovecraft had been a ghostwriter for literary
aspirants like Hazel Heald, Zealia Bishop, Harry Houdini, and others, but
here we have an example of one of Lovecraft's correspondents using
Lovecraft's ideas in his own work. This shows the trust that existed
between Lovecraft his literary circle of weird fiction writers. In addition,
stylometric analysis of Lovecraft's writing can provide new avenues of
explorations into his work.

Paul Neimann
University of Colorado, Boulder
"Naming the Unnamable: The Ethics of Lovecraftian Horror"

H. P. Lovecraft's tale "The Unnamable" (1922) has been taken as a meta-
fictive commentary on the supernatural in fiction. That description points
to elements of the story generally evident in Lovecraft's work and treated
in criticism: rejection of realism, baroque prose, obscurity in representation, and a conflicted relationship with commercialism. But that

reading, which fits Lovecraft's remarks in "Supernatural Horror in Literature," may prove too simple. The story—in remarkably programmatic fashion—examines and, I argue, apparently discards familiar aesthetic theory around Gothic and weird traditions, including perhaps Lovecraft's own statements on the suprasensory. The narrative effort to define "the unnamable" nearly settles on something like Freud's uncanny, or the socially repressed, as a source of true horror. References to oppressive Puritanism in Cotton Mather—whose lurid 1702 account of a human/animal hybrid informs the story—flirt with psycho-biographical hermeneutics commonly applied to Lovecraft himself. But the story also resists being read as an account of repression, often seen as horror fiction's clearest moral tendency. This paper tries to discern a theory of horror by looking at what Lovecraft rejects—and then poses questions about the ethical implications of insisting on the unspeakable.

Heather Poirier
Independent Scholar
"Dynamics of Detective Fiction in H. P. Lovecraft"

Scholars frequently treat H. P Lovecraft's narrators as agents to an extensive study of cosmic horror; few scholars have studied them characters as detectives. Even though some recent popular works feature Lovecraft himself as a detective, the critical literature does not offer much in the way of analysis of detective fiction elements in his works. This gap in knowledge prevents us from understanding the energy these elements bring to Lovecraft's fiction. Detective fiction dynamics are strongly present in Lovecraft's works. His narrators use, then subvert, the genre's conventions. In most detective fiction, a detective investigates a crime, then presents a clear-cut case with facts to support the conclusions reached. The criminal is caught, and justice is served. In contrast, Lovecraft's investigators are often unreliable, yet the reader comes to trust them. Investigations lead to the dire clarity of cosmic horror that must then be concealed. Truth and deceit are meaningless in the face of cosmic terror, yet that terror powers the investigator's pursuit of the truth. Evidence and facts have uncertain status. Confessions are disregarded, crimes are concealed, and investigators face incarceration while perpetrators cannot be caught. Justice cannot be served because no redemption is possible. This paper examines the role of detective fiction dynamics in Lovecraft's work and explores some of the implications. Specifically, this paper looks at how Lovecraft uses elements key to the genre; how the tripartite dynamics of detective fiction power Lovecraft's narrators; and how certain Lovecraft stories, when juxtaposed against traditional works of detective fiction, reveal the connections and disjunctions between popular detectives and Lovecraft's investigators, thus placing Lovecraft within the genre as a subverter. In doing so, this project provides a better understanding of the little-recognized intersection of Lovecraft and detective fiction.

Lúcio Reis-Filho
Independent Scholar
"Lovecraft out of Space: Influences of the American Weird Fiction on Brazilian Literature and Cinema"

By developing an oeuvre that has shown endurance for almost a hundred years, H. P. Lovecraft paved the way for a wide range of cultural products such as theatrical films, television shows, cartoons and games. Not by chance, Lovecraft became one of the most renowned horror writers in the twentieth century. By 1969, he was one of the biggest selling authors in the U.S. and had already reached countries outside the Anglo-Saxon world such as France and Brazil. In the latter, Lovecraft was first published in 1966 by Edições GRD (GRD Editions), an editorial venture based in Rio de Janeiro, focused on publishing authors who renewed universal literature. Translated by George Gurjan from *The Dunwich Horror and Others* (1963), the collection included the short stories "The Call of Cthulhu" (1926), "The Colour out of Space" (1927), and "The Whisperer in Darkness" (1930). A decade later, Lovecraft seems to have inspired Carlos Hugo Christensen's *A Mulher do Desejo–A Casa das Sombras* (*The Woman of Desire–The House of Shadows*, 1975), a piece of Brazilian horror cinema. The film is tied to significant themes of Lovecraft's work and shares similarities with two of his later stories, *The Case of Charles Dexter Ward* (1927) and "The Thing on the Doorstep" (1933). Through the analysis of Christensen's film, I observe the impact of Lovecraft's fiction outside the U.S., considering his appropriation/adaptation in Brazilian cinema of the 1970s.

Faye Ringel
U.S. Coast Guard Academy, Emerita
Jenna Randall
Independent Scholar
"Perspectives on Lovecraft and Racism:
Internet 'Facts' and Recent Metafictions"

In the period that saw Lovecraft ensconced in the Library of America (2005) and selected as a Penguin Anniversary Classic (2016), a chorus of voices criticizing Lovecraft's racism rose to a crescendo in 2015, campaigning to remove Lovecraft's image from the World Fantasy Award. Mainstream media coverage meant that readers to whom his name was unknown first heard of him as Lovecraft the Racist. The Internet turned this exaggerated, monolithic perception into games and memes. Perhaps the worst result: white supremacists and Neo-Nazis have come to his defense. When the white supremacist publisher Counter-Currents heard the WFA would no longer carry Lovecraft's likeness, it invented a "Counter-Currents H. P. Lovecraft Prize for Literature." Its website maintains a database of Lovecraft scholars, thus aligning them with Neo-Nazism. These events and controversies in popular culture are reflected and wrestled with in a group of recent metafictions by mainstream and genre authors. African-American author Victor LaValle dedicates his novella *The Ballad of Black Tom* (2016) to "H. P. Lovecraft, with all my conflicted feelings." Readers of this re-visioning of Lovecraft's "The Horror at Red Hook" (1925) are presumed to understand that his conflict is over whether the value of Lovecraft's art overcomes his racism. LaValle's novella employs a black protagonist to deconstruct one of Lovecraft's most problematic stories, part of a larger trend of authors commenting upon America's racist past and present using fantastic tropes. The most mainstream example, Colson Whitehead's *The Underground Railroad*, features a literal steam-driven railway linking states, each of which reflects a different aspect of American racism. Within the fantastic genres, Matt Ruff's *Lovecraft Country* does the same work, refracted through a Lovecraftian lens. Nick Mamatas uses the 2015 NecronomiCon Providence as backdrop for a murder mystery, *I Am Providence* (2016). These and other recent fiction, such as Paul LaFarge's *The Night Ocean*, join writers over a ninety-year period responding to Lovecraft, beginning in his lifetime before the term "metafiction" was coined, and continuing through references, shared worlds, pastiche, rewriting, and rejection of his influence.

Troy Rondinone
Southern Connecticut State University
"Lovecraft Meets the Mummy: Orientalism, Race, and Monstrous Egypt in
'Out of the Aeons' and Other Stories"

In this paper I discuss the figure of the mummy in works written by, or in collaboration with, H. P. Lovecraft. Since at least the 1800s, mummies have been compelling figures, surrounded by mystery and terror. The process of mummification, the enigma of a sprawling and advanced pre-Western civilization with bizarre gods, and the connections made in the popular imagination between Egypt and the currents of imperialism, all influenced weird fiction. Especially following the discovery of Tutankhamun's tomb in the Valley of the Kings in 1922, Americans became fascinated with the mummy and the ancient and gruesome technology of immortality. In this paper, I examine "Out of the Aeons" (a tale Lovecraft ghostwrote for Hazel Heald) and "Under the Pyramids" (ghostwritten for Harry Houdini), situating their themes and references in the broader context of Orientalism, xenophobia, racial ideology, and the production of knowledge. I include a brief contextual sketch of earlier popular mummy stories by Bram Stoker and others, and a look ahead to future mummy horror developments. I make use of the insights of Edward Said, Jackson Lears, Lynn Hunt, and other historical theorists in this discussion. The mummy, for Lovecraft and many other writers, was more than a mere monster—it was a symbol wrapped in contemporary fears.

Daniel Rottenberg
Independent Scholar
"Dreams of Lost Time and Space:
Lovecraft's Writings on Nostalgia and Home"

H. P. Lovecraft's body of work examines humanity's bleak position within the indifferent cosmos. This is illustrated by use of unnamable monsters, unmentionable tomes, blasphemous ventures into scientific terrors, and mysterious cults always trying to release horrors upon us which have been writhing perpetually just beyond our peripheries. These elements can be attributed to Lovecraft's own philosophies on horror, which he establishes in the opening of his essay "Supernatural Horror in Literature": "The oldest and strongest emotion of mankind is fear, and the oldest and strongest kind of fear is fear of the unknown." Lovecraft adhered to the idea that true horror is the unknown and unknowable, and he repeatedly demonstrated this through protagonists ending their own lives or going mad. While this may be true of Lovecraft's indifferent cosmos, it ventures into our closest liminal spaces, including childhood, nostalgia, and home, which empowers the horror to turn to wonder. This can be seen in "The Silver Key," in which Randolph Carter returns to his boyhood home, where he sets aside scientific dogma for the dreams and wonders of his ten-year-old self; in "The Outsider," in which a ghoul laments on the decay of the world and longs for companionship; and in *The Dream-Quest of Unknown Kadath*, in which Carter crosses the Dreamlands for his sunset city, only to have been pining for his home of Boston all along. Indeed, Lovecraft tends to depict the unknown as horrific dreamscapes of ichor-dripping tentacles, but many stories blur the lines of horror and wonder, conjoining the postmodern New Romanticism to the science fiction–Gothic horror he championed. Even the scientists and scholars are tempted through curiosity and wonder when exploring tomes and ancient cities. By equating the three subjects of strong emotion, fear, and the unknown, Lovecraft not only welcomed childlike wonder into his cosmos, but also delivered truths about confronting safeguards of memory through nostalgia and home.

Christian Roy
Independent Scholar
"Lovecraft's Accursed Share in Bataille's General Economy"

In writings such as *The Accursed Share* (1946–49), Georges Bataille appro-priated Einstein's distinction between general and special relativity for a non-anthropocentric recasting of cosmology and sociology, contrasting the "general economy" of the universe's boundless, pointless waste of energy with the "special economy" of living entities designed for self-perpetu-ation. Humans thus tend to economize for utilitarian motives of survival, security and profit, resisting or channeling the lure of loss in the profligate vastness beyond, to which they only give in on special, often ambiguously "sacred" occasions. Lovecraft's once-and-future gods, indifferent or hostile to mankind, moving in deep time on unimaginable scales, may well stand for Bataille's "general economy," where organic life, personal sanity and human civilization appear as insignificant marginal phenomena. This "economic" angle to cosmic horror seems literally translated in "The Shadow out of Time" (1934–35). For Nathaniel Wingate Peaslee, professor of political economy at Miskatonic University, his mind is displaced by that of an alien entity mid-sentence during a lecture he delivered in 1908. His "amnesia" shares the dates of Lovecraft's own bout of depression, until both recover five years later. Peaslee then completes the mind-blowing thought that "orthodox economist" William Stanley Jevons, who gave the theory of utility its mathematical features and thus "typifies the prevailing trend toward scientific correlation," could take it to its "apex" in tying "the commercial cycle of prosperity and depression with the physical cycle of the solar spots." As with Bataille's paeans to the sun's mad self-expenditure and the galaxies' swirling movement, Lovecraft's "economic" point is that "man must be prepared to accept notions of the cosmos, and of his own place in the seething vortex of time, whose merest mention is paralysing." The Great Race's social system reflects Lovecraft's interest in the New Deal with its emphasis on expenditure over savings, which would also fascinate Bataille in the Marshall Plan. However, Bataille sought radical outlets for the energies monopolized by capitalist accumulation, whereas Lovecraft, closer to Marcel Mauss's original anti-utilitarian retrieval of the gift economy, wanted reformist socialism to save civilization by spreading its energy gains to make noncalculative leisure generally available.

Daniel Schnopp-Wyatt
Lindsey Wilson College
"Human Sacrifice and Ritual Murder on the Bayou: Historical Antecedents of the 'Endless Bacchanal' in 'The Call of Cthulhu'"

Between 1910 and 1912, in the bayou country of Louisiana and East Texas, between 47 and 63 African Americans, mostly women and children, were ritualistically murdered in what the newspapers of the time referred to as "blood orgies." The bodies were hideously mutilated and displayed, their blood collected in basins. Only one person, a young Black woman named Clementine Barnabet, dubbed "the Ax-Woman of the Sacrifice Sect," was ever convicted. This presentation summarizes what is known of the murders, the trial, incarceration, sanctioned mutilation, and eventual disappearance of Ms. Barnabet. It speculates on the nature of cult responsible, placing it in the context of the flowering of esoteric Black religious movements in the Jim Crow era. The case, widely publicized at the time but now almost totally forgotten, likely provided the inspiration for "The Tale of Inspector Legrasse" in "The Call of Cthulhu." The character Legrasse was probably inspired by Sheriff Louis LaCoste, the lead investigator of the killings. This presentation outlines the murders, discusses connections to the *Xwetanu* human sacrifice ritual of the Mande and Fon peoples of West Africa from which most of the rice belt slaves were taken, and touches on the possibility that anthropomorphized depictions of Fon leaders as sharks influenced Lovecraft's depiction of the Deep Ones in "The Shadow over Innsmouth."

Elena Tchougounova-Paulson
Cambridge University
"Alexander Blok and H. P. Lovecraft:
On the Mythopoetics of the Supernatural"

In this paper, I analyze the vivid resemblance between the literary works of the Russian Symbolist poet Alexander Blok and H. P. Lovecraft from the perspective of their mythopoetics. Such an approach is entirely original; although scholars have studied both authors extensively, none has attempted a comparative assessment of their aesthetic worldviews. I address not only the writings of Blok and Lovecraft themselves but also their extra-textual substantiality, including the evolution of Blok's and Lovecraft's *Weltanschauung* as incarnated in their heritage. My analysis proceeds in two stages. First, I classify the most significant publications on which a comparative study can be based and second, I establish the actual conception on the structural and typological levels, using primarily comparative and intertextual methods as theoretical frameworks. Why these two writers? Because there is a striking similarity in the depth of their world perception and in their philosophical development. Given the extensiveness of this topic, I offer here only an introductory commentary. Works dedicated to Blok and Lovecraft (individually) are voluminous. Of the two, only Blok has received significant attention in both Russian and Western literary studies, largely as the key figure in the literature of the Russian *fin de siècle* (or Silver Age). Lovecraft's work has remained primarily the domain of Western scholars, who have addressed his influence on modern American literature, fine art, and cinema. Existing work in Russian is preoccupied with the artistic methods used in his fiction, the structure of the Cthulhu Mythos, and Lovecraft's substantial role in American neo-Gothic culture. Comparing the poetics of the supernatural in Blok and Lovecraft's works demands an examination of their oeuvres, including poetry, fiction, articles, and correspondence.

Michael A. Torregrossa
Independent Scholar
"Shadows over Camelot: Lovecraftian Motifs in Arthurian Fiction"

For just over a millennium and a half, the Matter of Britain, the massive conglomeration of stories dealing with the activities of King Arthur and his court, has remained a living and ever-changing tradition, one linked, for much of its history, with the monstrous, the supernatural, and the weird, a fact made most readily apparent in manifestations of the new Matter of Britain produced in the various multimedia of the present day. Some creative artists, their contributions not as yet fully surveyed, have added a further threat to this catalogue and have brought the Arthurian world into contact with preternatural menaces reminiscent of the horrors described in the fiction of H. P. Lovecraft to create, within the larger Arthurian tradition, a series of innovative intermedia subtraditions best labeled Lovecraftian Arthuriana. Borrowing heavily from Lovecraft's Cthulhu Mythos, the corpus of Lovecraftian Arthuriana remains relatively small, although its text base comprises various popular media, including fiction, film, television programming, and comics. Despite their relative rarity, the intermedia subtraditions that develop within these texts through the integration of both the Arthurian and Cthulhuvian mythologies represent unique contributions to the Arthurian legend. Furthermore, they display the continued vitality of both sources through the creation of a series of new narrative patterns for depicting the monstrous within the modern-day Matter of Britain. These motifs build upon two major themes in Lovecraft's work, both, as categorized by S. T. Joshi, "a wide array of extraterrestrials (deemed 'gods' by their human followers)" and "an entire library of mythical books containing the 'forbidden' truths about these 'gods.'" In Arthurian works, these themes are manifested as Cthulhuan menaces faced by Arthurian heroes (usually presented as reinterpretations of Arthur's role as the Once and Future King) and as a series of arcane tomes present at Camelot and used for various results. Works of Lovecraftian Arthuriana do not reflect a sophisticated engagement with Lovecraft's writings or the mythology that developed from them, but they do represent interesting appropriations of his ideas that deserve further reflection.

Faith Trowell
Independent Scholar
"Transhumanism, Monstrosity, and Modernity: Rhetorics of Abjection
in H. P. Lovecraft's 'The Whisperer in Darkness'"

This paper explores the ways in which H. P. Lovecraft engages with trans-humanist rhetorics in "The Whisperer in Darkness" (1930). It incorporates selections from Lovecraft's personal letters that highlight the places in which his strange blend of Enlightenment-era humanist and early twentieth-century Modernist discourses clash with what he saw as the monstrous, growing "machine culture" of the 1920s and '30s. Based on a close reading of "The Whisperer in Darkness" informed by Lovecraft's letters, what conclusions can we draw about his stance on and answers to transhumanist rhetorics? In what ways are the dynamics of power and powerlessness bound up in this figuration of the abject other? How does Lovecraft use specific rhetorical devices to produce horror and abjection in the transhuman subject? Placing Lovecraft within his own kairotic moment in the years between the two world wars prove fruitful to understanding his ethos as a writer of weird fiction and a rhetor. It is hard to believe that such a voluminous letter-writer who also styled himself as an antiquarian and classicist did not have a functional understanding of and use for rhetorical writing. I posit "The Whisperer in Darkness" as a story in which those two elements—letter writing and rhetorical discourse—are brought to bear in ways that create a unique opportunity to showcase horror and abjection set against the backdrop of contemporary proto-transhumanist discourses operating in the post–World War I and pre–World War II milieu. That was a time during which humanity was seriously re-evaluating its place in the universe and its relationship to machinery and modernity. Do developments in technology make humanity monstrous? Even more pertinent to this discussion is how humans become more monstrous, more horrific when they allow themselves to be molded by modern (and futuristic) contrivances.

Steve Walker
University of Central Missouri
"The Rats in the Trenches: The Gothic Horror of the Great War as
Revealed in the Writing of H. P. Lovecraft"

The year 2017 is a centennial for the Great War. Allusions to it appear in several Lovecraft stories, among them "The Rats in the Walls." An indirect reference may be found in the title creatures, since rats compose a frequent presence in some literature about trench warfare. How much does the presentation of the rat nourish Lovecraft's writing of the story? In the war literature, no less than Winston Churchill mentions the presence of rats, and an eyewitness account by a barber-turned-soldier together with an early nonfiction bestseller, *Over the Top*, features them prominently and may establish or refortify or extend conventions about them. Poetry and other sources that also include them are evidence. As a symbol the rat is an intermediary between this and the demonic world (to borrow from Northrop Frye), and as such negotiates an ambiguous status, embodying the bestial side of nature and of man, and appears in fiction of the era, including allegorical and fantasy. For example, the war literature portrays rats as, in effect, a placeholder for the ghoul that feasts on the endless supply of the dead, the fallen in battle. A reference in the story to the rats as a "ravenous army" (a pun?) may be traceable to the association of rats as an army and the identification of soldiers with rats. Since during the war the rat was known for eating corpses and destroying food, it may be an implicit synecdoche of consumption. Rats also provided sport for soldiers as targets for hunting and more practically helping to save lives through their ability to smell gas. Rats may also represent the manifestations of madness, the result of "shell-shock," now known as PTSD; breakdown of the mind corresponds to the breaching of physical barriers, the human form compromising on a were-rat. When Lovecraft's story first appeared, readers may have been more susceptible to the image of the rat as a creature that was a product of war, the connection being gradually effaced through the years.

Nathaniel R. Wallace

Independent Scholar

"The Cosmic Drone of Azathoth: Adaptation, Genre and the Sublime"

This paper examines musical adaptations of H. P. Lovecraft's fictional deity Azathoth by artists associated with the genre of drone music. In 1919, Lovecraft wrote the name "Azathoth" in his commonplace book of ideas for stories. He subsequently elaborated upon the concept in his fiction. Compiling all Lovecraft's descriptions of the fictional deity, one finds that the author ultimately characterized Azathoth as infinite concurrent reactionary processes rather than a singular entity, and its description closely aligns with Dionysian mystery rituals conducted in ancient Greece. In terms of specific qualities of sound, Azathoth is an aperture that mutters and blasphemes, erodes and undermines the order of the universe, while unnamed creatures accompany it with flutes and drums intended to induce a hypnotic and mitigated state within the deity. Although Lovecraft references instrumentation in his characterizations of the deity, his allusions to an ancient musical performance and a set of abstract processes make Azathoth a rather problematic object to adapt into a self-contained piece given its "untranslatable" qualities. Despite these adaptation-related complications, Azathoth has been the subject of at least 25 musical pieces, dating back to a composition by psychedelic British band Uriel in 1969. While there are some genre-related variations within these works, most are drone and metal based. This analysis of Azathoth adaptations focuses on works within the genre of drone music, a minimalistic and largely static music established in the mid-1960s with historical roots in various cultures throughout the world. Azathoth-based drone compositions have been prevalent because characteristics of the genre conform to Lovecraft's aesthetic as laid out in his letters and fiction, the Dionysian mystery rituals Azathoth is similar to have traditionally featured a drone instrument, the Aulos, and there are qualities of the genre that induce the sublime within audiences that have historical associations with divinity. These aesthetic influences are evaluated for their significance within a specific selection of pieces, including those by Uriel, the ambient drone band Ungl'Unl'Rrlh'Chchch, and the drone collective Cryo Chamber.

Index

CPSIA information can be obtained
at www.ICGtesting.com
Printed in the USA
BVHW041417120819
PP10180300001B/1/P